TO THE EDGES
OF THE EARTH

ALSO BY EDWARD J. LARSON

The Return of George Washington: Uniting the States, 1783–1789

An Empire of Ice: Scott, Shackleton, and the Heroic Age of Antarctic Science

A Magnificent Catastrophe: The Tumultuous Election of 1800, America's First Presidential Campaign

Summer for the Gods: The Scopes Trial and America's Continuing Debate over Science and Religion

Evolution: The Remarkable History of a Scientific Theory

Trial and Error: The American Controversy over Creation and Evolution

Evolution's Workshop: God and Science on the Galapagos Islands

Sex, Race, and Science: Eugenics in the Deep South

George Washington, Nationalist

On Faith and Science (with Michael Ruse)

TO THE EDGES
OF THE EARTH

1909, the Race for the Three Poles,
and the Climax of the Age of Exploration

EDWARD J. LARSON

WILLIAM MORROW
An Imprint of HarperCollins*Publishers*

HarperCollins books may be purchased for educational, business, or sales promotional use. For information please e-mail the Special Markets Department at
SPsales@harpercollins.com.

FIRST EDITION

Title page photograph Alinari Archives/Getty Images
Maps by Virginia Norey

Library of Congress Cataloging-in-Publication Data has been applied for.

ISBN 978-0-06-256447-4

18 19 20 21 22   LSC   10 9 8 7 6 5 4 3 2 1

TO MY WIFE,
LUCY,
WITH LOVE

Contents

Maps

Arctic Explorations Toward the North Pole

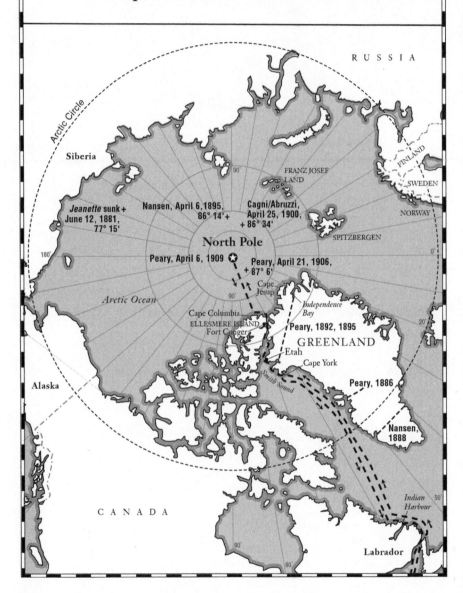

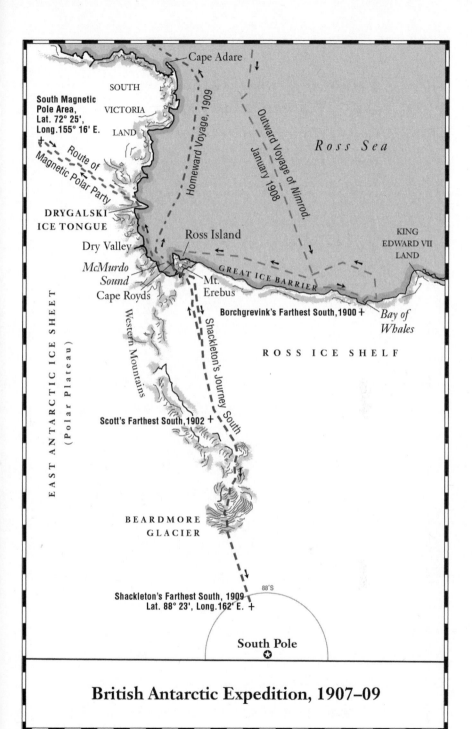

Cape Adare

SOUTH

South Magnetic
Pole Area,
Lat. 72° 25',
Long. 155° 16' E.

VICTORIA

LAND

Ross Sea

Route of
Magnetic Polar Party

Homeward Voyage, 1909

Outward Voyage of Nimrod.
January 1908

DRYGALSKI
ICE TONGUE

Ross Island

KING
EDWARD VII
LAND

Dry Valley

GREAT ICE BARRIER

McMurdo
Sound

Cape Royds

Mt.
Erebus

Borchgrevink's Farthest South, 1900 +

*Bay of
Whales*

ROSS ICE SHELF

Western Mountains

Shackleton's Journey South

EAST ANTARCTIC ICE SHEET
(Polar Plateau)

Scott's Farthest South, 1902 +

BEARDMORE
GLACIER

88'S

Shackleton's Farthest South, 1909
Lat. 88° 23', Long. 162' E. +

South Pole
✪

British Antarctic Expedition, 1907–09

Portion of the Karakoram Range
(Western Himalaya)

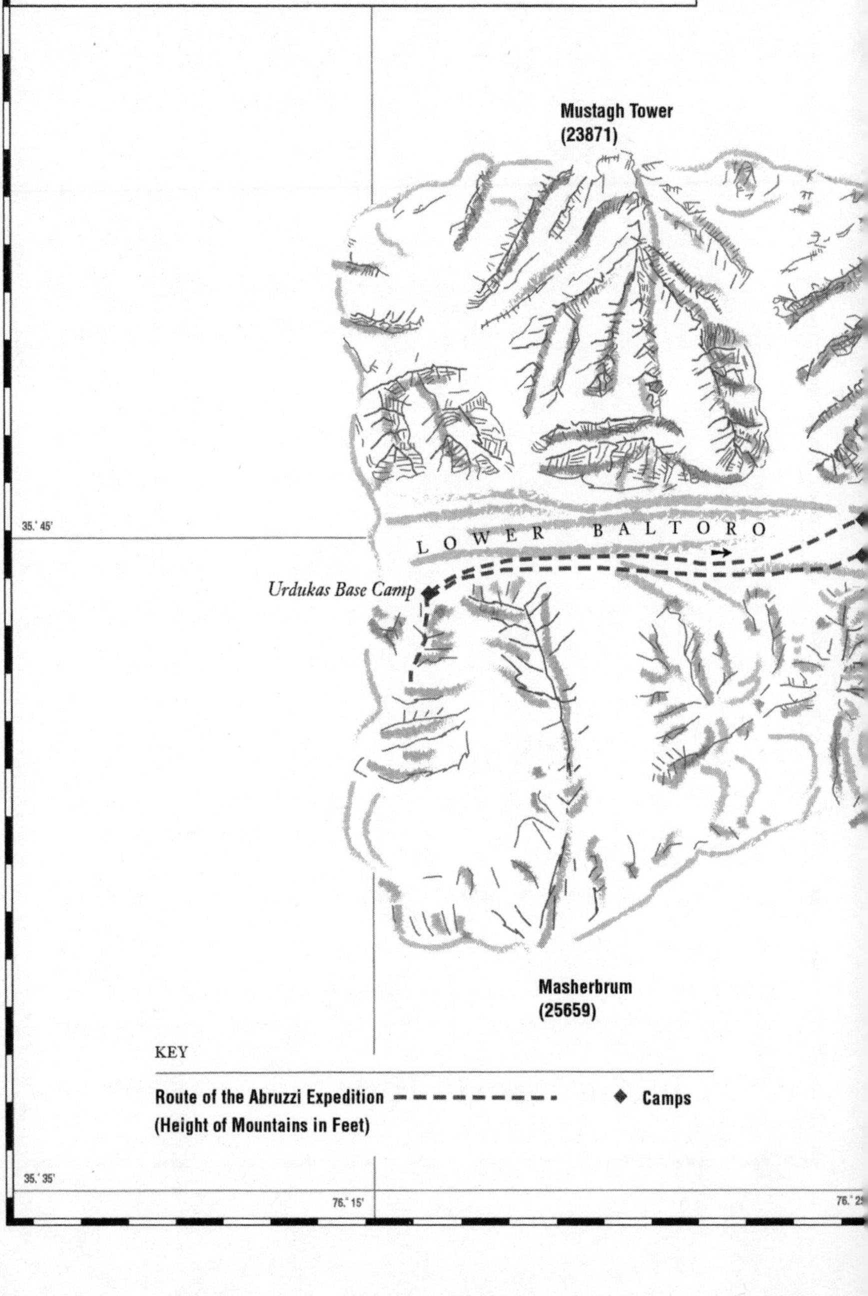

Mustagh Tower
(23871)

35.° 45'

L O W E R   B A L T O R O

Urdukas Base Camp

Masherbrum
(25659)

KEY

Route of the Abruzzi Expedition — — — — — — — —·   ◆ Camps
(Height of Mountains in Feet)

35.° 35'

76.° 15'   76.° 2

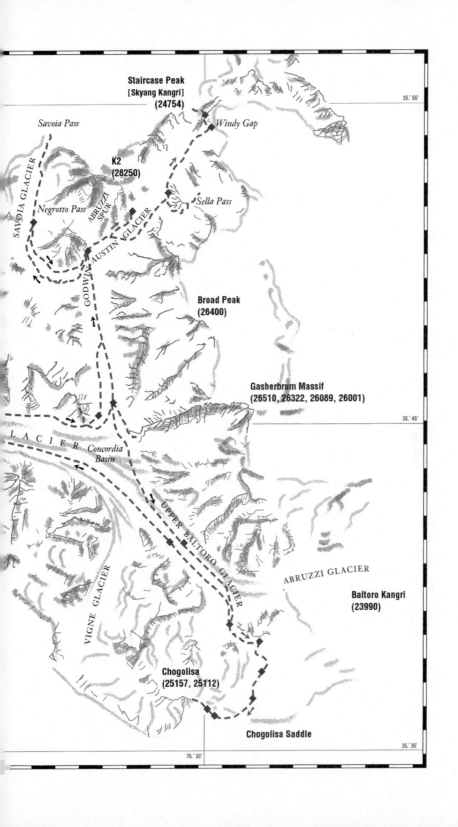

Staircase Peak
[Skyang Kangri]
(24754)

Windy Gap

Savoia Pass

K2
(28250)

Sella Pass

Negrotto Pass

ABRUZZI SPUR

SAVOIA GLACIER

GODWIN AUSTIN GLACIER

Broad Peak
(26400)

Gasherbrum Massif
(26510, 26322, 26089, 26001)

L A C I E R

Concordia Basin

UPPER BALTORO GLACIER

ABRUZZI GLACIER

Baltoro Kangri
(23990)

VIGNE GLACIER

Chogolisa
(25157, 25112)

Chogolisa Saddle

35.° 55'

35.° 45'

35.° 35'

76.° 35'

The Wonderful Year 1909

THE ADVENTURES DESCRIBED IN these pages carried the dreams
of the multitudes in Europe, America, and Australia. "Never in the
history of modern exploration have efforts so widespread and persistent as those of the present been made to uncover the mysteries
of the unknown parts of the world," the *New York Times* commented
in 1908. "Two explorers are seeking to solve the riddle of the North
Pole. Four parties have in view the ice-capped continent of the Antarctic. . . . In the heart of Asia are impenetrable mountain ranges and
vast deserts still unknown to modern geographers."[1] With the
adventure-enthusiast Theodore Roosevelt in the White House and
the like-minded though less active Edward VII reigning over Britain's far-flung imperial domains, new technologies easing access to
remote places, and empire in vogue, explorers vied to reach places that
previously seemed unattainable. Three unclaimed poles became the
ultimate goals: the North Pole, the South Pole, and the so-called Pole
of Altitude in the Himalayas, with the second sometimes divided into
the south geographic and south magnetic poles. With fame assured
to anyone bold enough to try and tough enough to succeed in reach-

ing them, 1909 was shaping up as a climactic year in the modern age of adventure-based exploration.

The expeditions of 1909 represented the culmination of long efforts in high latitudes and altitudes by explorers with notable track records. The lead American contender, Robert E. Peary, had mounted seven prior expeditions to the high Arctic, with the last three aimed squarely at the North Pole. British explorer Ernest Shackleton had tried once before for the South Pole. Then the most famous of the three, Prince Luigi Amedeo of Savoy, the Italian Duke of the Abruzzi, had made widely hailed first ascents on three continents as a mountaineer and once led an Arctic expedition that set a farthest-north record. Australia's premier field geologist, Edgeworth David, went along with Shackleton to try for the south magnetic pole, aided by future polar star Douglas Mawson. These were celebrities of the day chasing immortality at the edges of the earth.

The explorer's instinct was not new. It is probably as old as human life itself. Around 1500, with the emergence of improved naviga-tion and surplus population, European explorers began probing far beyond their own well-known regions of the world. From Christopher Columbus, Ferdinand Magellan, and Samuel de Champlain to James Cook, Lewis and Clark, and David Livingstone, to name but a few, Europeans and their transplanted progeny began exploring and colo-nizing long-inhabited lands across the globe. With Eurocentric pride, they called it "the Age of Exploration," and so it was for them. Never before had one people traveled so far and so fast from its homeland and reestablished itself in so many places so quickly.

With most of the world's inhabited places explored if not colo-nized by Europeans by the nineteenth century, the high Arctic and remote mountainous regions gained a central place in the Western imagination. They became new places to explore. Realms of ice fasci-nated romantic poets, gothic novelists, adventure-seeking aristocrats, and the rising middle class. Popular nineteenth-century writers from Charles Dickens and Jules Verne to Edgar Allan Poe and A. Conan

Doyle, drawing mainly on the long history of British efforts to find a Northwest Passage from the Atlantic to the Pacific Ocean, adopted Arctic settings for some works. Amid scenes of icy desolation, they showed humans thrown back on their own resources in the face of a hostile or indifferent natural world. Other authors, especially poets, looked to the Alps for inspiration. The latter scene might be portrayed as sublime or even spiritual in a pantheistic way; the former inevitably was a frozen hell—at best a testing place for human fortitude, at worst a site of desperation, madness, and death. Climbers might find their god in the mountains; polar explorers rarely did in the endless expanse of arctic ice.

In popular literature, the poles and high mountains exerted a strong and sometimes fatal attraction on heroes and antiheros alike. In the opening scene of Charlotte Brontë's 1847 novel, *Jane Eyre*, for example, the young and impressionable protagonist slips into a deserted room and reads wistfully of "the vast sweep of the Arctic Zone, and those forlorn regions of dreary space,—that reservoir of frost and snow, where firm fields of ice, the accumulation of centuries of winters, glazed in Alpine heights above heights, surround the pole."[2] In an oft-quoted sentence that would resonate with polar explorers and alpine mountaineers alike, the book later commented, "It is in vain to say human beings ought to be satisfied with tranquility: they must have action; and they will make it if they cannot find it."[3] Mary Shelley begins her classic 1818 horror story, *Frankenstein*, with her infamous title character chasing his monstrous creation across the arctic ice toward their doom at the North Pole. In *Persuasion*, Jane Austen depicts a polar explorer's homebound wife yearning to follow her husband to the Arctic. First-person narratives penned by returning Arctic explorers and extreme mountaineers sold as well as any novel during the Victorian era. They invariably related tales of struggle and sacrifice in the face of hostile natural forces beyond the bounds of civilized norms. Not all survived, and none ever attained the pole.

Having grown up with such stories and narratives, by 1909, explorers of a new generation were better equipped than their Victorian predecessors to reach their elusive goals. The public hung on every word as a series of extreme expeditions reached for the earth's still unexplored places. Their leaders became the lions of the season and the heroes of the age. By year's end, the *London Daily News* could write in its annual review, *The Wonderful Year 1909*, "Few events of the year 1909 have created more interest than the return to civilization of the explorers who, for a time, had been lost to the world in their endeavours to solve the mystery of the Polar seas."[4]

Within half a decade, however, an all-consuming world war had created new fields for glory and pathos, coupled with an altered understanding of heroism. Subsequent cultural, economic, and political developments kept the focus elsewhere for most of the twentieth century. With climate change, however, the shrinking sea ice, glaciers, and ice sheets had regained the attention of scientists, explorers, and the general public by the century's end. Private yachts and cruise ships now ply the Northwest Passage and the Antarctic coast. Mountain glaciers serve as indicators of global warming. The thinning of the Arctic sea ice opens new areas for commerce. Ice cores from the world's remaining ice sheets offer evidence of past temperature swings and testify to the remarkable rapidity of the current warming. The regions that the exploring parties of 1909 discovered, long frozen in time, are changing before our eyes, giving new meaning to the old accounts.

Conducting research in polar regions has always required collaboration, and this is true for my study of its history as well. This book especially benefited from my participation in the National Science Foundation's Antarctic Artists and Writers Program, which allowed me to go where the Antarctic explorers went, camp where they camped, and climb where they climbed. Always traveling with others, and frequently in the company of experts, through this program I saw much of what Shackleton, Mawson, and the other early visitors to the Ross Sea region saw, from the East Antarctic Ice Sheet and Ross Ice Shelf to the South Pole and summit of Mount Erebus. Extended stays at Shackleton's Cape Royds and near Scott's Hut Point and Cape Evans, where the explorers' primitive winter quarters remain intact down to their unused crates of hardtack biscuits and long-frozen meat in the larder, gave insight into how the parties lived beyond what I could hope to glean from archival research. Other trips took me to Elephant Island and the Antarctic Peninsula, the Himalayas, and the high Arctic above Norway and North America. Despite the changes of the past century, these coddled visits gave me a deep respect and appreciation for the explorers of 1909.

Many of the papers, field notes, diaries, and letters of these explorers are published. Some unpublished ones are held in public archives while others remain in private hands. For access to unpublished sources, I wish to thank the archives and archivists at Scott Polar Research Institute in Cambridge, U.K., the National Archives in College Park, Maryland, the Library of Congress in Washington, D.C., the Royal Geographical Society of London, the South Australian Museum in Adelaide, the British Library in London, the Victoria State Library in Melbourne, the National Museum of Scotland in Edinburgh, Museo Nazionale della Montagna in Turin, Byrd Polar Research Center at The Ohio State University, and members of the explorers' families. For published resources from their own collections and interlibrary loan sources, I received particular help from the UCLA, University of Richmond, University of Melbourne, and Pepperdine University libraries. Online sources now make some of these original published sources readily available from repositories around the world. Again, I owe a great debt to my editor at William Morrow/HarperCollins, Peter Hubbard.

The expeditions of 1909 at once drew on past traditions and forged new approaches. Looking back, these early twentieth-century efforts relied on human porters in Kashmir and the Karakoram, man-hauling on the Antarctic ice sheet, and sled dogs for the Arctic sea ice. None carried radios, so they remained out of contact with the outside world once they passed the reach of telegraph cables. Looking forward, they adopted new methods of organization, execution, and funding. In tackling K2, for example, the Duke of the Abruzzi set the modern standard for a supported mountaineering expedition. To reach his starting point in the far north, Peary employed a ship of advanced design and engineering. In as much a bow to a sponsor's self-serving request as to any anticipation of future means of Antarctic transport, Shackleton took along a motorcar refitted to run on ice. It did not go far.

The history of these three expeditions, overlapping in time and similar in ambition if not results, tells a shared story of struggle to reach the edges of the earth and draw them within the bounds of human experience. Peary captured their common spirit in a letter that he sent to President Theodore Roosevelt from Greenland's northernmost Inuit village in August 1908. "I have secured the necessary walrus meat, Eskimos, and dogs," the seasoned polar explorer reported. "From now on the real struggle begins, and the element of luck may play a stronger hand than experience, hard work, and most careful provision, combined. I shall do my utmost. I hope for success."[5] A restless, adventuresome spirit propelled Peary and other explorers of his day forward into 1909 and beyond. It still lives in many of the polar scientists and extreme mountaineers that I met in the course of researching and writing this book. The world of Shackleton, Peary, and the Duke of the Abruzzi is now ours, even at its outermost edges.

TO THE EDGES
OF THE EARTH

CHAPTER 1

The Aristocracy of Adventure, Circa 1909

THE YEAR 1909 BEGAN with the European and American press abuzz with rumors about a pending marriage between Prince Luigi Amedeo of Savoy, Duke of the Abruzzi, and the American Katherine Elkins. The dashing thirty-five-year-old duke, grandson of modern Italy's founding king, Victor Emmanuel II, was considered Europe's most eligible bachelor. Miss Elkins, the spirited twenty-two-year-old daughter of a wealthy coal baron who represented West Virginia in the United States Senate, was dubbed "The Belle of America." They had supposedly met at the White House in 1907 under the watchful eye of President Theodore Roosevelt, who admired the Italian aristocrat as one of the world's leading explorers, mountaineers, and yachtsmen, and esteemed Elkins as one of his daughter's closest friends. "From Rome to Washington the wires have been kept busy transmitting all the bearings of such an interesting match," the *Times* of London reported in 1908, "and the newspapers have greatly enjoyed making the fullest display of the affair."[1]

It had been love at first sight, every account agreed, but in a Romeo-and-Juliet twist relished by the media, the lovers' families stood in the way. Apparently intent on securing European alliances through royal marriages, Italy's tradition-minded king forbade the union, the press reported, even as his softhearted queen lobbied for it. "The publication of gossip about the engagement," the London newspaper noted, "has become so intolerable that [Senator] Elkins yesterday was compelled to a statement asking newspapers to cease printing dispatches and rumors on the subject."[2] At the dawn of modern celebrity journalism, with every major American city boasting multiple penny dailies in cutthroat competition for circulation as nationwide media empires were being born and broken, this plea served only to pique interest in the story. And when the senator ordered the post office to intercept and return all letters and packages from the duke to his daughter, including one reportedly containing an engagement ring, the press and public made the elder Elkins the villain. Some later accounts had it costing the ambitious senator the presidency.[3]

New York's *Evening Post* denounced the prying coverage as yellow journalism at its worst, and the *Times* of London agreed, but both reprinted the core of it, sent reporters scurrying after the latest scoop, and clearly sided with the star-crossed lovers, if for no other reason than that the union would sell papers.[4] "The mystery surrounding the Duke of the Abruzzi and Miss Elkins, so far as the marriage which an inquisitive Press is anxious to arrange between them is concerned, remains as deep as ever," the *Times* noted in late 1908.[5] "The Duke of the Abruzzi might, were he so minded, find a wife in almost any royal household in Europe," the *New York Times* added. "He has chosen to seek her in the mountains of West Virginia, and all students of his past history and the best-informed members of Washington society believe he will succeed."[6] Reports pointed toward a wedding on January 29, 1909, the duke's thirty-sixth birthday; some had him renouncing his title to marry a commoner. It was not to be.

Instead of renouncing his title or defying his king, early in 1909 the duke escaped the controversy by departing on another of the grand adventures that were the source of his fame. He would go to the Himalayas to make the first ascent of one of the world's highest mountains—the so-called Pole of Altitude. He had already participated in the second successful ascent of the Matterhorn by the snow-swept Zmutt Ridge, and in 1897, at age twenty-four, he made the first summit of 18,000-foot Mount Saint Elias, the second-highest peak in both the United States and Canada. Such were the logistical challenges of reaching and climbing the remote Mount Saint Elias that six efforts had failed before the duke's, and another one would not succeed for fifty years. Yet he had done it, along with dozens of other Alpine ascents, while serving as an active officer in the Italian navy and pursuing a spirited social life. During the year after the Mount Saint Elias climb, the duke's 89-foot yacht won more races in the European circuit than any other vessel. In 1906, he led the first expedition to scale East Africa's Ruwenzori Range, summiting each of its six 15,000- and 16,000-foot massifs. In his achievements, it surely helped that the duke had been born the son of Spain's reigning monarch and grew up as the nephew of Italy's king. Still, it took courage as well as privilege. No other European aristocrat of the era had embraced the outdoor life with such vigor and success, and among world leaders, only Roosevelt could compare.

In the public eye, however, these mountaineering exploits paled beside the duke's 1899–1900 assault on the North Pole. At the time, for popular acclaim, no extreme outdoor adventure—no "call of the wild," as novelist Jack London would term it—could compare with polar exploration, which may explain both why some began hailing the duke's new objective as "the Pole of Altitude" or "the Third Pole" and why he attempted to reach the North Pole even though his first love was mountaineering.[7] In 1909, the media could report that the duke's "trip to the Himalayas was the direct result of a rupture of his romance with Miss Katherine Elkins," but in reality it was probably the aura generated by his polar trek that had attracted her to him in the first place.[8] More than his prior climbs, his polar expedition's farthest-north claim had made him a global celebrity and object of international romantic intrigue. First ascents carried social cachet during the Gilded Age but were eclipsed by a farthest north.

OVER THE PREVIOUS HALF century, the North Pole had evolved from a geographic curiosity to an ultimate destination. Since the European discovery of America, interest in the Arctic had focused on finding a navigable northwest sea passage linking the Atlantic and Pacific oceans. This was an eminently practical goal, promising shortened trade routes between Europe and Asia. For three centuries, Britain's Royal Navy led the way north by northwest through the labyrinth of sea channels in the Canadian Arctic, but never made it all the way across due to the vicissitudes of ice, shortness of the summer season, darkness of the winter, uncertainty of the route, and limitations of sail and early steamship technology. Martin Frobisher launched this quest in the mid-1500s, with the likes of Henry Hudson, William Baffin, and others extending it into the next century. During the early nineteenth century, multiple major naval expeditions, commanded by John Ross, William Parry, and John Franklin, pushed ever farther westward, but never far enough, before ice beset them. By midcentury, following Franklin's horrific lost expedition in 1845 and the massive British effort to find it, everyone realized that a commercially viable Northwest Passage did not at that time exist.

Only then, with the rising appeal of adventure travel and increasing economic and technological means for Europeans to reach ever more remote locations, did interest in the Arctic shift from the pragmatic goal of finding a Northwest Passage to a romantic one of attaining the North Pole. Not that the notion of a North Pole was anything new. At least since the third century before Christ, when Greek mapmaker Eratosthenes laid a grid of parallels and meridians on the Pythagorean concept of a spherical earth, educated Europeans had known that a geometric point, or "pole," should mark the globe's northernmost spot. Even Eratosthenes portrayed the Arctic as a frozen realm, however, and no one seemed interested in seeking its northern limit for over two millennia. Yet something in the pristine splendor and primeval struggle depicted in the tales brought back from the Northwest Passage expeditions captured the English imagination at the dawn of the Romantic era. Arctic sea ice had become a feature of British paintings and literature by 1800.

Fittingly, a popular Romantic novel—a gothic tale of scientific hubris—first stamped the North Pole as an ultimate and potentially final destination. Mary Shelley's 1818 classic, *Frankenstein; or, the Modern Prometheus*, opened with its half-mad title character chasing his creature across the Arctic sea ice toward the North Pole, where the monster aimed to end its life. Four years later, the celebrated poet Lord Byron referred to the North Pole in his "Vision of Judgement." A flurry of literary uses followed, and the North Pole soon was fixed in the British mind. The first expedition expressly aimed at reaching it, rather than simply a Northwest Passage or Arctic discovery generally, was Parry's fourth and final one, in 1827, which resulted in spectacular failure when the floating pack ice north of Spitsbergen, which he hoped to cross with man-hauled sleds to get to the North Pole, carried his party south faster than it could march north. Thereafter, the race was on.

The North Pole was a fundamentally romantic goal promising glory to anyone who could achieve it. The winner might cash in through publishing contracts and speaking fees, as many returning Northwest Passage explorers had, and his country might gain prestige in an ever more imperialistic and nationalistic age, but no one expected a conquest of concrete value, because the North Pole was merely a point on shifting sea ice, then most reliably discerned in daylight by determining the sun's altitude at noon. Once reached, some asked, who would want to go again? Ah, but what a goal! At a time when machines were replacing men as the engines of production, and faceless bureaucrats seemed to be taking the place of principled leaders, here was an objective requiring invincible will, indefatigable drive, and indomitable courage.

The British took the lead at first but failed as miserably as they had with the Northwest Passage. In 1865, the Royal Geographical Society's Clements Markham, a veteran of the Franklin searches and explorer of Asia, Africa, and South America, set the tone by saying about the North Pole, "It is the only thing in the world that is left undone, whereby a notable mind might be made famous and fortunate."[9] Working in league with like-minded Victorians, Markham transformed the pole into an imperial obsession, culminating in the Royal Navy's British Arctic Expedition of 1875–76 commanded by Captain George Nares. "To reach the Pole is the greatest geographical achievement which can be attempted," Royal Society president Edward Sabine declared, "and I own I should grieve if it should be first accomplished by any other than an Englishman."[10] For Sabine, Markham, and their ilk, it had become a test of national character and fitness in a Darwinian age.

The plan seemed simple enough. During the summer of 1875, sail as far north as possible through the waterway separating the west coast of Greenland from the east coast of Ellesmere Island until stopped by sea ice. Here, at least in warm years, British whalers had found a sea-lane open in late summer to 82° north latitude, with the prospect of land extending farther north. Favoring the Ellesmere (or British) side, Nares's lead ship, HMS *Alert*, would anchor at the most northerly navigable point through the Arctic winter, with officers and scientists conducting scientific research as time permitted. The straight-line distance from this anchorage to the pole and back would be about 1,000 miles, or less than some Royal Navy teams had man-hauled sledges through the Canadian Arctic searching for Franklin. From this advanced position, which proved to be on Ellesmere Island's northern coast at 82°30' north latitude, a sledge party would head toward the pole with the return of daylight in early spring. At the time, no one knew how far north the land might extend. An archipelago of islands could reach to the pole.

The Franklin searchers had followed coastlines and frozen channels between nearby islands, and that was the hope again. Once Nares's expedition found that land did not extend much beyond 82° north latitude, it began man-hauling loads over desolate and often disrupted sea ice. Having described reaching the pole as "a certainty, so far as human calculation can make it so," Markham accompanied the expedition as far as Greenland, with his cousin Commander Albert Markham tapped to lead the sledge party.[11] "Never before has a Polar Expedition been so perfectly equipped, provisioned, and provided for against all conceivable perils," the *Times* of London informed its readers.[12]

And rarely had one failed so unexpectedly. Not finding land beyond roughly 82° north latitude sealed its fate, but an unwillingness to improvise made matters worse. Without the ability to cache supplies on land or follow the ice foot along coasts, Nares doubted whether Markham's sledge party could reach the pole but ordered it to try. It might have gone more than 60 net miles north if it had not traveled as a single group without support from the northernmost point of land. Because they could not lay resupply depots on sea ice, two officers and fifteen men pulled three large sledges loaded with everything they anticipated needing (including two small boats), for a drag weight of over 400 pounds per person. They did not use dogs. And unlike on the Franklin searches, which traveled on or near land where fresh game abounded, because they were heading out onto sea ice, Markham's men relied on tinned food, which became a contributing cause of scurvy.

Weather posed endless problems. Departing in early April, the party faced brutally cold temperatures at the outset. "As a rule," Markham complained, "we were assailed by an intolerable thirst, which we were unable to assuage for two reasons: first, that we could not afford sufficient fuel to condense extra water; and secondly, it was quite impossible to prevent the water in the bottles from being converted into ice."[13] In contrast to the bitter April chill, by the journey's end in June, the constant daylight and warming temperatures had made the softened ice surface virtually impassable. Between the winter darkness and the summer sea-ice melt, the Arctic provides a narrow window for polar exploration.

As Markham and his men found, even during this window, Arctic Ocean sea ice provides a poor footing for travel. It is not as smooth as the ice sheets that cover Greenland or Antarctica, which rest on solid land and have gradually accumulated from snowfall over epochs. Sea ice freezes mostly from below each winter and melts mainly from above over the summer. Some marine ice lasts for years in old floes and fields. Unlike shore ice, which is anchored to land, Arctic sea ice moves with the ocean's currents and the region's unbroken winds. These shifts create open-water channels, or "leads," where ice floes or fields split or pull apart, and pressure ridges of upturned ice where they push together. Leads can be narrow enough to sledge across, lakelike and readily circumvented, or wide and long like a river. Pressure ridges can reach 20 feet high or more and extend like a mounded wall of ice in any direction.

Both leads and pressure ridges greatly impeded Markham's advance, with his party sometimes forced to ferry across leads on small floes or cut paths through ridges with pick and shovel. Even on ice fields or large floes, deep snow sometimes forced the party to divide and relay the load. "It is a succession of standing pulls," Markham wrote of one day's work. "One, two, three, haul! and very little result." Some snowdrifts swallowed the sledges whole. "On several occasions," Markham reported, "the men found it not only easier, but they could make better progress whilst dragging the sledges, by crawling on their hands and knees, than by dragging in the more orthodox manner."[14]

Scurvy made the journey into a death march for some. The disease prostrated its first victim less than two weeks into the ten-week ordeal. From then on, some of the men were borne on sledges, increasing the drag weight and diminishing the pulling power. As more succumbed, Markham finally gave up at 83°20' north latitude, nearly 400 miles from the pole. It was farther north than anyone had gone before, but far short of expectations, and the return march became a ghastly ordeal. With spring, snow became slush, and sledges sometimes broke through the ice with sick men aboard. Finally, in early June, with fewer than half the men still in harness, the party's sole healthy member, Lieutenant Alfred Parr, sprinted ahead to the ship for help, where he found that scurvy had disabled half the crew.

By the time relief arrived on June 9, 1876, only six members of the shore party had strength enough to drag sledges, which they relayed with two men borne on each, the other survivors stumbling along on foot. For Nares, scurvy became a compelling reason to abandon the mission. "Pole impracticable," he wired from his first port of call with telegraph connection, and so it became for Britain.[15] Clements Markham and his colleagues within the Victorian exploring community would turn their faces south, to the Antarctic, where a continent with solid footing for man-hauling sledges offered better prospects for British polar discovery.

THE NARES EXPEDITION'S HARD-WON farthest-north record fell within a decade to an unlikely pair of Americans, James Lockwood and David Brainard, who had not even set out to beat it. They were part of a twenty-five-man U.S. Army Signal Corps expedition under the command of First Lieutenant Adolphus Greely, sent in 1881 to conduct weather research on northern Ellesmere Island, near to where Nares's expedition had wintered. The Signal Corps then operated the National Weather Service. Greely established his base at Fort Conger, about 50 miles south of Nares's winter anchorage on the Arctic Ocean, where his men erected a comfortable structure while the ship went south for the winter. During that first summer, while mapping the unexplored Arctic coast of Greenland that protrudes some 70 miles above the most northerly point of Ellesmere Island, Lockwood and Brainard passed a few miles beyond Albert Markham's farthest north without ever venturing onto the sea ice.

After two years of low sea-ice melt kept resupply ships from reaching Fort Conger, Greely marched his men 200 miles south in the fall of 1883 to an agreed-upon rescue site on Smith Sound. Ice blocked the American ships from even reaching that point, however. Suffering through an appalling winter in an exposed location on limited supplies, only seven men remained alive when a rescue ship reached them in June 1884. Lockwood had died two months earlier; Brainard had prayed for death. With Greely, he was among the survivors left to tell the tale. They were welcomed home as heroes, despite rumors of cannibalism.

By this time if not before, the polar north seemed as terrifying as it was alluring, which further enhanced its standing as a test of character, courage, and conviction. A succession of other expeditions had failed to reach the pole without even securing the fleeting fame of a farthest north. These included the doomed team aboard the American navy ship *Jeannette*, captained by George De Long, that sank in 1881 after being icebound for nearly two years in the Arctic Ocean north of Siberia on a fool's errand to find open water at the pole. And so Lockwood and Brainard's record held for over a decade until a remarkable Norwegian, Fridtjof Nansen, devised a novel approach to Arctic exploration that became part of the solution to reaching the pole. Massive, slow expeditions on the British model did not work. Light dashes drawing on native ways offered more promise. For his efforts, Nansen became the polar star of his generation and won international fame.

Nansen had leaped onto the world's stage in 1888 when, as a zoology graduate student and expert Nordic skier, he devised and executed a six-man crossing of the Greenland ice sheet—the first traverse of the island. Eschewing the hierarchical structure and large scale of standard Arctic expeditions, the party skied across the ice sheet towing small sleds and light equipment of Nansen's own design. And unlike the young U.S. Navy engineer Robert Peary, who had tried and failed to cross the island from west to east using native Inuit dogsledding techniques two years earlier, Nansen insisted on starting from the virtually inaccessible east coast so that there could be no turning back. "I demolish my bridges behind me," Nansen is noted for saying; "then there is no choice but to move forward." He returned to Norway a national hero. "Never keep a line of retreat," he reportedly added; "it is a wretched invention." Here was the resolute character and indomitable spirit that people valued in a polar explorer.

By 1890, Nansen had devised an even more audacious scheme for his next expedition. Based on the discovery of wreckage from the *Jeannette* on the Greenland coast, an ocean away from where the ship had been crushed in the sea ice, Nansen deduced that the Arctic ice pack must slowly rotate in response to underlying ocean currents. With a proposal that Greely dismissed as "an illogical scheme of self-destruction," Nansen secured Norwegian funding for a purpose-built, rounded-hull ship, the *Fram*, which he intentionally froze into the sea ice above eastern Siberia in fall 1893, with the intent of being carried north-by-northwest across the pole in the circulating pack.[16] The round hull would rise above rather than be crushed by the ice, Nansen reasoned. The expedition could take years, during which time Nansen and his crew would study polar currents and climate as they drifted.

The plan worked, to a point. The icebound *Fram* slowly rode northwest in a wide arc, besting the Greely expedition's farthest north in January 1895, after more than a year in the pack. Two months later, when it became clear that the arc would fall short of the pole, Nansen and one colleague, Hjalmar Johansen, set off with skis, dogsleds, and kayaks for the pole. They established a new record of 86°14' north latitude—or about 200 miles beyond the prior mark—before turning back for a death-defying sixteen-month journey home. No one could have gone farther and lived. As it was, Nansen and Johansen barely survived. After traveling for three months on skis and with dogsleds to the ice pack's southern edge and then by kayak across the open Arctic Ocean, they reached the remote western reaches of the recently discovered and still uninhabited Arctic Ocean archipelago called Franz Joseph Land. There they camped for the winter in a hut made of stones and moss, living on what they could catch or kill.

Setting out again by kayak in May 1896, Nansen and Johansen happened to encounter a British expedition to the archipelago on land a month later. "Aren't you Nansen?" the expedition's astonished leader, Frederick Jackson, asked. "Yes, I am Nansen," came the laconic reply.[17] Drifting with the circulating ice all this time, the *Fram* and its crew broke free of the pack near Spitzbergen a short time later and were reunited with Nansen and Johansen in northern Norway. Together, they sailed down Norway's coast to rising acclaim and into the capital, Christiania (now Oslo), where the king and the largest crowd ever assembled in Norway turned out to greet them. The pioneering British mountaineer Edward Whymper, the first to summit the Matterhorn and by then a world-renowned icon of Victorian manhood, proclaimed that Nansen had made "almost as great an advance as has been accomplished by all other voyages in the nineteenth century put together."[18]

RETURNING FROM HIS 1897 ascent of Mount Saint Elias, the Duke of the Abruzzi threw himself into preparing an expedition to succeed where Nansen had fallen short by reaching the North Pole. Of course, the duke admired Nansen greatly, as did all explorers and adventurers of the age, and drew heavily on Nansen's innovations in planning the expedition, including the use of Nordic skis, dogsleds, minimal equipment, and a civilian organizational structure. "I had comrades with me, rather than subordinates," the duke would say about the eleven Italians selected for the expedition and the nine Norwegians serving as the ship's officers and crew.[19] And each of them would come back singing his praises as a leader.[20] Reflecting the then-dominant gender views, as with all prior polar expeditions, every participant was male. The duke personally met with Nansen in Norway during the planning stages and traveled to Spitzbergen for Arctic training and to Siberia for sled dogs. In each of these preparatory trips, he was accompanied by his military aide and soul mate in adventure, Captain Umberto Cagni, ten years his senior, whom he had met on his first naval deployment in 1889 and who had served as his second on the Mount Saint Elias expedition.

The duke also drew on lessons from the American explorer Robert Peary, who by this time had followed up on his initial 1886 expedition to Greenland with two more to the island. In both, one in 1891–92 and another in 1893–95, Peary crossed a corner of Greenland's ice sheet from the island's northwest coast to a bay in the far northeast—journeys of over 1,000 miles by dogsled that Peary believed proved for the first time that Greenland was an island and did not extend farther northward. But at the terminus of his treks, he mistakenly reported seeing a channel and other land in the north. "It was evident that this channel marked the northern boundary of the mainland of Greenland," Peary wrote, and he added that the land beyond might offer an "Imperial Highway" to the pole—errors that fatally misled later expeditions.[21] The channel did not exist, and the land beyond was merely more of Greenland.

These two journeys by Peary, the first completed with only one other man and the second with two, each averaged about 13 miles per day (or over twice the rate of the skiing and sledding part of Nansen's polar trek). Such speed led the duke to believe that, if he traveled light like Peary but used more dogs and men, his team could sprint the 1,200 miles from the northernmost reaches of Franz Joseph Land to the pole and back in three months. This would allow the trip to be completed within the one-hundred-day sledging season between the return of daylight in late winter and the breakup of the Arctic icepack in late spring.[22]

"The plan, as thus conceived, had certainly its drawbacks," the duke readily conceded.[23] He did not know if the speeds Peary reported on the Greenland ice sheet could be duplicated on sea ice—certainly Nansen had not been able to achieve them. Nor did he know if more men and additional dogs would accelerate or slow the process. Yet it offered the prospect of achieving something grand. "The practical use of Polar expeditions has often been discussed. If only the moral advantage to be derived from these expeditions be considered, I believe that it would suffice to compensate for the sacrifice they demand," the duke wrote, in justification of an endeavor that offered little in the way of material reward, scientific purpose, or territorial gain. "As men who surmount difficulties in their daily struggles feel themselves strengthened for an encounter with still greater difficulties, so should a nation feel itself still more encouraged and urged by the success won by its sons, to persevere in striving for its greatness and prosperity."[24] Viva l'Italia!

EXECUTING THE DUKE'S PLAN, the expedition left Norway in June 1899, aboard the same ship Nansen had used for two Greenland expeditions, now refitted and rechristened the *Stella Polare* (or *Polar Star*). It steamed to Franz Joseph Land's most northerly island, Rudolph Island, where it wintered in an icebound bay at 82°47' north latitude. Damage to the ship from twisting ice forced the party to camp on shore in makeshift tents rather than sleep on board. In midwinter darkness, the duke and his men began training the dogs and learning how to drive them. "The first attempts were enough to make us despair," the duke wrote, yet it was on those dogs that all their hopes rested.[25] "Dogs are undeniably the most useful animals for man in his expeditions with sledges over the ice of the Polar Sea," the duke explained. "They have this advantage, too, that, unlike horses and reindeer, they readily eat their fellows."[26] But they are of no use if their drivers do not know how to mush them. Two days before Christmas, the duke severely frosted his left hand in a sledging accident caused by runaway dogs. This ultimately led to the amputation of parts of several fingers, putting the duke out of commission for the spring dash for the pole. Cagni would take his place as its leader while the duke remained in camp.

After one false start, the polar party set off on March 11, 1900, with ten men, four kayaks, thirteen sledges carrying about 550 pounds each, and one hundred and two dogs. According to the original plan, three of the sledges were to carry all the food for the first part of the trek and turn back at the 85th parallel with a detachment of three men. Three more sledges were to carry food for the next part and turn back at the 88th parallel with another three-man detachment. A final detachment of four men would then sprint for the pole. As it turned out, the sea ice posed relentless problems from the outset, with open leads, massive pressure ridges, and a southward drift that all but negated the party's forward progress. None of the preset goals were met.

After making only about 45 net miles in ten days, Cagni sent back the first detachment of three men. They were never seen again. Nine days later, having barely exceeded 83° north latitude, Cagni sent back the second three-man detachment. After nineteen days of heavy sledging, with the dogs having to eat other members of the pack after they ran out of dog food on the thirteenth day, one member of this detachment was able to kayak the last 6 miles of open water to the base and rescue the other two. Once the first two detachments left, and knowing that their own small party could never reach the pole due to their slow start, Cagni, with an Italian navy sailor, Simone Canepa, and two Italian mountain guides, Joseph Petigax and Alexis Fenoillet, gamely tried for the farthest north possible.

"We are alone on the immense plain, the northern boundary of which meets the sky," Cagni wrote in his diary, capturing the explorers' esprit de corps. "Behind us, the departure of our friends has severed the last link which united us to the world. . . . [Ahead,] the boundless desert seems to call upon us to perform our task, to fulfill our duty. It does not inspire us with a feeling of terror, but seems to say, 'Now, all depends on you.'"[27] They pushed on with forty-nine dogs and six sledges, carrying food enough for three weeks out and forty days back.

Their first week proved as maddening as the previous two, with four days trapped in place by a blizzard, two of modest advance amid what Cagni depicted as an "endless network of channels and pressure ridges," and only one covering more than the hoped-for average of 13 miles per day.[28] The open-water leads could be anywhere from a few inches to many hundred feet wide; Cagni estimated that some of the ice ridges reached 45 feet in height. Either could extend for miles, forcing long detours or slow crossings. In accord with the survival-of-the-fittest spirit of early twentieth-century polar exploration, from the first day they began butchering the weakest dogs to feed the rest, a duty Cagni depicted as "disagreeable but necessary."[29]

The next two weeks were a mixed bag. Some days the party raced forward over level fields of new ice and light snow; most days it dodged and weaved around leads and ridges for modest gain; and some days high winds and blinding snow kept it in camp. The rapid advances, when they occurred, exhausted the dogs. "We beat them to force them on," Cagni complained on one such occasion, "and it is very hard work, which hurts the back, to push the sledges forward every moment, because the dogs will not start when they are bid."[30] Temperatures of minus 30°C and below intensified the pain from Cagni's right forefinger, which had suffered frostbite in the same accident that had incapacitated the duke. Taking off the bandage for the first time on April 15, Cagni found the digit half putrefied. "I took away with forceps as well as I could the pus and dead flesh," he noted.[31]

Despite the obstacles, the men crossed the 84th and 85th parallels during this period and were halfway to the 86th when the third week ended and the prescribed turning point was reached. They had covered 16 miles the previous day, however, and Nansen's farthest north seemed so close. "Now, with six or seven days' marching like yesterday," Cagni urged his colleagues, "we might obtain, if not complete success, at least a very satisfactory result."[32] And so they voted to go on with reduced rations in the hope that, with lighter sledges and more experience, they could return to the base more quickly than they had come from it. "Will God abandon us just at this moment?" Cagni asked. "I am full of hope."[33]

The next three days provided near perfect sledging, with Cagni depicting the ice as "level and smooth, and later on undulating."[34] Pushing themselves and their dogs—"Never have I felt more weary," the famously indefatigable captain reported—the four Italians reached Nansen's mark at 10 P.M. on the second added day and stopped for the night to celebrate.[35] "We searched hastily in the kayak for our little flag; tied it to a bamboo pole and waved it to the cry of 'Long live Italy! Long live the King! Long live the Duke of the Abruzzi!'" Cagni reported in a passage giving voice to the glory then afforded to polar firsts and farthests. "For never shall a conquest won by sword, nor by the favors of fortune, adorn the Crown of the House of Savoy with greater lustre!"[36] They toasted their achievement with cognac: "We have conquered! We have surpassed the greatest explorer of the century!"[37]

Adding cushion to their record north, the men pushed on the next day until stopped at 6 P.M. by a broad lead, where they called a halt to their quest at 86°34' north latitude, 68° east longitude. "We have reached the end of all our fatigues," Cagni wrote on April 24, 1900.[38] Yet they still needed to make it back to the ship, which lay frozen in place some 280 miles away. And they had taken forty-five days to get from the ship to this desolate point on the sea ice but had only thirty days of full rations left for the return trip. Of course, fewer rations meant less hauling weight, yet they now had only thirty-four dogs left to pull, and these were culled frequently for dog food. Cagni's infectious optimism bordered on the irrational.

The return trip began even better than Cagni could have hoped. With generally clear weather and firm sea ice for the first two weeks, the sledges went so fast at times that the men occasionally jumped aboard just to keep pace. They covered over 20 miles some days and had crossed half the distance to the ship in the first ten. The men began guessing that they would get back by the end of May. The worst problems were medical, with snow blindness among the men and Cagni's finger reaching such a critical stage that he had to amputate the distal bone with the crude instruments available.

During the third week, however, the pack beneath them began breaking up with the spring thaw, and their troubles multiplied. Leads opened and closed around them. Pressure ridges rose and fell. Pools formed on the surface, and the snow became soggy. All this slowed their progress to a crawl and increased the work for men and dogs. "It is impossible to follow one [direction] continuously, and it is difficult to keep an exact account of all the windings and deviations which broken ice or channels force us to make," Cagni complained.[39]

Then, on May 10, when Cagni calculated their longitude, the party learned that the winds or currents had been pushing the pack westward, so that they were many miles farther from the ship than they thought and drifting still farther away. Cagni compared their plight to that of a caged squirrel running in a wheel: working hard but getting nowhere. "The difference between the ice-pack in March and that of the present time is remarkable; one might say they were the product of two absolutely different seas," he wrote on May 12, "and the ice-pack which we found to the north of the 85th degree might well be typically placed between the two."[40] Making matters worse, soon they began entering belts of upturned ice pinnacles, or "séracs," surrounded by soft, deep snow. "We find ourselves in the midst of such difficult *séracs* that we cannot advance 200 yards in an hour. We work without ceasing with the ice-axes, often carry the sledges, and are worn out and breathless by fatigue," Cagni wrote on June 7.[41] By this point, the men were alternating between slogging through ankle-deep slush and sinking waist-deep in snow, when not breaking through the thin ice altogether.

As day upon added day produced little or no progress, food and fuel became the overriding concerns. Daily rations dropped, biscuits ran out, horse-meat pemmican meant for dogs became food for men, and more dogs were killed, at first to feed other dogs but later the men too. "We sacrifice my personal friend Grasso (Fatty), because he is still worthy of his name; his flesh is plentiful and good," Cagni reported in June about a dog that Nansen had given to the expedition from among those born on the *Fram*.[42] When the fuel ran out, the men cooked by heat generated from burning sailcloth wicks in shallow tins of dog fat. No one ever managed to catch native wildlife, even though seals appeared in the open leads and bear tracks abounded. "At times it seems to me that it must all end by some catastrophe; our provision will be exhausted; we shall be unable to keep up this terrible struggle against the drift," Cagni lamented. "The terrible end of De Long, and still more that of Greely's expedition, comes to my mind with all its horrible details."[43] The men dreamed of food and what they would eat should they survive. The weather too turned against them, with persistent snow, fog, and wind.

"Our future is as dark as the atmosphere," Cagni observed in June.[44]

Slowly, however, the party made progress against the drift, which carried them southwest of their destination so that they ultimately had to aim for parts of Franz Joseph Land below Rudolph Island and work their way north over the shore ice and intervening channels to the base. One by one the men discarded their sledges as they consumed or cast off their supplies and ate their dogs until they had only two half-loaded sledges and seven dogs by the end. Their kayaks being useless by this time because of leaks, when they could not go around leads or channels they waited until they closed or ferried across on ice floes, once raising a kayak's sail on a floe to speed the crossing. Often the party had to backtrack before obstacles or circle back to where they had been. "It drives one to despair! After toiling for so many hours we find ourselves at the same place!" Cagni exclaimed on one such occasion.[45]

Yet on June 23, more than a month after it was due and one hundred four days after it left, Cagni's party reached Rudolph Island from the south and descended a glacier into camp, to the amazement and delight of their colleagues. "Captain Cagni, Petigax, Fenoillet, and Canepa had the appearance of suffering much," the duke noted. "Their clothes were in rags."[46] Their farthest north, however, became the expedition's defining achievement and the pride of Italy.

Following the party's return, it took nearly seven weeks to make the *Stella Polare* seaworthy and free it from the shore ice with explosives. Then, ice in the main channel through the Franz Joseph Land archipelago held it up for another two weeks and threatened to trap the expedition for a second winter. Finally, on September 5, at his first stop in Norway, the duke could wire to his cousin, Italy's new king, Victor Emmanuel III: "The steadfast courage and determination manifested by the leader of the sledge operation [Cagni] and by all those who composed it, in spite of immense hardships, assured its success, and acquired fresh glory for our country, by making its flag wave at the highest latitude which has hitherto been reached."[47] Stepping ashore, he still carried his left arm and hand with the amputated fingers in a sling.

Despite his readiness to ascribe credit where credit was due, the laurels inevitably went to the duke. After all, he was the organizer and leader; he was the aristocrat; he was the known celebrity whose name could sell newspapers. "The Duke of Abruzzi, head of the artic exploring expedition on the Stella Polare, was to-day the recipient of a splendid popular tribute in Christiania," the *New York Times* reported about the ship's arrival in Norway's capital on September 11, 1900. "This evening the students organized a grand torchlight procession and the streets were thronged with cheering and singing thousands. At the official reception earlier in the day Dr. Nansen spoke, saying that the Duke of Abruzzi not only had renewed the traditions of Italy, of Marco Polo, and of Columbus, but had given the youth of all nations a noble example." No mention was made of Cagni in that or other early articles in the *Times*.[48] Reaching for the pole was a story made for the media, and the media gave its spin to it.[49] History, especially popular history, perpetuated that story. No matter where one looks, the new century's first farthest north is attributed to Prince Luigi Amedeo, Duke of the Abruzzi.[50]

POLAR EXPLOITS HAVING ESTABLISHED the duke as an international celebrity of the first order by 1900, his fame grew over the ensuing decade. He was, of course, a royal in an age of royalty with access to the seemingly limitless funds of the House of Savoy. He excelled on the European circuit at racing both yachts and motorcars even as he chalked up widely publicized first ascents in mountaineering. Further, surely aided by his stature and status but also reflecting his leadership skills, the duke rose in rank within the Italian navy and received command of first the cruiser *Liguria* and then the battleship *Regina Elena*, which he took on global goodwill tours. Darkly handsome and devilishly suave, his star-crossed love affair with America's leading debutante generated headlines in Europe and the United States. By 1909, only an assault on the Pole of Altitude and a world climbing record could add to what the duke had already achieved in exploration and extreme adventure. This became his goal.

CHAPTER 2

The Audacity of Adventure, Circa 1909

IT SHOULD HAVE BEEN a proud man's proudest time, but he stood eclipsed in the limelight and allegedly forestalled in his twelve-year quest to reach the North Pole first. In August 1909, returning from the most recent of his three grueling expeditions in search of the pole and five other trips to the Arctic, U.S. Navy engineer Robert Peary sailed south to Greenland's northernmost settlements claiming success. On arrival, he learned that a former subordinate with a spotted reputation as an explorer, Brooklyn physician Frederick Cook, claimed to have beaten him to the prize.

Before leaving on this final expedition in 1908, Peary had warned anyone who would listen not to believe Cook should he claim the pole. No one could reach it in the impromptu manner proposed by Cook, who had set off with scant preparation and two Inuit sledge drivers on an effort that, by experience, Peary knew required intricate planning and a sizable support party. Now, rather than bask in his hard-won glory, Peary steeled himself to defend his priority.

"Don't let Cook story worry you," he wired to his wife from his ship's first stop with telegraph connection to the outside world. "Have him nailed."[1] And in telegrams sent to the press from the same site, Peary promised to return with proof that Cook "has simply handed the public a gold brick."[2] Who could have guessed that "the goal of centuries," as the press then dubbed it, would be claimed twice within a span of nine days?[3] The competing claims and the resulting controversy captured the world's attention.

Peary's 1909 dash toward the pole built on his prior Arctic expeditions. Almost on a lark, he had first gone north in 1886 during a summer leave from the navy in an attempt either to cross Greenland's ice cap or to reconnoiter such an effort—before the trip, Peary suggested the former; after, the latter. Three years earlier, already renowned for leading the first transit of the Northeast Passage above Siberia, Swedish explorer Adolf Erik Nordenskiöld attempted the island's first crossing. The local Inuit (or Kalaallit, as they call themselves in Greenland) shunned the interior. Instead, for assistance, Nordenskiöld took along three native Sami from Lapland. Reading about this attempt and the attention it generated, Peary wanted to succeed where Nordenskiöld had fallen short.[4]

By this point, as his private writings make clear, Peary hungered for fame. "I don't want to live and die without accomplishing anything or without being known beyond a narrow circle of friends," he wrote to his mother shortly after moving to Washington to work first as a draftsman for the U.S. Coast and Geodetic Survey and then as a civil engineer in the navy. "I would like to acquire a name which shall be an open sesame to circles of culture and refinement anywhere, a name which would make my Mother proud."[5] An only child whose father had died when he was four, Peary was devoted to his mother, who always remained his closest confidant. Arctic exploration offered a ticket to such fame, and Peary knew it.

Upon reaching Ritenbeck on Greenland's west coast, Peary encountered the town's young Danish assistant governor, Christian Maigaard, who convinced him that he should not make the trek alone. Together, they scaled the ice cap to over 7,500 feet above sea level and, by their own reckoning, proceeded 100 miles east before turning back. Because of the crude methods that Peary and Maigaard used for calculating their longitude, coupled with their lack of a working chronometer and the long distances claimed for their daily marches, Fridtjof Nansen later questioned the accuracy of this distance.[6]

Although far short of a complete crossing, this achievement was enough to draw attention to the charismatic thirty-one-year-old navy civil engineer when he returned to Washington. He boasted of having penetrated deeper inland "than any white person," a wording that allowed him not to include the Sami with Nordenskiöld, who had gone farther.[7] "My last trip has brought my name before the world," Peary now wrote home. "Remember Mother I *must* have fame & cannot reconcile myself to years of commonplace drudgery & a name late in life when I see an opportunity to gain it now."[8] Determined to a fault, Peary planned to go back for a complete crossing but was delayed by being posted to Nicaragua to survey the route for a canal that would never be built. In 1889, upon learning that Nansen had beaten him to the crossing, Peary refocused on discovering Greenland's northern limit. While he made no mention of seeking the North Pole, Peary knew that some geographers then thought that Greenland extended north to the pole. Two expeditions ensued in rapid succession.

The first of these two North Greenland expeditions launched Peary forward as an Arctic explorer of note and pioneered the techniques that he would later use in his polar quest. He planned to have a ship deposit a small party on the northwest coast of Greenland, where it would winter with support from the local Inuit, whom Peary invariably called by the American name Eskimos. From there, beginning in the spring, he would travel by dogsled with a small party across the ice cap to Greenland's unknown northeastern corner, returning in time to join the ship in late summer for the voyage home.

Lecturing widely about this plan, Peary secured support from various East Coast scientific and geographical societies. He also tapped some of the wealthy young men who wanted to join the expedition and others who simply asked to ride up and back on the ship without wintering. Money for the expedition also came from selling advance rights for the story to publishers, which was a common practice by explorers at the time. Earlier in the century, the American explorer of Greenland Elisha Kent Kane received up to $80,000 for his book, and the Anglo-American explorer of the Congo Henry Morton Stanley made $200,000 on his. Even Nansen, Peary explained in an 1891 letter to his mother, earned $10,000 for his account of an expedition that Peary viewed as borrowing from and forestalling his own work. "Fame, money, and revenge goad me forward till sometimes I can hardly sleep lest something happen to interfere with my plans," he wrote to her. At the very least, he expected that a published account of his expedition would net considerably more than his $2,700 annual salary.[9]

This 1891–92 expedition came off much as planned except that a wayward tiller broke Peary's leg on the outbound voyage, limiting his movement for much of the autumn. Seven members of the expedition wintered near Smith Sound in a hut made of planks and boxes; nine more went along for the round-trip voyage on a grimy commercial seal-hunting ship; and two—Peary and the young Norwegian skier Eivind Astrup—made the 1,200-mile trek with dogsleds over the ice sheet to an Arctic Ocean fjord that Peary named Independence Bay. An Inuit community gathered around the hut, supplying the dogs, food, clothing, and labor needed by the explorers in return for knives, tools, and useful supplies. Three members of this expedition had lasting ties to Peary. Two became his most trusted and devoted supporters—Peary's new wife, Josephine, or "Jo," who came along as the first non-native woman on an Arctic expedition, and the valet from his Nicaragua days, Matthew Henson, who went as his "body-servant" and became the first African-American to play a major role in polar exploration. The other, the expedition's able but independent-minded physician, Frederick Cook, would become Peary's later-life nemesis.

It was from a high cliff above Independence Bay after a punishing thirty-three-day journey with Astrup that Peary said he saw the northern coast, with more distant land beyond, which would establish Greenland as an island with an archipelago to its north. The claim to have determined the insularity of Greenland and to have found further islands north of it, although later disproved—and maybe doubted at the time by its maker—made Peary famous and his expedition a success.[10] Honors flowed his way.

"Civil Engineer R. E. Peary of the U.S. Navy has shown us what can be done in the way of traveling in the interior of Greenland by an energetic and persevering explorer," the 1875–76 Nares Expedition's famed sledge-team leader Albert Markham, by then an admiral, reported to the 1895 International Geographical Congress held in London.[11] This was the sort of acclaim in the highest circles of culture and refinement that Peary craved. A claim of discovery in the uttermost parts of the earth is only as good as its maker, however. Coming from a U.S. Navy officer (even though as a civil engineer Peary was not a line officer), American geographic societies uniformly accepted it. European institutions were less sure, especially after Astrup failed to back it fully, with some reviving the doubts Nansen had raised about the distance Peary had claimed to travel across the Greenland ice sheet five years earlier.

HAVING TASTED THE FRUITS of Arctic success, Peary was determined to go back as soon as possible to follow up on his discoveries and confirm them. When he and Astrup had first reached the cliff above Independence Bay in 1891, they had nearly exhausted their supplies. They could not go farther. Now Peary wanted to return to Independence Bay and explore the land north of it, which he claimed might offer an "Imperial Highway" to the pole.

Returning from his first North Greenland expedition in September 1892, Peary had little time to organize and fund a second voyage if he wanted to depart early enough in 1893 for his wintering party to settle in by autumn for what he planned as essentially a repeat of the previous expedition with an extended trek beyond Independence Bay. He made no mention of seeking the pole aside from suggesting that the best route to it might start with his chosen course.

"My stay north will be no longer than it was before, & am not after the North Pole nor planning any work that is not entirely simple, safe & non-sensational," Peary assured his anxious mother. "I believe little Mother that it will be but a short time before you have a son more famous than Stanley."[12]

To proceed, he needed to secure leave from the navy and quickly raise money for the trip because, unlike major polar expeditions from other countries, Peary's efforts never received government funding beyond his naval appointment. His leave from the navy was granted after one of Peary's new, well-connected supporters intervened directly with the secretary of the navy. Money was more uncertain, but here too his newfound fame opened both doors and checkbooks. Exploration was then the rage; exotic hunting trips were popular among the rich; and wilderness adventure was seen as a cure for the weaknesses of modern urbanized industrial civilization that were perceived as sapping the strength of the American character.

PEARY ESTIMATED THAT HE required $80,000 for chartering a ship and buying supplies and equipment. To raise money rapidly, he turned to the lyceum circuit, which then dominated popular entertainment in America. He delivered 165 lectures in 103 days—two per day in some venues—under the auspices of James Pond's Lyceum Theater Lecture Bureau, which at the time also managed national tours by Henry Morton Stanley, Mark Twain, and Booker T. Washington.

Over the course of the winter, Peary visited most of the nation's large cities and many smaller ones, regaling audiences with tales of the Arctic from a stage set to look like an Inuit village. He wore his hooded deer- and sealskin coats, dogskin britches, and Inuit-made boots. "With various combinations of this outfit, I could keep perfectly warm and yet not get into a perspiration," Peary noted.[13] On cue, Henson would come onstage driving a sledge pulled by the five dogs that had survived the expedition. "They would wait very patiently until the time for Mr. Peary to finish," Pond later recalled, "but if he happened to speak a little longer than the usual time, the dogs would set up a howl so that he would have to finish." Those dogs and Peary's projected stereoscopic images of Greenland proved the greatest draws. "Of all the tours I ever had the pleasure of managing, none met with greater success on a short notice than this one," Pond wrote of Peary. "If he succeeds in reaching the Pole, then he will be the biggest attraction in the world."[14]

Funds for the expedition came together quickly enough for an on-time departure in July 1893, with the final amount raised by charging admission for the public to view the ship before it sailed. It carried an even larger wintering party than before—eighteen in all. Thousands of applications poured in from people wanting to participate, but some familiar faces returned. Having published a popular account of the previous expedition in time for the advance to help pay for the next one, Jo was back, six months pregnant with the Pearys' first child, who was subsequently hailed as the first "white baby" born in the high Arctic. Henson and Astrup returned as well, but Cook bowed out after Peary refused his request to publish ethnographic material on the Inuit collected during the prior trip. All the men had signed contracts agreeing not to publish before Peary, and he waited to write up his own account until after the second North Greenland expedition. Peary made no exceptions.

ON THIS EXPEDITION, HOWEVER, nothing went as well as on the prior one. The wintering party built a spacious hut not far from the previous expedition's base, and again drew Inuits alongside, but a freak wave destroyed its fuel supplies and two whaleboats. Then fierce spring blizzards, which killed dogs and disabled men, forced Peary to turn back from his trek across the ice sheet after barely going a quarter of the way to Independence Bay. With dwindling supplies and unfulfilled purpose, the strong-willed leader allowed most of the party to return with the ship as planned but stayed on himself with two volunteers—Henson and Hugh Lee—to try again for Independence Bay the next year. Peary all but forced his wife to go. To salvage what he could of the summer, Peary bribed Inuits encamped at his base to reveal the location of three nearby iron meteorites that for generations had supplied local natives with hardened metal for tools. Found to be among the largest of such meteorites, at about 300 pounds, 5,500 pounds, and 34 tons respectively, they gave Peary something of inestimable value to sponsors back home.

Despite finding the second year bleak and lonely without his wife, Peary persevered and, beginning on April 1, with Henson, Lee, and forty-three dogs, again attempted crossing the ice sheet. Failing to locate the food caches left the year before, the party pushed on with insufficient supplies as far as Independence Bay but could go no farther and made no new discoveries. Forced to eat their dogs, they returned to the base after nearly three months, with one emaciated dog trailing warily behind. For companionship over the year, Peary took a young Inuit, Allakasingwah, whom he described at the time as "just beginning to develop into a woman."[15] Without revealing their relationship, Peary published a seductively posed, full-page nude photograph of her lying on coastal rocks, captioned "Mother of the Seals (An Eskimo Legend)," in his book on the Greenland expeditions.[16]

When Peary returned to the United States in 1895 after his second failed summer, he took with him the two smaller iron meteorites and loaned them to New York's American Museum of Natural History with the understanding that the museum could later buy them. It was not much to show for two years of grueling work. Without a new geographical discovery or even returning sled dogs, Peary's ensuing lyceum talks generated less popular interest than before, but lecture agent James Pond insightfully noted, "Peary is a nineteenth-century hero, and will continue to push on because he cannot stop."[17] Pond viewed supporting Peary as an investment in the future.

WITH NOTHING MUCH LEFT in Greenland to attract an explorer of Peary's ilk, he fixed on the North Pole as his next goal. Peary had been eyeing that prize for years without committing himself to it. With Nansen's announcement of a new farthest north in 1896, however, public interest in the pole increased and new entrants joined the race to get there first. With much fanfare, Swedish aeronaut S. A. Andrée tried to fly over the pole in a hot-air balloon in 1896 and again in 1897, but failed in his first attempt and died in his second. The globetrotting American journalist Walter Wellman launched much-publicized polar quests in 1894 and 1898, but never got far. Italy's dashing Duke of the Abruzzi announced his siege on the pole in 1897. Otto Sverdrup, the captain for Nansen's polar drift, sailed the *Fram* to Greenland in 1898 on a research trip that Peary wrongly interpreted as part of a second Norwegian assault on the pole. Swedish geologist Alfred Nathorst led an expedition to Spitzbergen and beyond that same year. And Russia was trying to build an icebreaker capable of plowing its way to 90° north.

For Peary to join the contest, he would need more paid leave from the navy and hefty financial support from donors. In the meantime, he had an engineering task to complete that could help on both counts: to retrieve the third iron meteorite and place it on display with the others at New York's donor-rich American Museum of Natural History.

Because it weighed 34 tons and was located in an isolated spot over one-eighth of a mile inland from the coast, moving the meteorite to a ship for transport to New York required Peary's skills as a civil engineer as much as his resolve as an explorer. It took two trips. During the summer of 1896, Peary used hydraulic jacks and a trolley to get the stone to the beach, but a furious storm prevented him from getting it on board before the ship had to leave or risk being iced in for the winter. The next summer, he completed the task. Both trips were funded by taking along paying passengers for what Peary described as "a summer outing" to see the Arctic coasts, with hunting stops along the way.[18] "The voyage this summer will, in addition to its attractions for scientific investigation, appeal to others, as, for example, sportsmen, artists, and lovers of the novel, grand, and picturesque in nature," Peary's promotional brochure promised. "For the sportsman, the Arctic region offers some of the most magnificent game, in the shape of the polar bear and the walrus, the 'tiger' and the 'elephant' of the North."[19]

Peary used these summer excursions not only to retrieve the meteorite but to gather furs, skins, tusks, and native artifacts for sale to collectors and loan to museums. He also dug up the remains of recently deceased Inuits and transported them to the United States as anthropological specimens. On his 1897 trip, in response to a request from the museum curator Franz Boas, a renowned expert on indigenous cultures, Peary even brought back six living Inuits for ethnographic study. He promised them warm homes in a land of sunshine, but they got basement rooms in the museum. Within a year, four of them had died from disease, their bodies dissected for science and their skeletons encased at the museum. Amazingly, Peary listed two of the four by name in his book on the North Greenland expeditions—"Nooktah, my faithful hunter" and "Kessuh, or the 'Smiler'"—and asserted about all those so named, "Fortunately for them, with no possessions to excite cupidity, with a land in which no one but themselves could conquer a living, they are likely to be left in peace."[20] Both were dead and dissected before these words were published. Their only peace came in their demise, but in Inuit culture, eternal peace required a proper burial, which none of them received.

PEARY'S ACTIONS ON THE two short summer trips served his long-term purposes. After the arrival of the third meteorite, American Museum of Natural History president Morris K. Jesup launched the Peary Arctic Club, which Peary depicted as "an organization of gentlemen prominent in the highest business and social circles of New York" committed to funding his future expeditions.[21] Each of the club's fourteen founding members pledged $4,000 to support Peary's work, and dozens more contributed lesser amounts. Also in 1897, Peary received gold medals from the New York–based American Geographical Society and the Royal Geographical Society of London, both of which boasted a silk-stocking membership of gentlemen interested in exploration. And of further importance that year, Charles Moore, a socially prominent New Yorker who had served as a presidential elector for William McKinley in 1896, intervened with the new president to secure a five-year paid leave for Peary after the navy had flatly refused to grant one. All these developments, plus the successful return of the third meteorite, made 1897 a very good year for Peary.

Plunder contributed as much as discovery to raising Peary's profile with Jesup and his friends. Underscoring this point, the Peary Arctic Club's constitution listed the group's principal objectives as "to promote and encourage explorations of the Polar regions, as set forth in Lieutenant R. E. Peary's letter dated January 16, 1897, and . . . to receive and collect such objects of scientific interest or otherwise as may be obtainable through Lieutenant Peary's present expedition or other expeditions of a like nature."[22] Indeed, in return for the club's financial backing, Peary promised that all the collections from future expeditions "would be turned over to the American Museum."[23] Yet, as reflected in this ordering of club objectives, firsts and farthests were still necessary, if for no other reason than to demonstrate Peary's fitness in an age that valued vigorous manliness, as personified by the rising New York patrician-politician Theodore Roosevelt, a darling of the Natural History Museum crowd, who went west after graduating from Harvard College to toughen himself on the frontier.

Peary's January 16 letter to the Peary Arctic Club coincided with his public announcement, made on the occasion of his receipt of the American Geographical Society's gold medal, that he would contend for the pole. "Nansen has wrested from the Stars and Stripes the record of highest north which it had held for a dozen years and placed the Norwegian flag far in advance," Peary told his wealthy, nationalistic audience. "The Pole is certain to be reached soon; it is only a question of time and money and not so very much of the latter; and unless we are alert we shall be left in the rear."

Peary proposed what he called a "common-sense" plan for reaching the pole. Use a strong ship "to force a way" north along the west coast of Greenland during the first summer, collecting Inuit (or Eskimo, as he called them) families along the way. Choose a winter base as far north as possible, with forward supply depots laid from there to the northernmost point of land. Then, in the spring, "with picked dogs, the lightest possible equipment, and two of the best of the Eskimos, the dash for the Pole would be attempted." If ice conditions prevented them from reaching the pole one year, they would try again the next. He estimated the expedition's cost at $150,000.[24]

Peary closed with his pitch to society members and their guests. "There is not a man or woman here to-night whose heart would not thrill with patriotism to see the realization of this project and know that it was American money, intelligence, energy and endurance that had scaled the apex of the earth and lighted it with the American flag," he said. "And no man could . . . obtain a more royal and imperishable monument than to have his name written forever across the mysterious rocks and ice which form the setting for the spinning axis of the globe—the North Pole."[25] Peary would name the capes, bays, islands, and glaciers that he found for his donors. It was a Gilded Age offer and received a Gilded Age response. Peary got his money, with

Jesup in the lead and publisher Herbert Bridgman, financier Henry Cannon, railroad baron James J. Hill, and banker Henry Parish close behind. Many others contributed. British publishing magnate Alfred Harmsworth donated *Windward*, the steam yacht that had carried Nansen home. It headed north on July 4, 1898. The United States had declared war with Spain eleven weeks earlier, but Peary did not offer to relinquish his leave from active duty. At age forty-two, he feared this might be his last chance to bag the pole.

WITH THIS PLAN AND its execution, Peary had returned to his original approach of using a small party and native techniques to succeed where large expeditions with modern technology had failed. Over the years, his expeditions had grown ever larger with the addition of more men, paying passengers, and his wife, but in 1898 he took only two others, Henson and a doctor, Thomas Dedrick. Once the ship dropped them off, Peary would rely on Inuit support. Leaving behind his again-pregnant wife also afforded Peary freedom to pursue his relationship with Allakasingwah, who at fifteen would soon be also pregnant with a child by him.

Personal motives aside, by this time Peary sincerely believed that small and simple were best for polar exploration. "Where three men will get along in safety and comfort, six would merely exist on half rations," he now observed. "The two-man party is the ideal one; both Nansen and myself have proved this."[26] As for technology, he later added, "Sooner or later—and usually sooner—any machine will fall down in polar work, and when it does so it is simply a mass of old junk which neither man nor dog can eat."[27] Peary used dogs for transport, igloos for lodging, animal skins for clothing, and Inuits as dog-drivers, hunters, and tailors. "The traveler who goes upon the ice-cap without fur clothing does so either from ignorance or because he is reckless," he wrote.[28] Like Inuits, Peary slept in his clothes and traveled without sleeping bags or tents.

Peary's attitude toward the Inuit reflected his time and place. In line with the romantic attachment that many late nineteenth-century Americans displayed for the waning frontier and its dwindling native population, Peary believed that the Inuit, through evolution, were ideally fitted to their natural environment. "Everyone will agree with me," he wrote on the eve of his 1898 expedition, "that there are no human beings on the face of the globe better adapted to form the rank and file of an Arctic party than that little tribe, the most northerly people of the world, whose fathers and grandfathers lived in that very region." Yet note the stress on "rank and file." In line with the so-called scientific racism of the day, which envisioned a progressive evolution of peoples and cultures with Western Europeans on top, Peary depicted Inuits as "children" and their ways as "primitive." They lived near the coasts, he noted, fearing the interior and the sea ice. But due to his regular visits, Peary believed, they had come to trust him like a generous father and would follow him across the sea ice to the pole. "It is interesting to note the childish delight with which they listened, as I told them how they were each to have a 'shake-her-up' (Winchester) rifle, and were to hunt musk oxen and bear, drive dogs, and eat biscuit and pemmican with me in the distant legendary *Oomingmuk Nunami* (Musk Ox Land) of their forefathers," Peary wrote about the coming polar trek.[29]

With the pole as his goal, Peary hoped to sail 250 or more miles north of his previous bases near Smith Sound to establish winter quarters at Greely's old Fort Conger, which had been left undisturbed for two decades, or even farther north to where the Nares Expedition had wintered in 1875–76. This would put him and his supplies less than 600 miles from the pole, or about the same distance as he had twice traversed from his old bases to Independence Bay. Since Inuits rarely live north of Smith Sound, Peary had planned to pick up some families there and take them to his winter quarters. As Greely had learned to his peril, however, the ice does not clear every year beyond Smith Sound, and, due to a machinists' strike in England, Harmsworth had not delivered on his offer to refit the *Windward* with powerful engines. It was a sturdy ship, but could not break ice. The combination of poor ice conditions and an underpowered ship forced Peary to stop just north of Smith Sound at Cape D'Urville on Ellesmere Island. Confronted with the same ice conditions in the *Fram*, a ship designed to drift in rather than cut through ice, Sverdrup made his winter quarters in the Smith Sound region as well. Although at the time neither knew of the other's location, their proximity would not prove a happy coincidence for Peary, who already feared that Sverdrup wanted to beat him to the pole.

Brooding about his inability to make it as far north as planned, Peary established his winter quarters at Cape D'Urville with his ship, sixty dogs, and a house made of packing boxes. In late August, Peary, Henson, Dedrick, and their Inuit supporters began hunting game and charting the coastline. A chance meeting with Sverdrup in October heightened Peary's baseless concerns about the Norwegian's designs on the pole and added new worries that he might also want to occupy Fort Conger as a forward base. Although no record of it exists in the writings of Peary or Sverdrup, Henson later recalled a second meeting between the two in December, after which he depicts Peary as becoming obsessed with getting to Fort Conger before Sverdrup. "I can't possibly afford to lose my one chance of a northern base to a competitor," Peary reportedly cried.[30]

Whatever the cause, with a waxing quarter moon on December 20, 1898, Peary began a reckless attempt to move his supplies 250 miles north to Fort Conger. Illness had already cut the number of his dogs in half. Departing on the winter solstice meant that the sun would not return for two months and the cold would most likely get worse—Peary reported that the daily mean low temperature during the trip was minus 52°F and the lowest reading was minus 66°F.[31] Nevertheless, Peary set out with Henson, Dedrick, four Inuit sledge drivers, and the remaining thirty dogs over a largely unknown route along the rough coastal ice foot on what polar explorer and historian

Wally Herbert later described as "the most ill-conceived and badly planned journey [Peary] ever made."[32]

Peary expected the trip to take about ten days, but it extended into a seventeen-day ordeal. Even the known first half of the route, over which Peary's men had blazed the trail and prepared shelters, proved surprisingly difficult due to strong winds and heavy snow. Running four days late by this point, Peary pushed on toward Fort Conger expecting a similar route ahead. In fact, it grew much worse as the ice foot deteriorated and the moonlight waned. "Just south of Cape Defosse we ate the last of our biscuit," Peary wrote of the three-quarters point on the trek, "just north of it the last of our beans."[33] The biting wind became so numbing by the next day that, to save them, Peary left two Inuit drivers and nine dogs buried in a snow-drift. "The moon had left us entirely now, and the ice-foot was utterly impracticable," he noted a day later. "In complete darkness and over a chaos of broken and heaved-up ice, we stumbled and fell and groped for eighteen hours."[34] They killed a dog for food and left nine more behind with a broken sledge.

Finally, Peary wrote, "At midnight on January 6, we were stumbling through the dilapidated door of Fort Conger," after which he felt "a suspicious 'wooden' feeling in the right foot." On inspection, he found that both feet were frozen. "It was evident that I should lose parts or all of several toes, and be confined for some weeks."[35] The sledding season for 1899 was shot.

TWO OR THREE TOES from each foot came off with Peary's rabbitskin boot linings, Henson recalled.[36] Other reports have Dedrick cutting off all or part of seven toes with crude tools at some time over the next few days. Although Peary must have felt excruciating pain as his feet thawed and the stumps healed, every report has him bearing it like a Stoic, and one has him writing in Latin on the wall above his sickbed Seneca's famous motto "I shall find a way or make one."[37] More dogs died at Fort Conger from eating meat left over from Greely's expedition. Once some daylight returned in late February, Henson, Dedrick, the two remaining Inuits, and twelve surviving dogs carried Peary back to the ship on a sledge. Henson later recalled lashing Peary to the sledge in a sitting position and lifting him into the igloo each night.[38]

Another operation on Peary's feet followed in March, when Dedrick removed all that remained of his toes except the two little ones, from which the distal phalanges were later removed. "Just leave me enough to stand on when I get to the Pole," Peary reportedly told the doctor.[39] After Peary could walk again, it was always with a shuffle, and accounts of his future expeditions leave it unclear whether he walked alongside his sledge or rode on it. Yet when an officer from the *Fram* visited him at his ship in March 1899, it was made very clear that Peary intended "to push northward, in spite of everything."[40] The still cabin-bound explorer waved off his visitor's condolences with the admonition "You must take your chances up here, you know."[41] That was Peary: driven and indomitable, sullen when crossed, and intensely private, with a proud Yankee exterior, coldly calculating mind, and stern Stoic soul.

Peary accomplished little that year, however. He returned to Fort Conger for the remains of Greely's records and sent them south with the relief ship in August—a feather in the cap for the Peary Arctic Club, he boasted—but his one attempt to push farther north stumbled on the rough ice when he attempted to cross from Ellesmere Island to Greenland. "Crippled as I was," Peary wrote, "and a mere dead weight on the sledge, I felt that the road was impracticable."[42]

Otherwise, he devoted his efforts and those of his men to preparing for another winter and a push for the pole in 1900. News of his plight and the expedition's limited achievements reached the world with the relief ship. So did a long letter from Peary to his wife making light of his lost toes—"when I come back I shall be able to wear a size shorter shoe"—and asserting about his effort to reach the pole,

"There is something beyond me, something outside of me, which impels me irresistibly to the work."[43] The relief ship brought Peary news that his wife had borne him another daughter. By the end of August, the *Windward* sailed south ahead of the relief ship, leaving Peary and his men at the Smith Sound Inuit settlement of Etah for the winter.

GIVEN HIS PHYSICAL CONDITION and his starting point at Etah, Peary led a remarkable sledge journey during the 1900 season, even though it did not end anywhere near the pole. With Henson, Dedrick, and a large party of Inuits, he first went 300 miles north to Fort Conger, near the Arctic Ocean. Then, with Henson and a small party, Peary crossed the ice to Greenland and followed its coast northeast along the route taken two decades earlier by Greely's northern party, James Lockwood and David Brainard. At the time, Peary believed that this route would lead to an archipelago north of Greenland, which he thought he had seen from the cliff above Independence Bay eight years earlier.

This effort took Peary and his party on a demanding, month-long, 250-mile passage across the rough sea ice to Greenland and then along the steep, slippery ice foot of Greenland's Arctic coast, simply to reach the point where Lockwood and Brainard had turned back. From there, Lockwood and Brainard had thought they could see Greenland's northernmost point in the distance and named it Cape Washington. By this point, after sending others back to Fort Conger, Peary was traveling with only Henson, one trusted Inuit, Ahngmalokto, three sledges, and sixteen dogs—his ideal sledging party. They pushed on along the unknown coast, still hoping for the pole.

Upon rounding Cape Washington a day later, Peary was happy to see the coastline still turning northeast. "I knew now that Cape Washington was not the northern point of Greenland," he wrote. "It would have been a great disappointment to me, after coming so far, to find that another's eyes had forestalled mine in looking first upon the coveted northern point."[44] Three days later, Peary reached this most northerly point and named it Cape Morris K. Jesup for his chief benefactor. At 83°37' north latitude, Peary believed it was the world's northernmost land, though a small offshore islet was later found to extend beyond it. Still, at 440 miles from the pole, it was not as far north as Peary had hoped. Neither Greenland nor any islands that Peary had supposed to lie farther north offered a highway to the pole. The trip would take sledging over sea ice of the type that had bedeviled Markham, Nansen, and all other prior explorers trying to cross it.

PEARY SURELY KNEW THAT, due to the lateness in the season, his dwindling supplies, and the condition of the ice, his party could not reach the pole. Yet he had never attempted to cross oceanic pack ice and he wanted to try. It did not go well. Leaving from the cape on May 13, nearly three months after his first teams had left Etah, Peary with his two companions headed north over the pack. The next two days' marches, he wrote, "were made in thick fog, through which we groped our way northward, over broken ice and across gigantic, wave-like drifts of hard snow."[45] The ensuing day brought a "frightful" mix of old floes, steep pressure ridges, open-water leads, and finally a large floe bounded by water. "A reconnaissance from the summit of a pinnacle of the flow," Peary wrote, "showed that we were on the edge of the disintegrated pack"—reason enough to turn back after having gone under 25 miles.[46] If this was the route to the pole, it would be tougher than anything Peary had ever faced. Although Peary did not know it, the Duke of the Abruzzi's polar party was struggling back over the deteriorating pack at exactly the same time as his own small group and having even more trouble.

Once regaining the land, rather than head back west, Peary led his party east for three days along the coast as it turned southward.

He hoped to reach the mouth of Independence Bay and thereby close the circle on his Greenland discoveries. His party did not make it that far, but on the last day Peary claimed to see from the north a mountain that he had first seen from the south on his 1895 trek to Independence Bay. Apparently, this was enough to close the circle, for at that point the party headed back the way it had come to Fort Conger, arriving nineteen days later.[47] Explorers and geographers have hailed this 800-mile trek as one of Peary's most worthwhile journeys.[48]

Having reached Fort Conger on June 10, 1900, Peary settled in with his entire expeditionary party for what became the least productive year of his time in the Arctic. On his orders, the Inuits that he had led there had demolished Greely's single large building and used the wood to build three separate huts. Living off the land, with abundant game to eat and furs to repair or replace their clothing and equipment, everyone stayed through the summer and following winter, with Peary having a private hut.

The next spring, Peary's only attempt to attain his stated goal of getting to the pole was a feeble march 40 miles north with Henson and Ahngmalokto that did not even reach the Arctic coast. I "do all I can without being rash," Peary wrote to his wife before departing on this dispirited trek. "I have no rose colored hopes. Am going about the job in a very prosaic manner."[49] Perhaps his memories of the frightful pack ice from the year before had knocked the poetry out of him—but what is an explorer without poetry? At some point over that difficult year, relations broke down between Peary and Dedrick, apparently over matters of loyalty, respect, and a doctor's place in the expedition's hierarchy. They never reconciled, and their former cordial relations soured into a deep distrust and animosity that neither man ever fully explained.

In late April 1901, Peary and his party finally headed south to Etah. Among the last letters that he wrote from Fort Conger was a long one to his wife, grieving that he had to stay away from her and his "babies" for too long without much to show for it. "A great slice out of our lives," he lamented, "and for what, a little fame."[50] Then, from Inuits that he met on his way south, Peary learned that his wife, Jo, and daughter, Marie, had arrived during the prior summer on the *Windward*'s relief voyage and been trapped by the ice in Smith Sound through the winter. These Inuits brought him letters from Jo informing him that a second daughter—born after his departure— had died soon after birth. "Oh, my husband, I wanted you, how much you will never know," at that time of our loss, Jo wrote. "Part of me is in the little grave."[51] Had he known, Peary could have been with her over the winter. She had spent it instead with Allakasingwah and her son, Anaukak, who was born about when the Pearys' second daughter died, and whose blue eyes and red hair proclaimed his parentage. Deeply hurt but never lacking courage, Jo still wrote in her latest-dated letter, "Come home and let Marie and me love you."[52]

After a layover at Cape D'Urville, perhaps to steel himself for the reunion, Peary returned to his family at Smith Sound on May 6, his forty-fifth birthday, determined not to yield to any entreaties that he go home. He had one more year of paid leave and, despite everything, wanted to make another push for the pole. Having received no word from the *Windward*, the Arctic Club had sent a second relief ship, the *Erik*, north in 1901 with news that Peary's mother had died. The ship carried Peary's former expedition physician, Frederick Cook, who had recently returned from serving as the doctor aboard the first vessel to winter in the Antarctic. Along with First Mate Roald Amundsen, Cook was credited with saving its crew from scurvy. Even after Cook conducted a physical examination of Peary and found him unfit to continue due to deep-seated anemia, signs of scurvy, loss of leg muscle (perhaps simply a gibe about his riding on sledges), and the amputation of eight toes, Peary refused to leave. "You are through as a traveler on foot on ice," Cook recalled telling him, to no avail.[53] After yet another winter, with the aid of Henson and the local Inuits, Peary would try again for the pole. So Jo, Marie,

The Duke of the Abruzzi, on a 1910 Hassan cigarette card from its World's Greatest Explorers series.

The duke climbing in Africa's Ruwenzori Range, 1906.

Popular accounts of the return of the duke's 1900 Arctic expedition, which set a new farthest-north record, and his 1906 Ruwenzori expedition, which claimed several first ascents in Africa.

The duke lecturing on the Ruwenzori expedition to the Royal Geographical Society in London with King Edward VII in attendance, 1907.

The duke's first encounter with American socialite Katherine Elkins, from an Italian magazine, 1908.

The duke's K2 expedition crossing a bridge over the Punmah River in Baltistan, 1909.

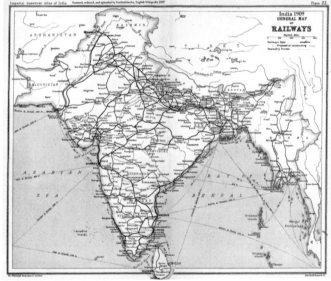

A railroad map of India in 1909, when the duke traveled by rail from Mumbai (Bombay) to Rawalpindi.

The K2 expedition crossing Zoji La on the way to the Karakoram, 1909.

The Upper Baltoro Glacier from the east, showing lines of glacial ice and debris, 1909.

The south face of K2 from the Godwin-Austen Glacier with the Abruzzi Ridge (or Spur) on the right, 1909.

The west face of K2 from the Savoia Glacier in one of Vittorio Sella's best-known Karakoram photographs, 1909.

The Duke of the Abruzzi's classic photograph of K2's east face from
Staircase Ridge, 1909.

Climbing Chogolisa toward setting a world altitude record, 1909.

The east face of 25,000-foot-high Chogolisa with the duke's route around on the left, 1909.

The view east from the Concordia basin with lines of glacial ice and debris, 1909.

LA TRIBUNA

ABBONAMENTI

Nel Regno, anno L. 5 — All'Estero Fr. 7.50
Il numero Cent. 10 — Arretrato Cent. 20
Si pubblica una volta la settimana — Dir. e Am. Via Milano, 37 - Telefono 27-25
Non si restituiscono i manoscritti

illustrata

Le inserzioni a pagamento si ricevono esclusivamente dalla Ditta Hassenstein e Vogler: Roma, Piazza S. Silvestro, 74, Bologna, Firenze, Genova, Milano, Napoli, Palermo, Torino, Venezia. - *Prezzo per ogni linea corpo 6, in 3ª pagina (3 colonne) L. 3, nelle altre pagine d'annunzi (1 colonna) L. 1,50*

N. 34 - Anno XVII   Roma - Domenica 22 agosto 1909   Anno XVII - N. 34

Il Duca degli Abruzzi raggiunge la vetta di Godvin Haustin nell' Himalaja

(*Disegno di M. Scagliarini*)

A popular account of the return of the duke's 1909 K2 expedition.

Author's photograph of a combination sledge and kayak used on the Duke of the Abruzzi's 1899–1900 polar expedition on display in a popular museum in Turin, Italy, celebrating the duke's many adventures.

Cook, and both ships sailed south that summer of 1901 while Peary and Henson stayed behind with some Inuits at a camp across Smith Sound from Etah, waiting for another spring—for another shot at glory. Dedrick remained as well, but in Etah, since Peary now refused his medical services even when illness broke out among the Inuits at his camp, killing seven.

UNLIKE THE PRIOR YEAR, Peary's 1902 trek was a full-throttle effort much like the one in 1900 except that it focused squarely on reaching the pole. Again Peary took a full party north to Fort Conger, and then a smaller one on to the Arctic Ocean. Upon reaching it, he turned northwest to follow the Ellesmere Island coast past Nares's old winter anchorage to Cape Hecla at 82°54' north latitude. From there, after already covering 400 miles in a month, his party headed onto the pack. "As the sledges plunged down from the icefoot," Peary wrote, "the dogs wallowed belly deep in the snow, and we began our struggle due northward."[54] It was the same route that Markham's 1876 sledge party had taken, but this time using dogs. In reality, however, Peary had as little chance of success as Markham had, because both of their expeditions were outfitted for their polar sledge parties to follow the ice foot along coasts rather than to cross open-ocean sea ice. Markham had hoped for islands north of Ellesmere; Peary for ones north of Greenland. Neither existed. It was over 400 miles of oceanic ice pack to the pole. Peary's only hopes now were that the pack was more stable north of Ellesmere than Greenland and that his party was tackling it over a month earlier than in 1900. Although this year Peary knew what to expect, that made little difference because he had to work with the same or similar men, supplies, and equipment.

On April 6, 1902, Peary, Henson, and four Inuits started across the sea ice. "Through the irregularities of this we struggled," Peary wrote of April 7, "now treading down snow round a sledge to dig it out of a hole into which it had sunk, now lifting the sledges bodily over a barrier of blocks; veering right and left; doubling in our track; roadmaking with snowshoe and pickaxe."[55] When they were able to travel, they covered about 5 miles per day compared with Peary's experience of 10 to 15 miles a day on glaciated or ice-covered land. On some days, storms kept them from moving at all.

After a week of start-and-stop travel the party reached the so-called Big Lead, or "Grand Canal," as Peary named it, where sea ice more or less attached to the coast grinds against the deep-water ice pack that circulates with the currents, winds, and tides.[56] The intersection often creates a wide, dark channel of frigid open water that can close rapidly should the two sides move together. Peary found it open, and sent back two more Inuits while waiting for it to close. When the Big Lead finally began narrowing on April 14 and the party dashed across it on moving fragments of ice, the far side proved worse for sledging than the near. A series of steep, parallel pressure ridges led to a sea of heavy, snow-covered old floes drifting slowly eastward amid a network of cracks, ditches, and open-water leads. "Frequently we were obliged to wait for the pieces to crush close enough together to let us pass from one to the others," Peary wrote.[57] Fog and storms delayed them further, reducing their net northward progress to a crawl.

"The game is off," Peary wrote in his diary for April 21. "My dream of sixteen years is ended." The party had reached a seemingly endless region of virtually impassable icy rubble and deep snow. "I have made the best fight," Peary added. "But I cannot accomplish the impossible."[58] Having reached 84°17' north latitude, they had covered less than 100 miles in fifteen days. It produced a new farthest north for the polar sector above North America, but fell 2 degrees of latitude short of marks set north of Europe by Nansen in 1895 and the Italians in 1900. Peary considered it a failure and headed for home.

"I think of 4 years ago when in spite of the set back of not getting my ship farther north, I looked full of life & hope & anticipation at this same shore mellow in the August sunlight, and dreamed of what I should accomplish," he wrote in a late May diary entry. "Now a maimed old man, unsuccessful after the most arduous work, away from wife and child, Mother dead, one baby dead. Has the game been worth the candle? And yet I could not have done otherwise than stick to it."[59]

The *Windward* arrived at Smith Sound in August 1902, to retrieve Peary. His wife and daughter were aboard to comfort him. They thought he would retire now, perhaps to the property he owned on Eagle Island, Maine.

By the end of the voyage, however, Peary's own resolve had revived him. "In spite of the amount of work which has been done in the north polar regions during the past few years, the work is not complete," he proclaimed in a lecture to the National Geographic Society upon his return to New York. "And the head of the Smith Sound 'gateway to the pole' is the central point from which to close this work . . . and the point from which the pole itself can and will be reached."[60]

The results of the Duke of the Abruzzi's expedition, which Peary learned of on his return, emboldened him. No earlier expedition had traveled so far as the duke's over the polar ice pack on foot, skis, or sledges—even Nansen had set his record by starting his trek from an icebound ship that, when he left it, was already farther north than anyone had ever been before. If a party of sailors and officers with no prior polar experience could travel nearly 300 miles north across the Arctic ice pack, then someone would surely reach the pole, and do so soon. Peary blamed his own failure on having started so far south due to an underpowered ship.

"The man who has the proper party, the proper equipment, and the proper experience, and can start fresh from the northern coast of [Ellesmere Island's] Grinnell Land with the earliest return of light in February," Peary told the Geographic Society, "will hold within his grasp the last great geographical prize that the earth has to offer, a prize that will rank with the prize which Columbus won; and will win for himself and his countrymen a fame that will last as long as human life exists." Of all the world's explorers, only Peary fit this description. He had already asked Jesup and the Peary Arctic Club to back him for one more grab at the brass ring. If anyone missed his meaning, Peary closed his lecture with a patriotic flourish aimed at Nansen, Sverdrup, the Duke of the Abruzzi, and other European challengers in what he now openly called a "race": "It should and must be won by American dollars, American energy, and American ability."[61] Peary was that American.

Two years earlier, drawing on the opinions of those who knew him best, a *New York Times* article on Peary reported, "Though his maimed feet form a decided handicap . . . he has shown such extraordinary energy and resolution in past journeys that he will overcome physical disabilities in the present instance, and make his way to the pole, even if he has to be hauled there on a sledge and at the last by the hands of his Eskimo servitors."[62] Toughened by adversity and driven by ambition, at forty-six Peary had not fundamentally changed from the fatherless child who wanted fame above all. And after six further years of struggles and setbacks, he would only be harder and more resolute by age fifty-two, when early in 1909 he set off on his final dash toward his elusive goal. In their efforts to reach a pole, if the Duke of the Abruzzi made manifest the aristocracy of adventure, then Peary personified its audacity. Others would show its allure.

CHAPTER 3

The Allure of Adventure, Circa 1909

AUSTRALIA HAD NEVER EXPERIENCED anything quite like the smooth-talking, high-energy, adventure-seeking Ernest Shackleton as he barnstormed across the island continent's southern coast during December 1907, raising funds and stirring interest on his way toward his planned 1909 march on the South Pole. He had started in London with a royal send-off by the king and carried the queen's flag to hoist at the pole, but Australia lay directly on his route south, and, short of money, he made the most of it. In a popular idiom from the era, the Anglo-Irish Shackleton "could sell ice to the Eskimos." He found a fertile market in Australia.

During the second half of the nineteenth century, Sydney, Melbourne, and Adelaide had expanded from obscure British outposts to brash commercial centers through mining. By the first decade of the twentieth century, the six Anglo-Australian colonies had federated into an independent dominion within the British Empire. With new mineral discoveries slowing, Australians were beginning to look offshore for further growth. Antarctica might provide that opportunity, Shackleton offered. Surely, it promised the prestige of discovery and the possibility of adventure. These arguments had been made before in Australia, most notably by the Australian Antarctic Exploring Committee, a group of Melbourne-based scientists interested in establishing research stations on the southern continent, but few Australians had listened. Due to his infectious intensity, Shackleton evoked a different response.

"Probably the Sydney Town Hall has never seen a bigger lantern lecture than delivered by Lieutenant Shackleton last night," the *Sydney Morning Herald* reported on December 7. "The lecturer's style throughout was discursive, colloquial, and breezy, departing entirely from the formal stereotyped lines which render dull so many discourses of the kind."[1] He began by speaking in modest yet self-assured terms about his experiences on a 1901–04 British National Antarctic expedition when he joined its young captain, Robert Scott, on a death-defying march toward the South Pole that, while setting a new farthest-south record, fell far short of its goal.

After relating the story of his past Antarctic exploits and disarming the audience with what one journalist described as his "happy way of relieving his more serious remarks with amusing anecdote," Shackleton turned to his future plans.[2] An overflow crowd some four thousand strong alternately laughed and cheered as Shackleton described his team—"the leader was after all only one unit in the game," he modestly observed[3]—and his equipment, including an Arrol-Johnston automobile supplied by a sponsor and modified to drive on ice.

While plainly declaring his intention to reach the pole, he never bragged or boasted. He simply vowed to do his best and left his rapt listeners to conclude that his best would be good enough.[4] "Those who had the pleasure of hearing and seeing Lieutenant Shackleton were soon convinced that if anyone could get to the Pole he would do so," the *Morning Herald* wrote.[5] Various newspaper reports spoke of his manifest humility, quiet humor, and sterling worth. One bestowed the apparent double compliment that Shackleton "sounded like an

Irishman, but he is really a Yorkshire man."[6] In fact, Shackleton was the former by birth and the latter by blood, and the English (wherever they then lived) cared more about blood. Several of these early articles from Australia observed what later biographers would stress: "He was a born leader of men."[7]

Shackleton delivered a similar talk in Melbourne and a shorter one in Adelaide over the course of a whirlwind week. "My main object is if possible the attainment of the Pole," he observed in Adelaide, "but there is a wide need for scientific research independent of that."[8] And he stressed the value of all this science for Australia: meteorological studies could explain hemispheric weather patterns, magnetic research would aid navigation in the Southern Ocean, and geological exploration might find gold. "Financially, this trip might be very easily justified," Shackleton assured his listeners in Melbourne. "The whole cost might be saved in the next few years by a correction in the variation of the magnetic pole."[9] Without government support from Britain, he had sailed on promises from private backers that had been only partly fulfilled due to a bank panic, Shackleton said. Now he needed £5,000 more to meet expenses, and asked the Australians to help. "[I myself] saw some 60 millionaires [in Britain], and impressed on them not only the value of the expedition, but the need to maintain national prestige, and they had turned a deaf ear," Shackleton explained to sympathetic Australians. "[I look] to this active growing country to help in a work that would go down in posterity as one of value to the world."[10]

Shackleton knew how to stir a crowd and play on passions. He repeatedly charged that other countries were plotting to reach the South Pole first and claimed that no other British effort was afoot, even though by then he knew that his former expedition leader, Scott, was planning one with the Royal Geographical Society's full support. At every turn he waved the Union Jack that the queen had given him to plant at the pole. "The Commonwealth was part of the backbone of the Empire," Shackleton proclaimed, and Australians would surely express their "enthusiasm for the glory of the Empire."[11] He was sailing for the empire, he now declared, not merely for England.

In line with his imperialistic tone, Shackleton invited Australia's leading geologist, University of Sydney professor T. W. Edgeworth David, and one of David's former students, University of Adelaide lecturer Douglas Mawson, to join the expedition's science staff. None proved more indispensable to the expedition's success than David and Mawson. Such was the allure of polar exploration that nearly five hundred persons had applied to go, despite the prospect of small wages, a hazardous journey, bitter cold, and long months of complete darkness.[12] In picking the fifty-year-old David, Shackleton noted, "I understand he is a man well capable of 'roughing it.'"[13] In recommending the twenty-five-year-old Mawson, David described him as "a most indefatigable person."[14]

Drawn to adventure, both David and Mawson had joined multiple trips to the Australian bush and one expedition each to the South Pacific. And each jumped at Shackleton's offer, which David, an elected Fellow of the Royal Society of London and holder of many other honors, called "one of the greatest compliments" of his life.[15] For his part, while in Australia, Shackleton gave as his own motive, "The fact of having been in the Antarctic Circle once always makes one want to go again."[16] Australians should appreciate this attitude, he noted. "If people had always gone for commercial good, Australia would never have been discovered, for that result was due to the spirit of adventure."[17] This spirit now drew David and Mawson from secure university posts to experiences that far surpassed their greatest hopes and worst fears, and made them national heroes.

David in turn seconded Shackleton's plea for funds in public letters that promised mineral wealth to a nation built on it, with a notable portion of this wealth attributable to David's prior geological fieldwork. "He quite believed there were goldfields in the Antarctic," one newspaper assured readers about David, and was certain "that miners would risk the rigours of the Antarctic" to work them.[18] Funds flowed in, first from individuals and then from the government, with the opposition leader supporting the request with the words: "If Professor David says he wants it, that ends it."[19]

By the time Shackleton left Australia in December 1907, he had collected enough money not only to proceed but also to expand his operations. His small ship, the *Nimrod*, headed for Antarctica's little-known Ross Sea coast, some 3,000 miles south-southeast of Sydney, which was the closest any ship could sail to the South Pole. Fourteen men would winter with Shackleton in a small hut on that coast in 1908 and venture forth from there in the spring, half of them headed to a pole. By then, it would be 1909.

ONLY A DECADE EARLIER, virtually no one knew anything about this sector of Antarctica except what James Clark Ross's 1839–42 expedition had discovered. During the late 1770s, blocked from reaching it by floating ice that he thought extended indefinitely southward, British explorer James Cook had looked in vain for the large landmass supposed by some to exist at the bottom of the earth. Yet by the 1820s, in their relentless search for new sources of supply after depleting old ones, whalers from Europe and America began encountering bits of land in Antarctic waters below South America, half a continent away from the Ross Sea. The whaling activity coupled with growing use of the deep southern sea-lanes of the so-called Roaring Forties and Furious Fifties led France, Britain, and the United States to dispatch navy expeditions to Antarctic waters in the late 1830s.

Among other tasks, all three of these expeditions sought to improve navigation in the Southern Ocean by charting the lines of terrestrial magnetic attraction in the deep south and locating the south magnetic pole. This drew them away from the whaling grounds around the Antarctic Peninsula to the region south of Australia, where the magnetic pole lies. As all navigators knew, compass needles do not point to the geographic poles but rather toward (though not necessarily directly at) the magnetic poles. Navigation by compass requires knowing the variation between the two northern and two southern poles, and thus the location of the magnetic ones.

Of these three expeditions, only Ross's British one aboard the HMS *Erebus* and the HMS *Terror*, two heavily built wooden naval vessels built to carry mortars but refitted to withstand ice, managed to sail through the belt of sea ice that had blocked Cook. To Ross's delight, his expedition discovered that the pack gave way south of Australia to water that was ice-free in summer. Entering it from the north, Ross found a vast open sea bounded on the west by a mountainous land that he named Victoria Land for his queen and on the south by a sheer wall, or "barrier," of glacial ice that rose vertically 200 feet out of the water, extended for 500 miles from west to east, and fronted an ice shelf. Far in the distance, Ross spied land to the east, giving three sides to what became known as the Ross Sea. Almost as striking as the Great Ice Barrier, which Ross called one of the world's wonders, he reported sighting two towering volcanos—one of them steaming—rising from an island at the barrier's western end, just across a bay or sound from the Victoria Land coast. He called the volcanos Erebus and Terror for his ships. Later geographers named the island and ice shelf (as well as the sea) for Ross.

In reaching the ice barrier, James Clark Ross set a new farthest-south record of 78°09' south latitude that stood for fifty-eight years, but he was barred by it from sailing any farther south. "We might with equal chance of success try to sail through the cliffs of Dover, as to penetrate such a mass," Ross declared.[20]

The magnetic pole, he determined, lay to the west, behind Victoria Land's so-called Western Mountains; the geographic pole lay south beyond the ice barrier. Ross could not reach either by ship. Indeed, sailing in wind-powered ships, he could only effect one brief landing, and it was on a rocky islet off the Victoria Land coast, which he presumptuously named Possession Island because on it he claimed possession of the entire region for the British Empire. After cruising twice along the barrier, Ross returned home to report on what he had seen. He could not gauge the ice shelf's southern extent or say if Victoria Land was part of a continent or merely a large island. No one went back for nearly six decades to settle these points. By then, popular interest in polar exploration had increased, and the Australians were positioned to play a role.

THE FIRST AUSTRALIAN TO do so was a Norwegian immigrant named Carsten Borchgrevink. Trained as a forester and inspired by his native countryman Fridtjof Nansen to seek adventure, fame, and perhaps fortune in polar exploration, by the early 1890s Borchgrevink had become a science teacher in a small mining town southwest of Sydney. His only prior record feat came in 1890, when he claimed to make the first ascent of Mount Lindesay, then thought to be the highest peak in Queensland. (It had actually been climbed at least once before.) At some point Borchgrevink heard about the work of the Australian Antarctic Exploring Committee, whose interests in a scientific expedition to Antarctica overlapped with his own. Borchgrevink also spoke about the possibility of finding mineral wealth in Antarctica's Victoria Land mountains and of the whaling, sealing, and fishing industry that could flourish in the Ross Sea. He simply could not convince anyone to back his scheme of leading an expedition there and did not have the resources to organize one independently. "It was up a steep hill I had to roll my Antarctic boulder!" he later said of these early years.[21]

Borchgrevink's initial opportunity to reach Antarctica came in 1894, after Australian-Norwegian entrepreneur Henryk Bull organized the first-ever sealing and whaling voyage to the Ross Sea. Borchgrevink tried to sign on as a scientist but was accepted as a sailor. Traveling from Melbourne aboard a steam-powered, metal-hulled Norwegian whaling ship renamed the *Antarctic* for the cruise, in 1895 Bull, Borchgrevink, and a few others briefly landed at Cape

Adare on Victoria Land's northeast coast. By virtue of having jumped off the dinghy before the rest, Borchgrevink boasted of being the first person to set foot on the Antarctic mainland. His claim was puffery. Whalers and sealers had landed on the Antarctic Peninsula for decades without knowing if it was an island or part of a continent. Further, two members of his own party said that they had disembarked at Cape Adare before him.

After returning to Australia, however, and then traveling on to the Sixth International Geographical Congress in London during the summer of 1895, Borchgrevink made the most of his boast. He was part explorer, part huckster.

Borchgrevink's timing was perfect. Before his arrival, the congress had already endorsed the importance of Antarctic exploration, particularly in the Ross Sea sector. Steam-powered ships made it feasible, one delegate observed, and who knew what might be found there? Some suggested that the land was prowled by polar bears; others said there could be plants or perhaps even a native people long cut off by ice from the rest of humanity. Supposing that Antarctica once had a warm climate, several delegates predicted that ancient fossils of foundational species would be discovered. "The key to the future knowledge of terrestrial magnetism lies in the determination of the exact position of the south magnetic pole," added former Royal Society president Joseph Hooker, the last surviving member of Ross's expedition.[22] Borchgrevink would never address a readier audience. His surprise appearance and bold assertions electrified the congress.

"Having spent thirty-eight days working through the ice-pack" south of Australia, Borchgrevink reported about his recent journey, the *Antarctic* reentered open waters and made for Cape Adare. "From there we saw the coast of Victoria Land to the west and south as far as the eye could reach, rising from dark bare rocks into peaks of perpetual ice and snow 12,000 feet above the sea-level." They were the first to do so since Ross's day. Cape Adare, Borchgrevink stated, protected a sheltered bay, featured a penguin colony, and offered a gradual incline rising into the interior beyond the coastal mountains, though he had no conception of what might lie there. "I strongly recommend a future scientific expedition to choose this spot as a centre for operations," he advised the congress. "I myself am willing to be the leader."[23] Following his address, the congress unanimously resolved that "the exploration of the Antarctic Regions . . . is the greatest piece of geographic exploration still to be undertaken" and urged "the various scientific societies of the world" to take up this work in earnest.[24]

A burst of Antarctic activity ensued. An official Belgian expedition sailed to the Antarctic Peninsula in 1897 for a planned summer of coastal mapping, with the American Frederick Cook serving as its physician and the Norwegian Roald Amundsen, on board for his inaugural polar venture, as first mate. Their party became the first one to overwinter south of the Antarctic Circle when the ship became trapped in the sea ice for thirteen months. Unprepared for the ordeal, scurvy and madness reigned until Cook and Amundsen wrested temporary control from the stricken captain, Adrien de Gerlache.

Britain, Germany, and Sweden began planning separate but coordinated expeditions to the little-known continent. Each expedition was charged with sailing to a particular quadrant of Antarctica's circular coastline late in 1901 to take synchronized magnetic and meteorological readings through the entire year of 1902 before returning north early in 1903. Further, each planned on conducting independent biological and geological research of scientific and commercial value. Organizers of the British expedition, particularly the polar-minded and record-obsessed Clements Markham (who still reigned over the Royal Geographical Society with an iron fist), also contemplated sending men on dashes toward the geographic and magnetic poles should conditions allow. With this contingency in mind, the British opted for the Ross Sea quadrant and commissioned a purpose-built research ship, the *Discovery*, under Commander Robert Falcon Scott and with Sub-Lieutenant Ernest Shackleton as third officer. Although not part of the coordinated international effort, expeditions from Scotland and France also prepared to sail for the Antarctic early in the new century.

THIS SNOWBALLING ANTARCTIC ACTIVITY threatened to sideline Borchgrevink and the Australians, until 1898, when London media mogul George Newnes agreed to foot the bill for a preemptive strike in return for exclusive newspaper, magazine, and book rights to the story. This left little time for planning and preparation, but neither meant much to the impulsive Newnes and overeager Borchgrevink.

At the time, articles about celebrated explorers and their thrilling exploits were a mainstay of popular journalism. David Livingstone's spine-tingling account of his first missionary journey to parts of Africa never before visited by Europeans became one of the best-selling books of the nineteenth century, for example. Moreover, when *New York Herald* publisher James Gordon Bennett Jr. sent reporter Henry Stanley to find Livingstone in the jungle after reports of the explorer's death reached Europe and America, the newspaper's circulation surged. By funding Stanley's exploits, Bennett learned that newspapers could both make and exploit news. He followed up by underwriting the *Jeannette's* quixotic 1878 voyage in search of an open Arctic Ocean. The expedition's catastrophic conclusion after pack ice crushed the ship and sent its crew members on a death march toward Siberia resulted in news stories and feature articles that gripped the world, with the *New York Herald* inevitably being the first to report the news that it had created.

Newnes hoped for similarly popular stories from Borchgrevink's venture. After all, it was the first expedition ever planned to winter in the Antarctic. That alone should generate compelling copy, Newnes believed, but he was wrong. The expedition's unspectacular failings generated little interest among readers, who by the time Borchgrevink returned were preoccupied by the Boer War and looking ahead to Scott's much larger and better-hyped government-sponsored endeavor. Even the aid of Newnes's best editors and ghost-writers could not transform the Norwegian-born explorer's mundane achievements, petty setbacks, and stilted prose into articles or a book with much appeal. Of course, other publishers helped to spike the story.

"New Year's Day broke bright and clear with the Union Jack flying merrily at the flag-staff," Borchgrevink wrote in a typical passage, regarding the first day of 1900 at his Cape Adare base. Then he added on behalf of himself and the eight surviving members of his shore party, "We looked back with sentiments of pardonable pride on the work accomplished by us during the year just spent, feeling that as the young century was rising above the horizon like the sun after the long Arctic night, so was the light of knowledge illuminating the hidden mysteries of the last *terra incognita* on the face of the globe."[25]

Of course, that New Year's Day did not break in any normal sense for Borchgrevink. The midsummer sun had not set for weeks and therefore did not actually rise above but rather circled the horizon. Moreover, these men would not look back with much pride on a year of dissension that failed to fulfill their leader's plans and included the death of the expedition's zoologist from an intestinal disorder. Some of them actively regretted the ordeal, and most had lost faith in their leader. Beyond surviving the winter, their few successes lay ahead. Scott and Shackleton would study Borchgrevink's failings and learn from them.

By establishing his base camp at Cape Adare, Borchgrevink isolated his party on a narrow peninsula at Victoria Land's extreme northeast corner. Once his ship, the *Southern Cross*, returned to Australia for the winter, the men had little to do and virtually no place to go. Cramped quarters in a small prefabricated hut, with few tasks to occupy their attention over the four-month Antarctic night, led to frayed nerves and growing bitterness. Forgetting to unload the smoking tobacco only made the grumbling of the expedition's many nicotine-addicted members worse. In addition, where Borchgrevink had promised easy access from Cape Adare to the interior, and a short sprint by dogsled to the south magnetic pole, followed perhaps by a long trek to the south geographic pole, he found steep mountains and impassable glaciers blocking the way.

Perhaps it was simply that conditions proved harsher than expected, but no part of the *Southern Cross* Expedition lived up to the advance publicity for it. Zoologist Nicolai Hanson conducted the most interesting work done at Cape Adare, but much of it was lost through improper labeling and storage after he died. Only the magnetic and meteorological data collected by Melbourne Observatory researcher Louis Bernacchi had much value to science, yet no one was more critical of Borchgrevink than Bernacchi. He damned him as an incompetent scientist and a poor leader. With few stirring achievements or thrilling adventures to relate, there simply was not much of a story worth telling about the expedition in the popular press other than the fact that nine out of ten men managed to survive in a hut on land through an Antarctic winter—the first humans to do so. Later leaders would learn that they must supply meaningful duties and engaging activities to fill the midwinter darkness, and no one would again try to base an Antarctic expedition at such an isolated place as Cape Adare.

Even Borchgrevink admitted on his return, "There was not much humour or fun in our experiences."[26] Nor was there much adventure or exploration. Simply being in the Antarctic does not guarantee a good story. It took leaders like Scott, Shackleton, and Mawson to make it an exciting and meaningful venture.

Borchgrevink's most noted success occurred after the *Southern Cross* picked up the party at Cape Adare for the second summer and briefly sailed south and then east along James Clark Ross's fabled ice barrier. Near the curved barrier's southernmost point, Borchgrevink found an inlet earlier observed by Ross. Here, the ice shelf's surface dropped nearly to sea level. Borchgrevink managed to disembark with two others and dash 10 miles by dogsled across it to set an anemic new farthest-south record of 78°50'.

In his expedition report, Borchgrevink rightly recognized the ice barrier as "nothing more than the northern extremity of a great ice sheet sloping northward from land near the South Pole."[27] As such, that ice sheet or shelf could offer a level route to the South Pole.

More interested in science than in records, Bernacchi feared the worst from Borchgrevink's discovery of the Ross Ice Shelf's level sledding surface. "A dash to the South Pole is not, perhaps, of very great scientific interest, but it is a goal for which most expeditions will strive," he predicted upon his return to Australia. "What is rather desired is a steady, continuous, laborious and systematic exploration of the whole Southern Region."[28] In saying this, Bernacchi displayed a deep knowledge of his fellow Australians, as well as of the British. They would go for the pole.

If his dreams of becoming a great polar explorer were not fully realized, at least Borchgrevink had more adventures than most Australian science teachers, and lived to tell the tale. Twice more, he proposed leading expeditions to the Antarctic, but nothing came of either offer. Yet speaking for himself and his men, he would write of his *Southern Cross* Expedition, "A young Antarctic day was born, and we saw a vision of many bold bands of explorers in our wake."[29] The first came quickly.

SCARCELY A YEAR AFTER the *Southern Cross* returned north, Scott's British expedition aboard the *Discovery* headed south from England to the Ross Sea region for two winters and three summers of polar exploration. It was scheduled to stop in Melbourne, but ultimately bypassed Australia for New Zealand, where added provisions were loaded and Bernacchi boarded as a last-minute replacement to serve as the expedition's physicist. To maintain the naval character of the undertaking, Scott planned for all its members to winter aboard the ship, anchored in some sheltered Antarctic cove rather than on land in the prefabricated hut that had been provided for that purpose. In contrast with Borchgrevink's bare-bones trip, the *Discovery* Expedition sailed on a state-of-the-art, purpose-built ship under orders from the Royal Navy in a venture cosponsored by the Royal Geographical Society and funded by both private donors and the British government. With Scott in charge, caution would be thrown to the winds in the pursuit of firsts and farthests. And although he chafed under Scott's military discipline, no one aboard was readier to take those risks and reap their rewards than Shackleton.

Unlike Borchgrevink, Shackleton had no deep-seated interest in Antarctica. An ambition for adventure drew him toward the pole and an addiction to the celebrity that polar exploration brought kept him going back. Seeking to escape the narrowing prospects open to him on land, as the scion of a declining middle-class family in late Victorian Britain, and hoping for adventure on the high seas, Shackleton joined the merchant marine as a cadet with officer potential. It did not prove as exciting as he hoped. Although he gained an officer's stripes, Shackleton soon was looking for an honorable way, as one of his fellow officers recalled, "Of breaking away from the monotony of method and routine" of serving as a subordinate on someone else's commercial ship. "He saw himself so slowly progressing to the command of a liner that his spirit rebelled at the thought of the best years of his life passing away in weary waiting."[30] That fellow officer further observed, "I do not think Shackleton had any preconceived inclination toward the Antarctic as a possible field for personal enterprise, but when the 'Discovery' expedition was planned he saw an outlet for the expansion of his concentrated vitality, and snatched at the opportunity for adventure."[31]

While working on a passenger ship ferrying troops to the Boer War in 1900, Shackleton befriended the South Africa–bound son of the *Discovery* Expedition's chief private benefactor, the wealthy English industrialist Llewellyn Longstaff. With the race for the North Pole intensifying and interest in Antarctica budding, Shackleton saw polar exploration as an outlet for his ambition and a means to adventure. He asked Longstaff to intervene on his behalf with the organizers of the expedition, and, although they had planned it as a strictly Royal Navy enterprise, they could scarcely refuse their benefactor's one personnel request. Shackleton became the *Discovery*'s third officer and a crew favorite. Charming, restless, and brimming with self-confidence, he won over everybody but Scott, who came to view him as a rival. Both led by example and acquired devoted followers. Even Antarctica was not big enough for both of them. Yet at first even Scott was charmed, and asked Shackleton along on the expedition's polar dash.

At the time, many geographers and glaciologists agreed with Borchgrevink that the Great Ice Barrier fronted an ice shelf that might extend to the pole. If it did, Scott reasoned, then while other expedition members were engaged in scientific work at or around the expedition's Ross Island base, a small, fast-moving sledge party conceivably could cover the 1,700-odd miles to the pole and back in the three months available during the brief Antarctic summer. At least the party could set a new farthest-south record. "It must consist of either two or three men in all and every dog we possess," Scott reportedly said about the southern party. "Our object is to get as far south in a straight line on the Barrier ice as we can, reach the Pole if possible, or find some new land, anyhow do all we can in the time and get back to the ship by the end of January."[32] The expedition's physician, Edward Wilson, joined Scott and Shackleton on the trek.

After wintering over at Ross Island, the southern party left its base on November 2, 1902, with five sledges, nineteen sled dogs, and nearly a ton of supplies, food, and instruments. Eleven days and 70 miles later, the men surpassed Borchgrevink's old farthest south.

"The announcement of that fact caused great jubilation," Scott noted in his diary.[33] Two days later he added, "We are already beyond the utmost limit to which man has attained: each footstep will be a fresh conquest of the great unknown. Confident in ourselves, confident in our equipment, and confident in our dog team, we can but feel elated with the prospect before us."[34]

Having virtually no experience on skis, driving sled dogs, or crossing an ice shelf, Scott should have felt less confident. Almost immediately, the dogs began to fail because of poor handling and tainted food. As they failed, Wilson butchered them one by one and fed them to the other dogs. None survived, leaving the three men to do the hauling. Having packed light for quick travel, they ran so low on food that they could think of little else. "Conversation runs constantly on food. We are all so hungry," Wilson noted while yet on the outbound journey.[35]

It grew much worse. Scurvy stalked them by the end, especially Shackleton. Wilson suffered extreme snow blindness as well. "I never had such pain in the eye before," he noted in his diary for the day after Christmas. "It was all I could do to lie still in my sleeping bag, dropping in cocaine from time to time."[36]

The party's route traced the Ross Ice Shelf's western edge, where it abutted the southern Victoria Land shore. No one had seen this coastline before. With magnificent mountains, inlets, and capes, it resembled the seacoast farther north, but glacial ice covered the sea, and the sea life had vanished. "We are now about ten miles from the land," Scott noted on December 19. "The lower country which we see strongly resembles the coastal land far to the north; it is a fine scene of a lofty snow-cap, whose smooth rounded outline is broken by the sharper bared peaks, or by the steep disturbing fall of some valley."[37] Glaciers had shaped the terrain into an awe-inspiring wonderland, and unlike most other places this was still a work in progress. An artist of considerable skill, Wilson captured the scene in sketches and paintings that, when later displayed, further fed popular interest in the poles.

Scott could not tell where the ice shelf ended in the south or how far the mountains extended, because, due to insufficient food, the loss of the dogs, and the sickness of all three men, his party advanced only about 300 miles south, or roughly two-fifths of the way from their base to the pole. The men reached their limit on the last day of 1902. "Observations give it as between 82.16 S. and 82.17 S.," Scott noted. "Whilst one cannot help a sense of disappointment in reflecting on the 'might have been' had our team remained in good health, one cannot but remember that even as it is we have made a greater advance toward a pole of the earth than has ever yet been achieved by a sledge party."[38] Then it was a race back on dwindling rations. First Shackleton collapsed with scurvy and either had to walk alongside the sledge or be carried on it, depending on who was telling the story. Then Wilson and Scott fell ill as well but managed to remain in harness pulling the sledge. By this time, all the dogs had perished, and the men suspected that much of their remaining food was tainted. It was touch and go by the end, with the party struggling back to their base on February 3, 1903, after some there had given them up for dead.

A gifted writer and storyteller, Scott made the most of this harrowing trek upon his return to Britain, where perseverance could matter more than success. "If we had not achieved such great results as at one time we had hoped for, we knew at least that we had striven and endured with all our might," he wrote in his account of the southern sledge journey.[39] A similar line punctuated his public lectures. These speeches and his popular book, *The Voyage of the "Discovery,"* described the expedition's other exploits as well, but Scott found the public desirous of records most of all. The polar trek supplied them in the context of an Edwardian tale of resolve in the face of adversity. The *Times* of London hailed it as the expedition's "most notable achievement."[40] Telling it in detail took up two long chapters of Scott's twenty-chapter book. Due to the weakness of his "constitution," as Scott termed it, Shackleton shouldered a disproportionate part of the blame for the party's failure.[41] "Our invalid," Scott called him in *The Voyage of the "Discovery,"* and claimed, regarding Wilson and himself, "we carried him" on the sledge for part of the way back—a claim that Shackleton vehemently denied and that Wilson never affirmed.[42] No matter what the truth of Scott's charge, Shackleton's troubles on the trek served as an early warning of the heart problems that would later kill him.

Shackleton never forgot the slight and complained bitterly when Scott sent him home on the relief ship after one year while the expedition remained south for two. Returning to Britain before the others, however, allowed Shackleton to take the spotlight alone for a season and begin planning how he could return south to try for the pole with an expedition of his own. It took five years of effort, but the 1907–09 British Antarctic Expedition to the Ross Sea on the *Nimrod*, with Edgeworth David and Douglas Mawson along from Australia, would elevate Shackleton to the first rank of polar explorers.

DAVID HAD FOLLOWED NEWS of the *Discovery* Expedition and eagerly read Scott's description of Victoria Land's glaciated Western Mountains. Although best known in Australia for fieldwork that had uncovered the South Maitland coalfields, which established the coal industry in New South Wales and brought incalculable wealth to the state, David's principal interest in geology was glaciation. As a young geologist in Britain, before immigrating to Australia in 1882 for a position with the New South Wales Geological Survey, he had used the location of erratic boulders, supposedly moved by ice floes from their place of origin, to study the extent and impact of the last ice age on the landscape of his native Wales. Once in Australia, in between his duties for the Geological Survey, David found evidence of an earlier ice age having molded a now virtually ice-free land. He extended this research after joining the University of Sydney's faculty in 1891. Soon his favorite haunt in New South Wales became the Snowy Mountains, the only place on the Australian mainland with anything like an alpine character. He frequently took his students there for field trips. One of those students, Douglas Mawson, learned to love it as well.

As the only continent still experiencing an ice age, Antarctica held a special interest for David. He volunteered to examine Antarctic rock specimens brought back by Borchgrevink in 1895, finding them similar to Australian ones. The continents were related, David surmised, except one was still ice covered. This further fed his curiosity about Antarctica, which was apparent in a letter that he sent to Scott prior to the *Discovery*'s departure from Britain, expressing support for the effort and interest in its geological work.

At that time, David thought that the University of Melbourne's new geology professor, John Walter Gregory, would serve as the *Discovery* Expedition's shore leader and chief science officer. This would have put the focus squarely on glacial geology because, while doing postgraduate work for Britain's Natural History Museum, Gregory participated in the first-ever crossing of Spitzbergen, where he studied the effects of glaciation on the terrain. He then topped this by leading an early scientific expedition to East Africa's Great Rift Valley—he gave it that name, and its major eastern branch is named for him—and the glaciated equatorial Mount Kenya—his expedition was the first to reach its glaciers, one of which is also named for him. In addition, Gregory had surveyed glaciated peaks in the Alps and Rockies. He knew the power of ice on rock firsthand, viewed Australia and Antarctica as kindred continents, and had a gift for writing popular books about his scientific findings.

By 1900, when many geographers still thought that the south polar region might consist of a large ice cap grounded on an archipelago of islands, Gregory wrote in his prospectus for the *Discovery* Expedition's science program, "There is little doubt that Antarctica is *geologically* a continent, consisting of a western plateau, composed of Achaean and sedimentary rocks like those of Australia, and of an eastern volcanic chain." Further tying the expedition's geologic work to Australian interests, Gregory proposed investigating whether Victoria Land's Western Mountains represented a southern extension of the mountains that ran along the Pacific Ocean's western rim, and whether they linked across the interior to the mountains of the Antarctic Peninsula, which he saw as an extension of the Andean range. "In that case," he wrote, "the great tectonic lines which bound the Pacific to the east and west are connected across the Antarctic area; and if that can be proved the unity of the great Pacific depression will be completely established."[43]

With this and his other research aims, Gregory offered a scientific program worthy of a great national expedition and one that could have shed new light on Australian geology. Scott, however, saw Gregory as a threat to his control of the expedition, which he would retain as the ship's captain only so long as the men were based on the ship. When the Royal Geographical Society took Scott's side by authorizing the *Discovery* to winter in the Antarctic with the men based on board, Gregory stepped aside, along with much of the scientific staff. The controversy became the talk of Britain's science community. Established researchers were reluctant to take Gregory's place. (Gregory went on to become a chair at the University of Glasgow and embarked on a succession of other expeditions. These would take him to the remotest reaches of Asia, Africa, and the Americas, and ultimately to his death, in 1932 at the age of sixty-eight, when the canoe that was carrying him to a volcanically active region of the Andes overturned in rapids on the largely uncharted Urubamba River in the Peruvian jungle.)

To fill the *Discovery* Expedition's geologist position, Scott eventually settled on twenty-two-year-old Hartley Ferrar, who had graduated with second honors in natural science from the University of Cambridge only one month earlier. It was neither an inspired nor an inspiring choice. By all accounts, Ferrar had spent more time playing sports at college than studying science. Early on, Scott privately dismissed him as a "conceited young ass."[44] Ferrar knew little about glacial geology and was not a quick study. After two largely wasted years, Ferrar salvaged something of his part in the expedition by doing some credible geologic mapping of the Western Mountains in the final summer along with bringing back a representative collection of rock specimens. Still, much remained for a glacial geologist to do in the region. When word of Shackleton's plans reached Australia, David immediately began lobbying to go along.

For his part, in addition to multiple treks into the Australian bush, by 1900 David had notched a notable overseas expedition of his own to Funafuti, a then little-known coral atoll in the South Pacific some 2,500 miles northeast of Sydney. A circular strip of land rarely more than 1,000 feet wide and barely a few feet high surrounding a lagoon roughly 10 miles across, Funafuti offered a classic site at which to test Charles Darwin's 1842 geological theory that atolls were formed by the subsidence of coral-ringed volcanic islands. As the volcano sank below the sea, Darwin reasoned, living coral built upon the remains of older coral to sustain a ring of land above the water. Of course, like Darwin's unrelated theory of evolution by natural selection, the process required vast amounts of time. After gaining favor over other scientific explanations for coral atolls, by the 1880s, Darwin's subsidence theory began meeting resistance from creationists opposed to all things Darwinian. This led his supporters within the Royal Society to propose proving Darwin's theory by drilling into a coral atoll to its supposed volcanic base. They turned to the growing Australian scientific community for help. David threw his weight behind the project.

At first for David this simply meant soliciting funds from New South Wales for an expedition mainly organized and supported from Britain. When the first attempt failed at 100 feet due to faulty drilling methods, David signed on to lead a second effort in 1897. His expertise as a geologist coupled with his experience drilling shafts for the New South Wales Geological Survey made him a perfect candidate to finish the job.

Though unmentioned at the time, David also welcomed the chance to defend science and the scientific method from religiously motivated critics. The son of a Welsh minister and a direct descendant of James Ussher, the seventeenth-century Anglican bishop best known for calculating the date of creation from the timeline provided in Genesis, David had a religious upbringing. Then, in what his authoritative biographer depicted as "a real crisis of faith" while a science student at Oxford, he rejected biblical Christianity in favor of a spiritual sense of a guiding providence.[45] With the Funafuti drilling project, he could lend support to scientific progress over religious traditionalism while leading a potentially significant and exciting expedition. "It was the duty of every man," David said in a public lecture given before his Funafuti venture, "to pursue truth, and if religion were not true man should modify it, or hold himself open to some fresh inspiration to lead him to a higher idea of what was called truth."[46] At least until Antarctica came along a decade later, Funafuti offered the opportunity of a lifetime to the forty-year-old David.

Once on the island, David threw himself into the drilling project, displaying the same traits that would mark his time on Shackleton's *Nimrod* Expedition: dogged perseverance, boundless enthusiasm, and a ready willingness to do more than his fair share of even the most menial tasks. He would persist at drilling until long after dark and begin again well before dawn. "Twed would eat ship biscuit if I were not here, and would eat that standing over his drill," his adventuresome wife, Cara, noted in her travel diary, using an acronym for David made from his four initials.[47] By jury-rigging the equipment as he went, David managed to drill down over 500 feet by the time he had to depart, with the core still showing coral. While this did not strictly prove Darwin's subsidence theory, it disproved every alternative hypothesis and won David election to the British Empire's premier scientific association, the Royal Society.

After returning from Funafuti, David resumed his work in glacial geology, leading to a breakthrough that cinched his place on the *Nimrod* Expedition. Building on the work of University of Adelaide geologist Walter Howchin, he developed and publicized evidence from South Australia of a third global ice age that had occurred eons before the two previously known ones. Howchin placed it in the Cambrian era; David thought it was Precambrian. In either case, it rocked the geological world and led to an invitation to speak at the World Geological Congress held at Mexico City in 1906—the first Australian so honored.

Stopping first in India to view glacial deposits of the second ice age and then in England to speak at the annual meeting of the British Association for the Advancement of Science, David arrived in Mexico for the congress near the end of a five-month journey around the world. There, he gave the keynote address on "Climate Changes in Geological Change." The trip secured David's standing as one of the world's foremost glacial geologists. This international recognition added luster to his well-established local reputation as a trusted and well-connected geological surveyor, scientist, and teacher. In 1907, when David asked to travel south on the *Nimrod*, the cash-strapped and status-hungry Shackleton could scarcely refuse. Indeed, he eagerly agreed.

While Shackleton cared little about science, he knew that donors and the British exploring establishment did. And when David secured a £5,000 grant for the expedition from the Australian government, on top of wresting donations from local philanthropists and the University of Sydney, Shackleton also agreed to David's request that Mawson go along too. "Shackleton himself would never have got this [financial] help," Mawson wrote about the grant; "it was David's appeal that secured it."[48] David could "charm a bird off a bough," Shackleton noted.[49] Birds of a feather in this respect, Shackleton and David took an immediate liking to each another.

ONLY TWENTY-FIVE YEARS OLD in 1907, Douglas Mawson was already fast on his way to becoming David's most accomplished student. Like David, who was then twice his age, Mawson was born in Britain, but unlike his mentor, who was educated there and always retained the willowy appearance and polite formality of a Victorian squire, Mawson was reared in New South Wales from the age of two and had the brawny look and breezy manner of a twentieth-century Australian. Both were tough, but only the tall, ruggedly handsome Mawson outwardly showed it. After hearing that David would go south with Shackleton but before learning that he could go too, Mawson, a hearty eater, was probably only half joking when he wrote to his semivegetarian former professor urging him to practice "swallowing and retaining blubber." Instead, more in line with his character, David had headed off to the Snowy Mountains to learn how to cross-country ski and build igloos. Perhaps recalling his earlier treks with David, Mawson concluded his letter, "Above all, may I be permitted to ask you to be careful in matters pertaining to your personal safety, which you always place in such light regard."[50] Mawson would learn firsthand the futility of giving such advice to David.

Notwithstanding his cautionary words to David, Mawson was not beyond risk-taking himself. Indeed, he seemed to relish such exploits more than David, for whom they seemed mostly a matter of doing his preordained duty.[51] This facet of Mawson's character developed early and never wavered. Upon his high school graduation, his headmaster reportedly said, "What shall we say of our Douglas as an acknowledged leader and organizer? This I will say—that if there be a corner of this planet of ours still unexplored, Douglas Mawson will be the organizer and leader of an expedition to unveil its secrets."[52] Late in life, Mawson reportedly affirmed, "I worship God through nature,"[53] and, for him, this nature demanded risks to worship it. Men with him would die in this quest, and twice he barely survived. For Mawson, it was never a conventional Christian faith but more an austere Stoic philosophy imbued, as it was for David, with a profound sense of providence. When leading his own Antarctic expeditions, Mawson read to his men from Marcus Aurelius's Stoic *Meditations*, which places humans squarely within the natural cosmos and gives them meaning through it. "No religion, not even Christianity, could circumscribe [Mawson's] God," his biographer observed.[54]

A top student, Mawson was embarrassed by his father's failings in business, which forced his mother to take in boarders. Driven to better himself, he entered the University of Sydney in 1899 to study mining engineering and, coming under David's sway, stayed on to earn a second degree in geology. His passion became fieldwork, with a particular interest in glacial geology, but never to the exclusion of looking for mineral deposits and mining sites. While still a student, Mawson helped to survey the iron-rich Mittagong region southwest of Sydney and later was the first to identify and describe a commercially viable uranium-bearing mineral in Australia. He named it Davidite in honor of his former professor. Soon he was also trekking in the Snowy Mountains.

In 1903, even before Mawson completed his geology degree, David recommended him to serve as the geologist for the first British scientific expedition to the New Hebrides Islands. This volcanic island group, now called Vanuatu, with mountains over 6,000 feet high, rises in the South Pacific roughly 1,600 miles northeast of Sydney. "Although the existence of the New Hebrides has been known to Europeans for 300 years," Mawson wrote in his report, "yet on account of the extreme hostility of the natives, and the prevalence in many parts of malaria of an acute type, this group long remained a *Terra Incognita*."[55] At least it suited him to see it that way.

While by 1900 Presbyterian missionaries had converted most of Vanuatu's native people to Christianity, some interior parts of the outer islands had not yet been visited by Europeans. Mawson was warned that head-hunting was still practiced in some regions, and himself wrote of the archipelago's second largest island, "The Natives of Malekula are the most uncertain of any inhabitants in the Group, having not yet abated from cannibal habits."[56] Despite the risks, he traveled widely surveying the rock strata and looking for minerals, first with armed guards but, as he grew more comfortable, alone or with local guides. He found lofty mountains that he attempted to climb, dense jungles that he crossed, and rugged countryside that he mapped. Nothing deterred him.

Once, in a particularly remote location, while he was knocking off a rock sample with a hammer, a sharp sliver struck his leg and lodged below his kneecap. As he and two guides paddled his skiff back to the survey ship for thirty-six hours without stopping, Mawson's leg became badly infected. "For Douglas each movement was agony, especially when he was rowing and had to bend his injured knee," his wife later reported. "His leg became puffed, red and then blackish up to the groin. He had all his life a stoic attitude toward pain: if nothing could be done to help, one just bore it."[57] Nearly unconscious when he reached the ship, Mawson was told that the leg should be amputated, but the infection abated after the knee was opened and drained. Two weeks later, he was back in the field. Mawson never even mentioned the incident in his field notes or diary, which simply and otherwise unaccountably jump from entries made before the accident to ones about his next excursion. As much as possible, he ignored adversity.

Mawson's New Hebrides exploits became the stuff of local lore in Sydney, at least among his classmates at the university. In those years, University of Sydney students celebrated graduation with a rowdy procession through town. "As on former occasions," a local newspaper reported about the festivities for the year that Mawson received his geology degree, "the various schools tried hard to outrival each other in grotesque make-up, in the methods of vehicular transit, and in their powers to make the most hideous noises."[58] Geology's float featured the 6-foot-3-inch-tall Mawson in Polynesian garb boiling a howling missionary in a large pot. If these accounts are accurate, then they reflected an aspect of Mawson's character that would appeal to Shackleton's lighter, sometimes ribald side. "He was a dear old chap," one of his Australian classmates said of Mawson, "serious as a rule but had a good sense of humour."[59]

By the time Shackleton reached Adelaide in 1907 on his passage to Antarctica, Mawson was living there as a university lecturer in mineralogy. David had helped him get the post. Despite being in the first year of his teaching position, Mawson asked Shackleton if he could go along. "In South Australia I was face to face with a great accumulation of glacial sediments of Pre-Cambrian age, the greatest thing of the kind recorded anywhere in the world," Mawson later explained. "So I desired to see an ice age in being."[60] By this point, however, Shackleton was inundated with applications. He gave Mawson the usual reply: no. It was only after Shackleton reached Sydney and David intervened on Mawson's behalf that a way opened. Shackleton then invited Mawson to join the expedition as its physicist, one of the few available positions. He would be responsible for astronomical, meteorological, and magnetic observations. Mawson lacked training in any of these fields, but that apparently did not bother Shackleton. It certainly did not deter Mawson, who was willing to serve the British Antarctic Expedition in any scientific capacity. Drawn by the allure of adventure and the chance to see an ice age in being, he accepted Shackleton's terms, and a polar star was born.

CHAPTER 4

The Great Game

ON DECEMBER 20, 1907, the Royal Scottish Geographical Society feted the Duke of the Abruzzi in a Glasgow ceremony that helped to launch his 1909 assault on the world's highest accessible mountain. With the thirty-four-year-old duke already a global celebrity for his multiple feats, a reception committee composed of landed aristocrats, middle-class professionals, and local officials chose to highlight his 1903 polar expedition. "The fact that your Royal Highness has penetrated nearer the North Pole than any other explorer will at all times—whether or not the final goal be ever reached—count amongst the greatest achievements ever accomplished," the society's official address to the duke declared.[1] Never mind that he was not part of the expedition party that actually set the mark, such was the enthusiasm engulfing farthest-north and -south records during the Edwardian era that a leading geographical society could depict setting one as among the greatest achievements of all time.

What could be next, those in attendance breathlessly asked the duke. What could top the North Pole? The duke was first and foremost a mountaineer, and his response was telling: an altitude record in the Himalayas, the so-called Third Pole.[2]

Just as farthest norths and souths had become the rage during the second half of the nineteenth century in Europe and America, mountaineering and first ascents of notable peaks were highly esteemed. These fashions carried over into the early twentieth century. It was part of a cult of extreme adventure linked to the wealth and leisure flowing from industrialization; a Darwinian sense of struggle against nature; and eased access to once-remote locales due to imperial conquest, steamships, railroads, and telegraphs. Accordingly, in addition to hailing his polar exploits, the Scottish Geographical Society's 1907 address to the duke expressed "unqualified admiration" for his "efforts to conquer the summit of Mount Kangchenjunga" in Asia, his "splendid achievement in scaling the peak of Mount Elias in Alaska," and his "ascent of the Ruwenzori Range" in equatorial Africa.[3] These were achievements of the age, and, while they set the duke apart from the average aristocrat in what he actually did, they were typical of what an increasing number of wealthy Europeans and Americans sought to do.

As with the duke, so too for modern sport mountaineering generally, the style was set in the European Alps and radiated out to ever more far-flung and challenging peaks. Mountain ranges in general, and the Alps in particular, typically stood as obstacles rather than objectives for travel until the dawn of the Romantic era in the late eighteenth century. Then they became sublime, and soon adventurers wanted to climb them. Earlier mountaineering manuals, if they could be called that, about the Alps were written for travelers crossing the range and thus focused on passes and ways around the steepest parts. No one reached the 15,777-foot-high summit of Mont Blanc, then considered Europe's highest peak, until 1786, but a crush of climbers followed, though only forty-five parties had made it to the top by 1850. Chamonix, the rustic, remote rural village at its base, blossomed into a tourist destination where mountain guides outnumbered working farmers. It became a popular stop on a cultured visitor's Grand Tour of the continent.

In 1787, the pioneering English mountaineer and naval architect Mark Beaufoy, aided by six guides and a servant, made the first ascent of Mont Blanc by a British climber. As customary at the time, he got the credit; they did the work. Three years later, as a twenty-year-old University of Cambridge student, the budding Romantic poet William Wordsworth joined a fellow "pilgrim," as they called themselves, on a walking tour of Europe that drew them to the place. "From a bare ridge we also first beheld / Unveiled the summit of Mont Blanc," Wordsworth later wrote in a poem titled "Cambridge and the Alps." "The wondrous Vale of Chamouny stretched far below." This scene, he observed, "was fitted to our unripe state / Of intellect and heart. With such a book / Before our eyes, we could not choose but read / Lessons of genuine brotherhood."[4] Countless British climbers, writers, artists, and travelers followed, seeking physical challenge, spiritual inspiration, and natural beauty. Their visits captured the growing appeal of mountains and mountaineering.

Responding in part to Wordsworth, Samuel Taylor Coleridge published "Hymn before Sun-rise, in the Vale of Chamouni" in 1802. Borrowing from Danish poet Friederike Brun's work on the same subject, Coleridge wrote of "O Sovran BLANC" that "I gazed upon thee, / Till thou, still present to the bodily sense, / Didst vanish from my thought: entranced in prayer / I worshipped the Invisible alone."[5] With Coleridge here extolling the "secret ecstasy" he felt from a mystic identity with Mont Blanc, others flocked to Chamonix for transcendental raptures through viewing, hiking, and climbing. Beginning in the same year, the English artist J. M. W. Turner exhibited a series of dramatic paintings featuring Mont Blanc that further impressed the Alps onto the European cultural consciousness. And unlike earlier generations, by the Romantic era, such works were not made solely for aristocrats and the landed gentry. They reached a growing educated, middle-class audience. Coleridge's "Hymn before Sun-rise," for instance, first appeared in a widely read London daily newspaper, the *Morning Post*.

Then, in 1816, the married English poet Percy Shelley and his eighteen-year-old lover and future wife, who traveled under his last name as Mary Shelley, toured Chamonix while summering with the poet Lord Byron in Geneva. It was during this unusually wet, cold summer that she conceived and commenced her gothic novel *Frankenstein*. Percy Shelley, in contrast, was drawn to Mont Blanc and its glaciers. Hiking to one of them during a storm, he exalted, "Lines of dazzling ice occupy here and there their perpendicular rifts, and shine through the driving vapours with inexpressible brilliance: they pierce the clouds like things not belonging to this earth."[6]

These comments reflected an obsession with ice that both Shelleys shared with an expanding number of nineteenth-century British polar explorers and Alpine climbers. Reflecting this fixation, Mary Shelley framed *Frankenstein* as a tale related by an Arctic explorer who meets Victor Frankenstein and his Creature on their way to the North Pole, where the Creature plans to destroy itself. "I shall quit your vessel on the ice-raft that brought me hither," the Creature tells the explorer, "and shall seek the most northerly extremity of the globe; I shall collect my funeral pile, and consume to ashes this miserable frame."[7] In the English mind, the North Pole thus became an ultimate destination, but, given nineteenth-century cultural norms, the Creature might as well have sought Mont Blanc's summit for its self-immolation. Either it or the pole would have equally served Shelley's artistic purposes.

For the Shelleys, the Alps were the icebound destination of choice and, within a year of his visit to Chamonix, Percy Shelley penned his famous poem "Mont Blanc: Lines Written in the Vale of Chamouni" in praise of them. "[W]hen I gaze on thee / I seem as in a trance sublime," he wrote of his trip to the valley. "Thou hast a voice, great Mountain, to repeal / Large codes of fraud and woe; not understood /

By all, but which the wise, and great, and good / Interpret, or make felt, or deeply feel."[8] The same year, 1817, Lord Byron published the dramatic poem *Manfred*, which included a melodic, often quoted, and separately reprinted sixteen-line tribute to the mountain. "Mont Blanc is the monarch of the mountains," it began. "They crowned him long ago / On a throne of rocks, in a robe of clouds, / With a diadem of snow."[9]

By the nineteenth century, mountains had gained meaning in the modern mind beyond what they previously held. In their respective poems, Wordsworth, Coleridge, and Shelley related different reactions to viewing Mont Blanc, but each presented his experience as intensely personal and transformational. Innumerable less poetic visitors reported feelings of wonder, awe, or reverence at Chamonix. Of course, such responses to seeing Mont Blanc need not lead one to climb it, but for some they did. Others were simply drawn to the physical challenge or psychological exhilaration of scaling monumental peaks.

For serious nineteenth-century climbers, who became known as Alpinists for the mountain range where their passion originated, Mont Blanc crowned but one of many massifs worthy of attention. For the most obsessed, the goal became pioneering new and more difficult routes on that or any similarly challenging mountain or, better yet, making first ascents of major unclimbed peaks. The Alps became the playground of Europe, with Zermatt and the Matterhorn region vying with Chamonix and Mont Blanc for prominence. No one in Britain seized on or fed this mountain mania more than the popular satirist, playwright, and entertainer Albert Smith, an impresario for the middle class.

ON AUGUST 12, 1851, almost on a lark during one of his annual overseas trips, the thirty-five-year-old Smith climbed Mont Blanc, ostensibly because it was there but surely also as fodder for his popular travel commentaries. He was already well known for his articles and one-person shows satirizing Brits abroad and the people they encountered, typically drawing on stereotyped parodies of different nationalities, races, and religions. In his humor, Smith particularly targeted the rich and privileged in a manner that delighted middle-class audiences without offending wealthy patrons. In an earlier, bestselling book, he had defined a "gent" as a presumptuous clotheshorse that anyone could spot by his stylish shawl and alfresco cigar "even if you meet him at the top of Mont Blanc," so it was only fitting that, when given the chance, he climbed the mountain to fact-check his work.[10]

At Chamonix's chic Hotel de Londres, Smith fell in with three Oxford students intent on climbing the mountain during their summer holiday and, attended by thirty-four guides and porters, they set themselves to the task. The caravan, "for by no other name can I call our company," one of the students wrote at the time, proceeded by the then-customary route across the heavily crevassed Bossons Glacier to the Grands Mulets rock outcrop, where the party camped. During this first part of the climb, the porters laid ladders over crevasses so that the climbers could safely cross. Later that day, along the same sector, though attended by "only" three guides, another British climber nearly died in a fall. For their part, the students reveled in what one of them called "the really awful grandeur of the scene."[11]

Reaching Grands Mulets put the party about halfway to the top before nightfall, with 1 mile of altitude gain to go. To this point, using English collegiate slang of the day, the students had hailed Smith as "a tremendous brick." By the light of a full moon, the caravan started again at midnight and virtually stair-stepped up the ice and rock to the summit on a trail cut by guides. "I found the walk," one student wrote, "by far the most unearthly I ever saw." By sunrise, however, he complained, "Smith was perfectly done up, and had to be dragged the rest of the way."[12] The party certainly had enough guides and porters to do so, and everyone reached the top around nine. "I believe we formed the largest party ever assembled before on the summit," Smith noted. Then it was cigars and champagne for the gents before they dashed down—"walking, running, sliding, crouching, advancing in all possible ways"– to reach Chamonix by evening, where bands and cannon fire welcomed the climbers like conquering heroes. Given mules for the ride into town, Smith teased the others about being "once more on the Grands Mulets," and so began a decade of his spoofing the episode. Mountain climbing would never be the same.[13]

Early in 1852, Smith opened a one-person show, "The Ascent of Mont Blanc," at a 430-seat London theater. Expecting a short run, he booked the hall for only a few weeks. Attracting full houses from the outset, however, the show ran for over six years and two thousand performances—a record for a production of its kind—with attendance approximated at a hundred thousand persons per year. On a stage set like an Alpine chalet and with artwork depicting the passing scene moving behind him, Smith related his expedition in a light, instructional lecture laced with comic patter songs of the type later featured in Gilbert and Sullivan operettas. "Nobody but Albert Smith could give a description of such an enterprise so entirely suited to the appreciation of Londoners," one review commented. "He is quite as intent upon the fun and slang with which he meets as upon the grandeur of nature."[14] Within the first few months, Prince Albert, the queen's consort, and the eleven-year-old Prince of Wales, the future King Edward VII, attended. Soon Queen Victoria called for a command performance at court, and, by the end of the run, the young prince was being guided across glaciers at Chamonix by Smith. "He has, in truth, identified himself with Mont Blanc," a reviewer wrote about Smith, "and no Londoner can think of its snow-capped summit without seeing our adventurous author serenely seated at its loftiest apex."[15] His performances made the mountain seem suitable for climbing by any number of Britons.

And climb Britons did, by the thousands. Where only about forty parties had reached the top of Mont Blanc before Smith, over twice that number completed the climb over the next five years alone. One of those groups included the first Englishwoman to reach its summit: "a lady," the *Times* reported, accompanied by her husband and nine guides "who paid her the utmost attention during the whole route."[16] Many British climbers now wrote in letters back to the *Times* that everything looked much as Smith had said. He was both their inspiration and their interpreter. In 1857, Smith cofounded the Alpine Club, the first association "for gentlemen who also climb," as one officer later depicted it, with most members drawn from London's rising professional class of barristers, bankers, and businessmen.[17] Nearly three hundred such gentlemen had joined by 1862, all with at least some alpine experience. More than five hundred signed up over the next three decades. Women were excluded until 1975.

By the time of the Alpine Club's founding, the editors of the *Times* had heard enough about climbing Mont Blanc. Noting that "the feat has now been accomplished so often that it is scarcely worthwhile to register its reoccurrence," the editors announced that the *Times* would no longer print letters about it because they all read the same and sounded of Smith. "If any more daring traveler will try his fortune at Chimborazo or Mount Everest, and his efforts are crowned with success, we promise him all the immortality which it lies in our power to bestow," the editors declared.[18] In so saying, England's newspaper of record was following an emerging trend. With most of its major peaks quickly falling to climbing enthusiasts, mountaineers were already looking beyond the Alps for adventure.

IN 1865, THE MOST prominent unclimbed peak in the Alps was the dramatically pointed, nearly symmetrical Matterhorn, which was fast gaining the prestige that climbers once reserved for Mont Blanc. Situated on the border between Switzerland and that portion of the Kingdom of Piedmont-Sardinia incorporated into Italy in 1860, it had foiled every attempt to scale. Alpinists began calling it unclimbable.

With the mountain's four sheer faces appearing particularly hopeless, attention focused on the four ridges where adjoining faces meet, yet even these were steep and had rotten sections and overhanging ledges. The growing mystique of the mountain's invincibility served to attract more climbers, and soon it became the focus of a fierce international competition for the first ascent, with Italian mountaineers seeking to conquer it for their newly unified nation and British climbers striving to extend their country's global reach in exploration and geographic discovery.

Unified Italy's first king, Victor Emmanuel II, came from Piedmont-Sardinia's House of Savoy, which counted many hikers and climbers among its members. In this sense, the Duke of the Abruzzi, the king's grandson, followed a family tradition in mountaineering, though he far surpassed any of his relatives in this respect. Further, in the 1860 accord that made Victor Emmanuel king of Italy, Piedmont-Sardinia gave up Chamonix and much of old Savoy to France, lending added symbolic meaning to the Matterhorn over Mont Blanc for Italians. Certainly, the duke would make it a prime target for climbing once he came of age. In the meantime, however, an earlier generation of well-known climbers fought over making the first ascent of the Matterhorn, the so-called mountain of mountains in the Alps.

Among the many British contenders for the crown, Edward Whymper was the most determined. The son of an engraver and an engraver himself, Whymper first went to the Alps in 1860 at the age of twenty to make a series of scenic engravings for an Alpine Club member. He hoped that experience on glacial terrain might win him appointment as an illustrator on a future British Arctic expedition. Whymper had a lust for adventure, a passion for travel, and a fascination with the exotic at a time when all of those magnets pulled toward poles or mountains. Reading about the Arctic searches for Franklin's lost expedition and attending Smith's "Ascent of Mont Blanc" had set his compass. One visit to the Alps made him a mountaineer, and the challenge posed by the Matterhorn proved irresistible. Seven times Whymper tried between 1861 and 1865, and seven times he failed, but always by a southern (or Italian) route. Successful ascents of other mountains made his name, yet he kept coming back to the Matterhorn. Arranging for another attempt in 1865, however, he found Italian guides refusing to work with him because by then the international competition had heated to the point where they would only assist Italians. So Whymper went to Zermatt and tried a northern approach from the Swiss side, on the northeast, or Hörnli, ridge.

On some of his earlier efforts, Whymper had engaged the Italian guide Jean-Antoine Carrel, who in 1857, with two relatives, made the first attempt to climb the Matterhorn. By his repeated attempts, Carrel proved as determined to succeed as any Englishman. Living near the mountain's base, sometimes as a guide and sometimes as the principal climber, Carrel tried again and again from the southern side, once reaching nearly 14,000 vertical feet on the southwest, or Lion, ridge—about 700 feet short of the summit—before being blocked by an unpassable cleft. Whymper sought to hire Carrel again in 1865, but by then, two deeply nationalistic founders of the Italian Alpine Club, geologist Felice Giordano and Italian finance minister Quintino Sella, had already secured his services, in an effort to assure that an Italian would get to the top first.

"That fellow whose life seems to depend on the Matterhorn is here," Giordano wrote to Sella about Whymper from the Italian mountain town of Breuil-Cervinia in July. "I have taken all the best men away from him; and yet he is so enamored of the mountain that he may go with others."[19] When Whymper realized Giordano's plan, the race was on. "I had been bamboozled and humbugged," Whymper complained, but by taking the Hörnli ridge by way of Zermatt, he expressed his hope that "the wily ones might be outwitted after all."[20]

Rushing to Zermatt from Italy, Whymper encountered two small British climbing parties with their guides. They made common cause. This brought the total to four British climbers—Whymper and Charles Hudson, who had made the first guideless ascent of Mont

Blanc ten years earlier, the eighteen-year-old Scottish lord Francis Douglas, who had also done some notable climbing, and Hudson's inexperienced nineteen-year-old companion, Douglas Hadow, son of a shipping magnate—plus three guides, including the renowned Michel Croz from Chamonix. While going only a short way up the Hörnli ridge on the first day, July 13, they found it easier than it looked from Zermatt. Starting before dawn on the 14th, they swung around to the east face, which Whymper described as "rising for three thousand feet like a huge natural staircase," but stayed near the ridge and twice resorted to it.[21] Still, the way remained easier than expected and the party made it to within 700 vertical feet of the summit by 10 A.M. Having reached the perpendicular portion that makes the east face appear unclimbable from below, the party shifted to the icy, snow-covered north face and then back to the ridge for the final stretch. Whymper described only this last part of the climb as difficult. "At 11:40 p.m. the world was at our feet and the Matterhorn was conquered," he exclaimed. "Hurrah!"[22]

Now they looked for the Italians, and spotted them over 1,000 feet below struggling up the same southwest ridge that had frustrated so many earlier climbing parties. Whymper and Croz shouted to them at first, but, after getting no response, both men began hurling stones down the mountain toward them. From this assault, Whymper reported, "The Italians turned and fled." They regrouped two days later and, led by Carrel, fought their way up the Lion ridge to the summit, if only to show that Italians could climb the mountain from the Italian side. "He was *the* man," Whymper later said about Carrel, "of all those who attempted the ascent of the Matterhorn, who most deserved to be the first upon its summit."[23]

For the British party, catastrophe struck on the way down. Roped together for the icy, difficult part near the summit, Croz led the way with the inexperienced Hadow next in line. Whymper and the two local guides brought up the rear. Hadow, who had been the only one having trouble climbing up, needed close attention from Croz. Having

laid aside his ice ax to assist Hadow in setting his feet, Croz was turning around when Hadow slipped onto his back and slid forward with
his feet hitting the unprepared Croz in the small of the back, sending
both hurling down the slope. Without an ice ax, Croz could not self-
arrest. The jerk on the rope dislodged Hudson and Douglas, sending them downward too. The two local guides and Whymper braced
themselves to hold the rope, but it snapped between Douglas and
the lower guide. "From the moment the rope broke it was impossible
to help them," Whymper wrote. "For two or three seconds we saw
our unfortunate companions sliding downward on their backs, and
spreading out their hands endeavouring to save themselves; they then
disappeared one by one, and fell from precipice to precipice on to the
Matterhorn glacier below, a distance of nearly 4,000 feet in height."[24]
Only limbless torsos were later found, and no part of Douglas.

SUCH WAS THE PRESTIGE of mountaineering and the celebrity
status of climbers that the first ascent of the Matterhorn and its tragic
conclusion made front-page news, and Whymper's later book about
the episode became a worldwide bestseller. Some commentators used
the occasion to condemn climbing as a wanton waste of civilization's
finest youth. The death of Douglas, who was described in the *Times*
of London as "the heir presumptive to one of our noblest titles,"
the Marquess of Queensberry, and "one of the best young fellows
in the world," drew particular lamentations. "Is it common sense?"
the *Times* asked about mountaineering. "Is it not wrong?"[25] Charles
Dickens agreed, writing about the selfish spirit of climbers, "We shall
be told that 'mountaineering' is a manly exercise. It is so, inasmuch as
it is not womanly. But it is not noblemanly."[26] Moved by the deaths,
Queen Victoria asked her prime minister about ways for the government to discourage the craze or make it safer.

But risk was an essential part of mountaineering, defenders
of the sport shot back in the ensuing public debate, and this was

good for Britain. The leading Victorian essayist and art critic John Ruskin, who had once denounced "the English mobs in the valley of Chamouni" and berated "shrieking" climbers for despoiling the quietude of nature,[27] now wrote in defense of climbing, "Some experience of distinct peril, and the acquirements of quick and calm action in its presence, are necessary elements, at some period of life, in the formation of manly character."[28] Arguing that mountaineering made men courageous, novelist Anthony Trollope expressed his hope that the "accident on the Matterhorn may not repress the adventurous spirit of a single English mountain-climber."[29] Oxford historian and alpine enthusiast H. B. George added, "The climbing spirit, like the love of all kindred pursuits, is essentially a form of that restless spirit, that love of action for its own sake, of exploring the earth and subduing it, which has made England the great colonizer of the world."[30] In short, hailing "the pure love of adventure" that motivated climbing, the *Illustrated London News* concluded, "It has given us the empire."[31]

Like polar exploration, mountaineering had become part of the culture in Britain and much of the Western world by the late nineteenth century. Zermatt sharply increased in popularity as a tourist destination *after* the accident, with ever more people seeking to climb the Matterhorn. For example, noting that the mountain "possesses a certain somber interest from the number of people that have lost their lives on it," Theodore Roosevelt, scarcely a year after graduating from Harvard College, left his young wife behind to scale the Matterhorn on his honeymoon in 1881. "I was anxious to go up it because it is reputed very difficult," he wrote home to his sister. "There is enough peril to make it exciting."[32]

Roosevelt's words spoke for a generation. In 1894, fresh out of boarding school at Harrow, a young Winston Churchill toured Zermatt but chose to climb nearby Monte Rosa because it was higher than the Matterhorn. That same year the legendary British climber Albert Mummery, who in 1879 had made the first ascent of the Matterhorn by the northwest, or Zmutt, ridge, led the twenty-one-year-old Duke of the Abruzzi up that same treacherous route. By this time, the duke had already climbed Mont Blanc and Monte Rosa. He was the son of a king; Roosevelt came from a long line of wealthy businessmen; Churchill was born in a palace to an aristocratic family. The children of privilege yet with driving ambitions to make their own names, each of them sought adventure and found it in climbing. From middle-class families, comfortable but not rich, Whymper and Mummery did so as well and gained admission to the gentlemanly Alpine Club.

In climbing, or at least while climbing, the era's rigid class barriers broke down between upper- and middle-class mountaineers, and even among them and their working-class guides such as Carrel and Croz. With a few notable exceptions, however, the gender divide persisted in mountaineering, much as it did on polar explorations, at least in part because manly danger was part of their appeal and male comradery was perceived as one of their virtues. These pursuits, their proponents maintained, built a man's character in a supposedly decadent age and thus, by convention, were reserved for men. While hiking in a high alpine region of Switzerland during the 1880s, German writer Friedrich Nietzsche was inspired to pen *Thus Spake Zarathustra*, which contained the line that called to his age: "Two things are wanted by the true man: danger and play."[33]

THE FIRST AND SECOND ascents of the Matterhorn, the last remaining prominent unclimbed alpine peak, marked the end of one era in mountaineering and the start of another. Climbing enthusiasts had already started to look beyond the Alps for new challenges, and now the trickle became a tide. With all the Alps' major peaks climbed, English writer and Alpine Club president Leslie Stephen wrote in 1868, "One great inducement of climbing [them] has all but disappeared." And "when there is a railroad to Timbuctoo, and another through the central regions of Asia," he added, a later generation "will feel on a large scale the same regret for the old days, when the earth contained an apparently inexhaustible expanse of unknown regions, as the Alpine traveler now feels on a very diminutive scale."[34] If he had added the Andes to this list of little-known regions, Stephen would have neatly summarized where Alpinists began looking for adventure: Africa, Asia, and South America.

Well into the nineteenth century, Europeans believed that the Andes were the world's loftiest mountain range, and, although it had lost its preeminence to the Himalayas by midcentury, it was there that many climbers looked for the next challenge. After his first ascent of the Matterhorn and two expeditions to Greenland, for example, in 1880, Whymper, with former rivals Jean-Antoine and Louis Carrel, made the first ascent of Ecuador's 20,000-foot-high Chimborazo, which Europeans once deemed the world's tallest mountain. When some doubted the feat, Whymper did it again by another route later in the same year. Between these two climbs, along with several other first ascents in the Andes, he summited Cotopaxi and spent a night on top to study the effects of altitude sickness.

Whymper then turned to the Canadian Rockies for first ascents. The Duke of the Abruzzi looked this way too in 1897 for his first ascent of Mount Saint Elias, which straddles the border between Canada and the United States and is the second tallest mountain in both. Other leading Alpinists resorted to the Caucasus and Norway during the period. Both Whymper and the duke considered tackling the Himalayas prior to 1900 but on-and-off political restrictions on access pushed them elsewhere. For the duke, equatorial Africa came next.

PRIOR TO 1850, FEW Europeans had ventured beyond the coasts of equatorial Africa to explore its vast interior. Those who tried usually succumbed to disease. As long as there were other places to explore and exploit, Westerners stayed away. On Western maps, it was terra incognita or filled in with features drawn from myth and legend. One of the oldest such legends held that snow-covered mountains—the ancient Greek geographer Claudius Ptolemy called them "the Mountains of the Moon"—fed the Nile River from a lake district in central Africa. In the 1850s, imperialist-minded Europeans began looking beyond their nations' coastal trading posts toward the African interior for further exploration and expansion. The ancient accounts of mountains and lakes offered hope that something other than malarial jungles and barren deserts lay there.

No one nurtured those hopes more than the wealthy former British army officer who then headed the Royal Geographical Society, Roderick Murchison. "The adventurous travelers who shall first lay down the true position of these equatorial snowy mountains," Murchison declared in his 1852 presidential address to the society, "and who shall satisfy us that they not only throw off the waters of the White Nile to the north, but some to the east, and will further answer the query, whether they may not also shed off some streams to a great lacustrine and sandy interior of this continent, will be justly considered among the greatest benefactors of this age to geographical science!"[35] The race was on to find the source of the Nile and, hopefully, a fertile, temperate interior highlands in East Africa suitable for European settlement, which drew them toward Uganda.

In 1856, the Royal Geographical Society asked Richard Francis Burton, a master linguist already known for his Middle Eastern travels, and his sometime companion John Hanning Speke to seek the Nile's source in east-central Africa. Departing from coastal Zanzibar, their first attempt ended with an attack by Somalis that saw a thrown spear pierce Burton's face and Speke stabbed over a dozen times. On their second attempt, they reached the large, central Lake Tanganyika in the heart of equatorial Africa before Burton grew too weak to continue. Partly deaf after cutting a burrowing beetle from his own ear and temporarily blinded by disease, Speke pushed on alone to find a lush highlands around an even larger lake that he named Victoria.

Speke and Burton were the first Europeans to see either lake. They split over whether Lake Victoria fed the Nile, and failed to find anything like the Mountains of the Moon, but their efforts laid a basis for British colonization of the region.

To mount an 1866 expedition to confirm the Nile's source, the society tapped fifty-three-year-old David Livingstone, who had gained worldwide fame for his earlier journeys in southern Africa. Also entering by way of Zanzibar, but no longer up to the rigors of such travel, Livingstone was sick, disoriented, and low on supplies somewhere in the eastern Congo River basin by 1870. Henry Morton Stanley, a Welsh-born journalist sent by the *New York Herald* to find him, reached the explorer in 1871. "Dr. Livingstone, I presume?" Stanley reported asking in an affected British understatement. "Yes, that is my name" came the reply that echoed around the globe.[36] Hooked on the fame and money it brought him, Stanley returned to the region once more for the *New York Herald* and twice for Belgian King Leopold II, who wanted to claim and colonize the Congo. In 1889, on the last of these expeditions, Stanley sighted the snowcapped equatorial peaks that he identified as the fabled Mountains of the Moon but called by their local name, the Ruwenzori Range. Virtually straddling the equator, they rose on the border between Uganda and the Congo 150 miles east of Lake Victoria, their crystal-white summits gleaming with glaciers. Stanley did not climb or visit them, but his reports renewed their fame. Alpinists took note.

"I have been wishing and hoping and praying that some sensible man would go into Africa and explore that region of Ruwenzori thoroughly," Stanley told the Royal Geographical Society twelve years later. "Some lover of Alpine climbing," he stressed, who "would take Ruwenzori in hand and make a thorough work of it, explore it from top to bottom through all those enormous defiles and those deep gorges."[37] Here was a challenge fit for a royal climber and naval officer from a country with colonial ambitions in Africa. The duke set sail from Italy on April 16, 1906, to make thorough work of the unconquered range.

Many key members of the duke's earlier Saint Elias and North Pole expeditions went with him, including Umberto Cagni and Joseph Petigax from the farthest-north party and photographer Vittorio Sella from the Saint Elias expedition. One of the duke's favorite alpine guides, Cesare Ollier, went too. In all, there were twelve Italians on an expedition that grew exponentially to over four hundred porters, guides, soldiers, and servants by the time it left Lake Victoria and headed toward the mountains. Even some of the servants took servants. The porters carried nearly 10 tons of supplies in wood-covered tin cases. This was a right royal expedition with nothing wanting: it literally traveled with beds, baths, and beyond.

After having journeyed for twenty days by ship, boat, and train as far as Entebbe, the colonial capital of Britain's Uganda Protectorate on the shore of Lake Victoria, the duke's caravan headed on foot and horseback 180 miles to Fort Portal, the final British outpost on the western frontier. That took another fifteen days. Already nearly a mile high in altitude, the duke now wrote that the way became steep and the trail "detestable." A "beating rain," as he put it, left them "wading in mud" and "sinking to the knees" in swamps. "The Bakonjo, with 40 lbs. or more on their heads, walked like so many squirrels, bending so as to pass their loads under the trees, or leaping from trunk to trunk with such agility that we had difficulty to follow them," he wrote in admiration about the native porters.[38] Still, most of them were sent back or remained behind after reaching the edge of the snow slopes and glacial ice at 12,461 feet in altitude, where the duke established his base camp. Then the climbing began.

Finally reaching a ridge at some 14,000 feet on June 10, the duke and a small climbing party assessed the situation. "Opposite us," he wrote, "appeared four distinct mountains, with snowy peaks far loftier than our standpoint."[39] Two more massifs rose behind him, making a total of six in the range, each with multiple peaks connected by saddles. All six rose over 15,000 feet; two topped 16,000 feet. Ridges ran between them easing access from one to another. Ancient glaciers clung to the sides of each but were small and clearly in retreat. New snows fed them only above about 14,600 feet. Over the next five weeks, the duke set out to make a circuit of all six mountains, map the terrain of each, and achieve as many first ascents of their multiple peaks as possible. In the end, his party claimed sixteen first ascents, including the range's highest massif, the 16,800-foot Mount Stanley, whose twin summits (classified as separate peaks) he named Margherita and Alexandra after the Italian and British queens.

The duke made the three-day trek from his base camp to the glacier below the two highest peaks with two Italian alpine guides, one Italian porter, and nine Bakonjo porters, but only the Italians summited. An overhanging cornice of snow appeared to block the way just short of the top. "We climbed up by a very steep snow-slope to the cornice," the duke reported. "The slope was so steep that my head almost touched the feet of the guide in front of me." After searching among the pillars of ice melting from and supporting the cornice, he added, "We found at last a sort of ice chimney 6 feet high. Petigax, to climb up it, had to plant his nailed boots on the head and shoulders of the unfortunate Ollier." Once up, Petigax lowered a rope for the rest. "The ridge was ours, and at the same time the top," the duke exclaimed. An Italian flag with the embroidered motto "Dare and hope" was unfurled and planted upon the peak, which "up to that time had known only the breath of the tempest." In a bit of imperialistic bravado typical of the age, the duke envisioned that the flag raising would serve "as an encouragement and support to all the hearty explorers who, among the still unknown and savage wilds of Africa, labour among hardships and perils for the advance of civilization."[40] The duke gave ideological meaning to mountaineering. He climbed for empire and later, as an admiral and senator, would participate in Italy's conquest of Libya and colonization of Somalia.

ALREADY A CELEBRITY BEFORE the Ruwenzori expedition, the duke returned to global acclaim. Italians could speak of little else. "The victories that he and his companions have won over the forces of nature in the Arctic circle, as well as in Africa, will be valued in Italy not so much for what they add to the sum of human knowledge as for the noble example they set of enterprise and fortitude," one correspondent reported from Rome.[41] A leading Italian newspaper agreed, describing the expedition's immense "moral" value to the nation and its people.[42]

Praise came from all quarters. With nearly a half million Italians living in New York City at the time, and Italians everywhere taking evident pride in the duke's achievements, the *New York Times* cobbled together a full-page article celebrating the expedition even before the duke issued his first public statement about it.[43] The duke's initial lecture on the expedition filled Rome's historic opera house. The entire royal family, ministers of state, and much of the diplomatic corps attended. The Royal Geographical Society hosted his second speech five days later in London's twenty-five-hundred-seat Queen's Hall with King Edward VII and the future King George V present, the first time a reigning monarch had attended one of the society's programs. Both lectures were oversubscribed and punctuated with loud and repeated cheers. "He possesses great courage, great coolness, and great will," the British king said of the duke.[44] These were canonical virtues of the Edwardian era. Leading mountaineers joined in hailing the duke, less for the technical difficulty of the climb than for its organization and execution.[45] Much as with Mount Saint Elias, the greatest obstacles to climbing in the Ruwenzori range lay in reaching the base and having sufficient dry, clear weather to gain the summits.

The Italian government capitalized on the duke's stature by promoting him to the command of a naval squadron and sending it on worldwide goodwill voyages beginning in 1907. In that window between the spread of far-flung global empires in the mid-1800s and the advent of effective military aircraft in the early 1900s, surface warships became a marker of national power, and publicly displaying them served a significant role in peacetime diplomacy. In the same year, for example, President Theodore Roosevelt dispatched America's first blue-water navy, the so-called Great White Fleet, composed of sixteen white battleships with support vessels, on a fifteen-month-long circumnavigation of the globe designed to strengthen alliances, encourage trade, and reinforce overseas holdings. Now an admiral in the Italian navy, the duke had much the same mission, and indeed one of his first stops was to call upon Roosevelt, a fellow outdoorsman who had closely followed his exploits.

This 1907 American visit coincided with tricentennial celebrations for the founding of Jamestown, with the Italian squadron joining the festivities in and around the Chesapeake Bay. Roosevelt met with the duke at Jamestown and invited him to a state dinner at the White House, where he reportedly first met the smart and spirited American who became his love interest, Katherine Elkins. The duke also sailed on the presidential yacht to Mount Vernon, where he laid a wreath at George Washington's tomb. By some accounts, the U.S. president and the Italian duke talked more about mountaineering than foreign policy. From the Chesapeake, the duke's flagship, the *Varese*, proceeded to New York City for a courtesy call that equally excited the local Italian American community and the elite American Alpine and Arctic clubs.

"The arrival of the *Varese* had been anticipated for days by New York's large Italian population," the press reported one day after the ship sailed into port, "and a great crowd of them stood alongshore and watched the ship as she rode at anchor."[46] Lines formed for tours of the *Varese*, with people waiting hours for launches that would take them to the ship. "In the crowd of enthusiastic Italians were hundreds of women," another article noted, "every one of whom fought for the chance to get on board."[47] All hoped for a glimpse of the duke, and perhaps that he would catch a glimpse of them. He was the celebrity who drew them to an otherwise ordinary navy cruiser. Newspaper reports inevitably described the duke as olive skinned and appearing much younger than his thirty-four years. Some mentioned his elegant dress, good looks, and stylish Italian cigarettes.

The response was much the same on shore. Besieged with social invitations, among those that he accepted was one to a banquet in his honor hosted by the American Alpine Club in the grand ballroom of the newly opened Hotel Astor. The long guest list included members of the Peary Arctic Club; Robert Peary himself, recently back from his 1905–06 polar expedition, during which he claimed to have beaten the Italians' farthest-north mark by some 30 miles; and David Brainard, the surviving member of the Greely expedition's farthest-north party. The only woman present was the wealthy mountaineer Annie Peck, who could then claim the western hemisphere altitude record for her 1904 assault on Bolivia's Mount Illampu and would confirm it at age fifty-eight with her 1908 first ascent of Nevado Huascarán's 22,000-foot northern peak. At the time, the duke still held the altitude record for the United States and Canada unless one credited polar explorer Frederick Cook's disputed claim to have summited Denali in 1906. "His Royal Highness was not content with the rank and wealth which came to him by birth," Peary said of the duke in the evening's closing remarks. "He went out to meet the forces of nature, and, strong in his self-reliance and courage, matched himself against them and triumphed. His noted achievements have won him a high place among the explorers of the world."[48]

Upon its commissioning later in 1907, the duke was given command of the Italian navy's sleek new *Regina Elena*, then the world's fastest battleship, and directed to continue his goodwill touring. In December, it took him to Glasgow and his gala reception at the Royal Scottish Geographical Society, as word began spreading that he would aim next for a world altitude record in the Himalayas or Karakoram.

BY 1900, THE TWO words *Himalayas* and *Karakoram* had merged together in the Western mind, or the second was subsumed by the first, to denote a single place of untold wonder and natural splendor. It was only as Britain gained effective control over India during the mid-1800s and extended its Great Trigonometrical Survey of the subcontinent north that Europeans recognized the Himalayas and Karakoram as the rooftop of the world and measured many of their tallest peaks from a series of lower-level observation stations. And it was not until near the century's end that first ascents in the Alps and elsewhere became sufficiently passé for top European mountaineers to begin looking toward these spectacularly tall and exotically remote mountain ranges for new challenges.

The duke first considered making a Himalayan climb after seeing the world's third-highest mountain, Kangchenjunga, from a viewpoint near Darjeeling during an 1895 goodwill visit to India, but an outbreak of the plague and famine in the area compelled him to set aside this plan. By then, with British dominance pushing north across the subcontinent and Imperial Russia expanding south into central Asia in what became known as the Great Game between those two powers for geopolitical influence over the region, Tibet and Nepal had long since sealed their borders to outsiders, cutting off access to Mount Everest and leaving K2 in the Karakoram Range northwest of the central Himalayas as the highest accessible peak for European mountaineers. At 28,281 feet, it is the world's second-highest mountain. Climbing K2 became the duke's goal for 1909.

CHAPTER 5

The Peary Way

JULY 4, 1908, INDEPENDENCE Day in New York City, and everything stood ready for Robert Peary's final assault on the North Pole.
Peary's custom-built ship, the *Roosevelt*—named for the nation's
young, vigorous president, then in his final year of office—was heavily
loaded, decked out in holiday bunting, and receiving a steady stream
of visitors at the 24th Street Recreation Pier on the East River.

"There is no doubt about it," Peary's longtime aide and sledging
companion Matthew Henson told reporters about the expedition's
prospects for reaching the pole. "I am not a weather prophet, and I
don't know much about science, but something in me—I don't know
what it is—tells me that the Commander will get there this time."[1]

Cheering crowds lined the shore and a flotilla of yachts with
whistles tooting filled the river as the *Roosevelt* cast off, heading to
nearby Oyster Bay Harbor where the president himself waited to inspect the ship at his Long Island estate, Sagamore Hill.

"It's going to be just a bully trip," Roosevelt told the crew following his inspection, "and I'd like to be with you when you find the
pole."[2]

OVER THE PRIOR DECADE, Theodore Roosevelt had become Peary's most visible booster. Before Roosevelt's ascension to the presidency following William McKinley's assassination in 1901, Peary had enough backers in political circles to secure a succession of paid leaves from the navy for his Arctic expeditions despite objections from his superiors. Indeed, he had spent half his navy career on leave. After the disappointing results of the 1898–1902 venture and his physical disability, Peary feared that the navy would harness him to a desk. Instead, with Roosevelt's support, he was promoted to the rank of commander in 1902 and assigned the following year to head a commission studying naval facilities in Europe, where he met with fellow explorers, learned about the latest Antarctic expeditions, and received honors from various geographic societies.

"All that I can do as President to give Peary a free hand and hearty backing for his next effort to go to the Pole, will be done," Roosevelt assured a friend in 1903.[3] The American Geographical Society chose Peary as its president that year, and he presided over the International Geographical Congress when it met in Washington a year later. A further operation on his feet, removing parts of his two remaining toes and shifting his soles forward, allowed him to walk with a less visible shuffle. He appeared capable of another polar trek.

Roosevelt's role was crucial at this juncture. Even as some long-time backers resisted Peary's pleas to fund yet another expedition, Roosevelt directed the navy to grant Peary further paid leave. "It was a great pleasure to issue the order. I feel you have rendered service not only to America, but to all the world, by what you have done, and any way I can help you I am desirous of doing so," he told Peary.[4] "The attainment of the Pole should be your main object. Nothing short will suffice," the order read. "Our national pride is involved in the undertaking."[5]

The leave was for three years beginning in September 1903.

Much of it would be spent raising funds and supervising construction of a ship, because Peary's new plan called for his most elaborate effort yet. Gone were any hopes of reaching the pole with a small party living off the land. Peary now knew where the land ended in the north, and that the route to the pole lay over shifting sea ice from roughly 83° north longitude on. One party could not carry enough supplies to get from the land to the pole and back. Support parties were needed, and sledging must begin as far north as possible.

Peary blamed the failure of his last expedition on having his base so far south that he needed to sledge 400 miles just to reach the Arctic coast. In 1899, he had lost his toes sledging from that base to Fort Conger, which itself was still over 60 miles from the coast. Now he was determined to sail past it, winter on a well-provisioned ship at the northern end of Ellesmere Island, and sledge north over the sea ice in early spring with multiple parties shuttling supplies in support of one final push to the pole. He would require a strong ship capable of forcing its way through ice to the Arctic coast, and that meant more money than ever before. All that Peary could offer donors was the "imperishable monument," as he once put it, of having their names placed "forever" on newly discovered geographical features, much as he had given the name Cape Morris K. Jesup to the northernmost point of Greenland during his last expedition.[6] But an expedition over the sea ice from a known point of land, as this one promised to be, would not offer many naming opportunities. So Peary relied more on the type of nationalistic appeal that moved Roosevelt. His was an American adventure to prove the country's manhood and establish the young nation's place in the world alongside the likes of such old-world powers as Britain, France, and Germany.

Roosevelt lent Peary additional assistance by urging his wealthy friends to back the project and by giving it public credence. A vigorous, visionary, and well-born public servant in an era known for weak and corrupt politicians, the president was one of the most popular and trusted persons in the nation and enjoyed a strong following among the sort of Gilded Age, adventure-seeking philanthropists inclined to support Peary. New York's American Museum of Natural History stood as a temple to the Rooseveltian spirit that knew no limits for the individual or the country, and Morris Jesup, its president and chief benefactor, had been brought into Peary's orbit in part by Roosevelt.

After receiving a letter from Roosevelt, Jesup had formed the Peary Arctic Club in 1898 to support the explorer's last expedition and in 1904 took the added step of incorporating and expanding it with the principal goal of supplying Peary with a suitable ship for his next expedition.[7] In the end, Jesup and his friend George Crocker, heir to a West Coast railroad fortune, supplied most of the funds for Peary's ship, which was launched in March 1905. Only about twice the size of a New York harbor tug, with curved sides, thick hull, flared prow, and oversized shaft and propellers, this ship was designed both to cut through the ice pack and to rise above it when trapped. More than any Arctic ship since the *Fram*, it was built for its mission.

Peary's determination to try again for the pole at age forty-nine, and his nationalistic calls for the United States to claim its destiny in the Arctic and elsewhere, captured the spirit of the age—or at least the spirit that the likes of Jesup, Crocker, and Roosevelt had willed upon the age. Jesup had given millions to promote Horatio Alger–type opportunities for immigrants and the poor in America. Peary's humble origins, manifest courage, and fierce determination appealed to him.

Roosevelt felt much the same way. "I am simply unable to make myself take the attitude of respect toward the very wealthy men which such an enormous multitude of people evidently feel," Roosevelt wrote privately following a visit with Peary. "I am delighted to show any courtesy to Pierpont Morgan or Andrew Carnegie or James J. Hill; but as for regarding any of them as, for instance, I regard [the Cambridge classicist J. B.] Bury or Peary, the Arctic explorer, . . . why

I could not force myself to do it even if I wanted to." Roosevelt went on to note, "The very luxurious, grossly material life of the average multimillionaire whom I know, does not appeal to me in the least," adding, "I should selfishly prefer my old-time ranch on the Little Missouri to anything in Newport."[8] Peary was his man, and for his champion, Peary named his ship. Portraits of Jesup and Roosevelt hung over the player piano in Peary's cabin on board what some reporters hailed as the strongest ship afloat.

DURING THIS PERIOD OF full-time preparation for his 1905–06 expedition, a confident, calculating Peary took center stage at the International Geographical Congress. There, he received a gold medal from the Paris Geographical Society "in recognition of his many and valuable contributions to the world's knowledge of Arctic regions."[9] He also secured passage of a resolution that, while recognizing "the importance of forthwith completing the systematic exploration of [both] polar areas," all but reserved the Arctic to American explorers and urged "that the expeditions now being prepared will be so supported as to secure early and complete success."[10] No one could miss its meaning: the North Pole was Peary's preserve.

"Only two great prizes now wait the present-day explorer—the north pole and the south pole," Peary declared in his presidential address to the congress. He went on to explain why, of these two, the North Pole should come first. "There is no higher, purer field of international rivalry than the struggle for the north pole," Peary stated. "Uninfluenced by prospects of gain, by dreams of colonization, by land lust, or politics, the centuries' long struggle of the best and bravest . . . has made this field of effort classic, almost sacred." Hailing the Duke of the Abruzzi for the Italians' recent farthest north, Peary maintained that their results "eliminated Franz Josef Land from further consideration as a polar base," leaving only his so-called American route to the pole as an option.[11]

Peary's address went on to survey the state of exploration at the dawn of the twentieth century. Climbers were beginning to ascend the Himalayas—"the roof of the world," Peary called it—but "the culminating peak of Asia remains to be won." He placed this third, behind only attaining the two poles, in his list of "geographical feats of primary magnitude yet to be accomplished." Otherwise, Asia and Africa were well known to Western geographers, Peary opined. Lhasa, "the mystery and secret of Central Asia," is occupied by an English military expedition and "a mystery no longer," he declared with imperialistic conceit. "In Africa, once 'the Dark Continent,' the work of large exploration is at an end, and has been succeeded by the work of division and colonization." The Americas were fully explored, he added, save only that "the culminating point of North America remains yet untrodden by human foot."[12] By rounding Ellesmere Island's northern coast, Peary had this feat in mind for his next expedition. Turning to Antarctica, which he depicted as the world's only unexplored area other than the Arctic, Peary praised the six national expeditions then out to or recently back from the region and saw them as precursors to reaching the South Pole. Either ignorant of or insensitive to modern developments in the field, Peary's address equated geography with exploration and reduced exploration to discovery. His own expeditions fit this mode.

At least two of the busy congress's other presentations held special interest for Peary. In one, an oceanographer used evidence from tides and currents to hypothesize that undiscovered land lay northwest of Ellesmere Island.[13] He was wrong, but the idea intrigued Peary. In another, Peary's former expedition physician and future rival, Frederick Cook, gave a comparative view of the Arctic and Antarctic based on his travels in both regions. "The fascination of the north-polar dash will increase rather than diminish, and with it will grow a similar enthusiasm to reach the South Pole," he predicted.[14] An affable self-promoter with a penchant for adventure, Cook clearly had not renounced his interest in these endeavors.

In a second lecture, Cook related his 1903 attempt to make the first ascent of North America's highest mountain, Denali, which he called by the then-popular (if not yet official) name Mount McKinley. Describing the difficult entry through rain-soaked brush, the steep climb, and Arctic conditions on the 20,000-foot mountain, he concluded, "The prospective conqueror of America's culminating peak will be amply rewarded, but he must be prepared to withstand the tortures of the [mosquito-infested] torrids, the discomforts of the north-pole seeker, and the hardships of the Matterhorn ascents multiplied many times."[15] Cook's four-person party had made it only to the top of a spur about 11,000 feet high before being blocked by a sheer cliff, but, addicted to the rewards of fame and glory that would flow to whoever first summited what he called "the top of the continent," Cook would try again in 1906 and claim success.[16] The poles held similar appeal for him.

By this point, Peary surely recognized Cook as a competitor for fame and glory as an American explorer. Indeed, Cook gave a third paper at the geographical congress—the only presenter to give so many—on his role in the first expedition to winter in the Antarctic.[17] He was a relentless author of popular articles and books about his own exploits, and a frequent public lecturer too.

While somehow maintaining his medical practice in Brooklyn, Cook had followed up on his role in Peary's 1891–93 North Greenland expedition by leading or guiding a series of "expeditions" to the Arctic, mostly involving paying guests, sightseeing, and big-game hunting, as well as by his stint as physician on the Belgian Antarctic Expedition of 1897–99. In 1906, Cook would claim the first ascent of Denali and be elected to succeed Arctic pioneer Adolphus Greely as president of New York's elite Explorers Club. It was possibly only Peary's looming 1905–06 assault on the North Pole that kept Cook from looking in that direction rather than to a Pole of Altitude for his next feat, but if so, it put further pressure on Peary to succeed this time or face an American challenger for the pole with almost as much renown, nearly as good connections, and at least as much audacity as himself.

ON THE OUTBOUND LEG of its maiden voyage, the *Roosevelt* lived up to its advance billing. It departed New York on July 16, 1905, with Henson, expedition physician Louie Wolf, a newly graduated Cornell engineering student named Ross Marvin, and a crew of thirteen Newfoundland sailors plus a few New Englanders under the command of Captain Robert Bartlett, a British citizen of Newfoundland. In three weeks, with brief stops in Maine and Nova Scotia, the ship had steamed to the northernmost Inuit villages on Greenland's west coast. There, Peary rounded up "my Eskimos," as he called them, with their dogs.[18] He had over forty Inuits, many in family groups, and some two hundred sled dogs aboard within three days, and on August 16 steamed north into the surging channel ice of Smith Sound and beyond.[19]

"Deep and heavy as the ship was," Peary wrote, "she rose on the opposing ice with no pronounced shock, no matter how viciously she was driven at it, and either split it with the impact, or wedged it aside by sheer weight." The *Roosevelt* had more trouble with heavy old floes, but managed to dodge and weave through Nares Strait to Robeson Channel above Fort Conger before a swirl of current, "which at times runs like a mill-race in this deep channel," Peary noted, drove the ship sideways into fast, firm shore ice, twisting the rudder and damaging the steering gear.[20]

After five days spent on makeshift repairs, the ship returned to the "battle," as Peary called it. "The *Roosevelt* fought like a gladiator, turning, twisting, straining with all her force, smashing her full weight against the heavy flows whenever she could get room for a rush," he wrote of this part of the voyage. "'Give it to 'um, Teddy, give it to 'um!'" the captain muttered to his ship. Twice it was driven ashore by ice floes and grounded till high tide before crawling around

Cape Union and steaming "with thick black smoke pouring from her stack" into the Arctic Ocean's Lincoln Sea.[21]

Maneuvering along the coast, by September 5 the *Roosevelt* had pushed 2 miles beyond the Nares Expedition's 1875 anchorage. At this most northerly point never before attained by a ship under its own power, Peary moored for the winter beside the shore ice below Cape Sheridan. "By a hard-fought struggle we had successfully negotiated the narrow, ice-encumbered waters which form the American gateway and route to the Pole," he crowed, "and substantiated my prophecy to the [Peary Arctic] Club, that with a suitable ship, the attainment of a base on the north shore of Grant Land was feasible almost every year."[22]

FOLLOWING A WINTER AT Cape Sheridan, where the Inuits lived in igloos on shore and the Americans stayed on board with the ship's crew, Peary began his poleward march in mid-February with Henson, Bartlett, Marvin, Wolf, two members of the ship's crew, twenty-one Inuit dogsled drivers, some one hundred twenty dogs, and twenty sledges. Eighty dogs had died since September from tainted whale meat, but the number of Inuits rose with the birth of a baby girl in January. Following the well-established "Peary style," or way of living off the land, hunting teams composed mostly of Inuit men had added over seventy musk oxen and nearly thirty caribou to the larder during the winter months.[23] Unlike most polar expeditions of the era, and in sharp contrast to those conducted by Nansen, Scott, Nares, or even Shackleton, no scientific records were kept or research done during this period of midwinter darkness.

Once they set out, the explorers traveled northwest for three days along the coast to Cape Hecla, where they established a supply base. Then they divided into seven small parties, each with two or three sledges, a non-Inuit leader, and three Inuit drivers. While he readily acknowledged the key contributions made by Inuits to his expeditions, and often singled out individuals for praise, Peary never promoted any Inuit to a leadership position or mastered the ability to talk in their language.[24] For any long or complex conversation, Henson served as a translator.

From Cape Hecla, each party traveled separately, with Henson's cutting the trail, Peary's in the rear, and the rest shuttling supplies to ever more forward depots without any intention of going the whole way. A day or more might separate them at times, but the seven parties inevitably bunched up at open-water leads, which irritated Peary because it backed up the entire operation. Accustomed to traveling in one small group, he had never encountered delays of this sort. Hampered by leading from the rear, Peary relied on Henson to set a good pace and keep on the right course. After four expeditions together, Henson understood Peary's demands but could not always meet them. Conditions on the shifting ice pack proved too difficult.

From a point on land 20 miles west-northwest of Cape Hecla, the evenly spaced parties set off north over the Arctic sea ice beginning on March 1, with later parties using the igloos built and supplies left by earlier ones. No prior expedition had staggered its parties in this supply-train manner as a means to cross moving sea ice—certainly not Peary, who typically traveled in one small group—but support parties were common in mountaineering, and the British would use them in their pursuit of the South Pole. The shifting nature of pack ice limited their effectiveness in the Arctic, however, as movements of the ice could collapse or carry away supply depots and igloos, disrupt trails cut by advance parties, and disorient returning groups. In the end, Peary's party needed to cut a new track back, and it led them to Greenland rather than to their Ellesmere Island base. In the Antarctic or when mountain climbing, explorers could cache supplies with a realistic hope of recovering them on the return trip. Advance parties could safely depot supplies as well. On shifting sea ice, this was less feasible. There, explorers needed to carry virtually everything they used or consumed, and support parties were using and consuming scarce resources too.

For Peary, the problems began at the outset and grew worse over time. For some reason, Henson's advance party veered about 10 degrees west of due north from the start, and later parties followed its track, including Peary's final one. At the time, Peary placed the blame on Henson for having always turned left to get around rough ice and open leads, but polar explorer and historian Wally Herbert later surmised that the fault lay with Peary for using the wrong variance factor to correct compass readings made in a region close to the magnetic pole.[25] Whatever the cause, the mistake added miles to an already hopelessly long journey and was not discovered until March 30, when the parties stood full stop at the Big Lead, where the sea ice near shore meets the midocean circulating pack ice. Taking this opportunity to compute the longitude and latitude, Peary found the group some 10 degrees of longitude west of where it should have been and less than 2 degrees of latitude, or about 120 miles, north of where it started. In this direction and at this pace, with nearly one-third of his allotted round-trip travel time now expended, he could not hope to reach the pole, which still lay 370 miles away, and return safely to his ship.

Some of the cause for being so far from the pole was attributable to veering left, but not most of it. At the outset, Peary had hoped to average 10 miles per day to get to the pole and back in the one hundred or so days between the midwinter darkness and the late-spring thaw. From the coast to the Big Lead, he averaged less than 6 miles a day. One cause was the awkward array of parties making the journey, but the terrain also presented significant problems. Everywhere, it seemed, the ice was in motion. In places it was heavily rafted, and the advance trail quickly faulted. While in one camp, Peary wrote, "The floe on which my igloos were built split in two, shattering the igloos, and the ice, evidently under heavy pressure, rumbled and groaned continuously."[26]

Temperatures often fell below minus 60°F at night and rarely rose above minus 50°F each day. At least this caused seawater to freeze over rapidly, but detours were still needed around some thin ice, pressure ridges, and open leads. Then, just as the pace began to improve, "bang up against it," Peary wrote on March 26, "a black eye to all my hopes of speedy success."[27]

They had hit the Big Lead or, as Peary now called it, the "Hudson River." Three parties were already backed up at its bank, including Henson's advance team, and now Peary joined them, overlooking what he described as "a broad open lead extending east and west across our course, farther than we could see." He had hoped to find the lead either narrow enough to raft across or temporarily closed, but instead it was as wide as ever. On the second day, he sent back two of the supporting parties, claiming, "I could not afford to feed all these teams and people here during what might be a several days' wait."[28] Only Henson and his advance team now remained with Peary's party.

It was not until April 1 that seawater in the lead became suitably still to skim over with ice just thick enough so that, as Peary judged it, "a man 'walking wide' as a polar bear does, could cross it." A day later, he wrote, "Across the 'Hudson River' at last, thank God, after a loss of seven days of fine weather."[29] He crossed gingerly by relaying light loads in multiple trips. From here, Peary hoped, it would be a dash north with Henson, six Inuits, five sledges, and some thirty-five dogs.[30]

Regarding the teams that Peary sent back, critics charge that, with little chance now of setting a new farthest-north record and virtually none of reaching the pole, he did not want any witnesses along who could credibly challenge whatever claims he might make. Certainly, his own writings at this point reveal an obsession with setting a record rather than reaching the pole and complain that, but for the seven-day delay at the Big Lead, "We would have been beyond Abruzzi's highest now." After a few good days going north beyond the Big Lead, he added, "On this date Nansen reached his highest, and but for the accursed lead, I should have been ahead of him."[31] As it was, Peary remained roughly 100 miles south of the Italian mark and only slightly less shy of the Norwegian one.

From here on, Peary's account becomes increasingly sketchy. Whatever he accomplished, however, he did so the Peary way, without support parties or relief from the rear. Even as he pushed himself and his men north from the Big Lead, Peary knew that, to use his own words, there was a "certainty of eating dog again before I got back to land."[32] To Roosevelt, such heroic pursuit of a worthy goal embodied American ideals.

HENSON'S PARTY LEFT THE Big Lead on April 2 to cut the trail, with Peary and his team following a day later. Snow squalls and biting winds blew initially from the north, the direction of travel, frostbiting Peary's face, then shifted to the west and gained force. "It was going that would seriously discourage an ordinary traveler, but my little brown children of the ice cheerfully tooled their sledges through it," Peary boasted about his Inuit sledge drivers, all of whom were fully grown and at least some of whom had traveled with him before.[33]

On April 5, Peary's party caught up to Henson's party in camp, with Henson complaining that the weather was "too thick to travel" and his men, according to Peary, "belly aching about being so far away." Peary blamed Henson: "He has fallen down badly on his job," Peary wrote in his diary. But the weather worsened, and both parties hunkered down until the gale spent itself. As days passed in what Peary later called his "storm camp," he mulled over his prospects for glory upon his return "and then, I run against the blank wall," he wrote, "unless I win *here*, all these things will fall through. Success is what will give them existence." This second multiple-day delay frustrated Peary more than the first because now he saw even his farthest north slipping away. "The wind continued its infernal howling past the igloo," Peary wrote on the third day in camp. "It seemed as if we had been here a month." He tried to go outside two days later, "partly for exercise, partly because I could no longer keep quiet," but could barely stand against the wind. "*No* party could travel in this gale."[34]

It was not until April 12 that the weather cleared enough for Peary to calculate his position. What he found surprised him. During the seven days in camp, while nothing seemed to have moved, winds and currents had carried the igloos en masse with the surrounding ice over 60 miles eastward. They now stood due north of the ship at slightly over 85° north latitude, or about 90 miles south of the Italian record. Here Peary faced a choice for himself and his men. He could try to push north on limited supplies or return south to his ship and safety.

Peary's harshest critics say that he turned south, and everything else he wrote about the journey was rank fiction. Comparing Peary's published account with what survives in a transcript of his sledging diary, and factoring in his fanatic determination, Wally Herbert concludes that Peary headed north for the record but probably exaggerated how far he went.[35] Having reviewed the same records, I side with Herbert but concede that, unless more evidence emerges, no one now can know for sure.

According to his account, Peary sent Henson's party north on April 12, with his own team following on the 14th. "We started after abandoning everything we did not absolutely need, and I bent every energy to setting a record pace," Peary reported. The first day, he claimed 30 miles and writes that his drivers put it at 40. Passing Henson's party around noon, he claimed 30 miles again the next day, with Henson struggling to keep pace. If correct, both distances were over five times the daily average of his prior travel days on this expedition and would have left Peary only about 30 miles short of a record farthest north. After another good day of perhaps 20 miles—Peary only gives a mileage rate for this day, not the total mileage or hours traveled—violent winds and driving snow forced the combined party to lay over on April 17. "While here," Peary wrote, "six worn-out dogs were killed and fed to the others."[36] The delay offered another point where Peary might have turned back. His drivers urged him to do so, but if his published claims are believed, Peary decided he was too close to give up. Yet the mileage estimates in his diary are less for each of the three prior days than in his published account, and if the lower figures are correct, he still had some 30 miles to go for the record rather than the implied 10.

According to both his diary and his published account, Peary resumed his trek north after the storm subsided on April 18. Here the former becomes truly muddled and the latter largely vacuous beyond the assertion that, at about noon on April 21, after three and a half more days of sledging, "When my observations were taken and rapidly figured, they showed that we had reached 87°6' north latitude." Peary had beaten the Italian mark by over half a degree—some 35 miles—or so he said. After hoisting his flags on the nearest hummock and taking a group photo, Peary, Henson, and their combined party hastily headed south, reaching their last camp by the day's end.

Peary's claim raises questions. Although the critical page for April 21 is missing from the diary transcript, the prior page suggests that the party was trapped "in a perfect mesh of leads" about 10 miles short of the record on April 20. The published account mentions these leads but asserts that the party hurried between them on "a forced march."[37] In either event, it strains credibility to think that he made it beyond 87° north latitude by noon on the 21st and then back to his last camp in one day—a distance of perhaps 60 miles or more. Maybe Peary padded his claim to make himself the first to reach within 3 degrees of the pole. Yet it was the record alone that allowed him to return home with enough acclaim to loosen his sponsors' purse strings for one last grasp at the ultimate prize.

ALREADY PHYSICALLY SPENT, THE men faced a hellish return trip. They had sprinted over the last stretch north with the barest essentials and had even less left for the long march back. Fierce headwinds now came from the southwest. A full-scale gale struck as they approached their former storm camp, driving them inside the old, now-snow-filled igloos where they had endured days of anxious waiting on the way north. A prisoner's return, it must have seemed. One by one, their weakest dogs were cooked over fires built from the broken-up sticks of their empty sledges.

Finding the Big Lead up to 2 miles wide, they were forced to lay over on its north side for two or more days before a portion skimmed over with a film of new ice just thick enough for them to glide across, widely spaced and wearing snowshoes to distribute their weight. One firm footfall would have doomed them to the frigid ocean's depths. Even as it was, a toe would break through here or there, causing a shriek. Peary now called it the River Styx rather than the Hudson.

"It was the first and only time in all my Arctic work that I felt doubtful as to the outcome," he wrote. Making matters worse, both sides of the Big Lead were marked by zones of wrenched, upheaved, and shattered ice requiring a pickax to break through. Peary termed it a "frozen Hades."[38]

Once across the Big Lead, the Inuits hoped the *Roosevelt* lay dead ahead, but Peary knew that the ice pack's eastward drift would make it Greenland's desolate Arctic coast. There, much to everyone's surprise, Peary's group met one of the supporting parties, utterly lost, wandering in the wrong direction, and with its members near death. Peary added them to his band, which now numbered twelve. Once on shore, the men foraged for Arctic hare, which they ate raw, before finally felling a small herd of musk oxen and feasting for two days. Then they faced the long slog over coastal shore ice to the ship.

After three months on the Arctic ice, the men staggered onto the *Roosevelt* during the final week of May. The other support parties were already present or accounted for, with no one lost. Only forty-one out of some one hundred twenty dogs survived.[39] Regardless of any padding of the record, it was an epic journey.

Yet Peary was not satisfied. In his address to the 1904 Geographical Congress, he had noted that a portion of Ellesmere Island's northwest coast had never been explored. Now he set out to map this 65-mile-long stretch by sledging west with a small party of Inuits around the island's northern shore to the farthest point that earlier explorers had reached from the opposite direction.

Still bruised and footsore from his northern journey, Peary departed on June 2 for a trek that covered more than 200 miles over fifty-eight days. Traveling in summer, the party faced wet snow, thick fog, broken ice, streaming meltwater, and knee-deep slush. "My clothes are now literally rotting from the constant wet," Peary complained partway through the ordeal. "I have got used to the disagreeableness of the wet, but not yet to the stench."[40] At some places, the route became virtually impassable. Forced by open water and shattered shore ice to cross a steep ice foot, for example, Peary wrote of the sledges being "pushed, dragged, hauled, hoisted and lowered by all of us, and sometimes unloaded and backed over the roughest places."[41]

For Peary, however, the trek offered a chance to chart newfound land and name its features for his sponsors. "*Mine,*" he wrote upon reaching the previously unexplored stretch, "mine by right of discovery, to be credited to me, and associated with my name, generations after I have ceased to be."[42] His greatest boast came at the journey's farthest point when he claimed to spy an unknown island in the northwest. He named it Crocker Land after George Crocker, who had given more money to the expedition than anyone else. Much like the islands that Peary claimed to see north of Greenland during his 1891–92 expedition, Crocker Land proved to be an illusion or a fabrication. Peary never mentions the sighting in his sledging diary, even though, in his later published account, he places it second only to his farthest north among the expedition's main results.[43] Once back in the United States, the finding and naming helped to prime the pump for funding his next expedition.

As Peary neared Cape Sheridan in late July, following his western journey, he learned that the *Roosevelt* had slipped its moorage three weeks earlier and floated south beyond Cape Union, where it had been pinched between the moving pack and the ice foot's vertical face, ripping a blade off the propeller and wrecking the rudder and stern post. Captain Bartlett later told the story somewhat differently, but all accounts agreed that ice had crushed the ship in early July, ruining the propulsion and steering, with Bartlett adding that it punched a hole in the hull the size of a small child.[44] The ship would have sunk then and there but for being held aloft by ice on both sides.

After makeshift repairs but still leaking in the stern and lacking full steam propulsion and proper steering, the *Roosevelt* began inching its way south, using its sails when possible. Twice it was trapped in ice for days, raising the prospect of another Arctic winter. Repeatedly it halted for repairs or caulking. With a jury-rigged rudder, it often ran aground or into the ice foot. Bartlett feared that the ship would sink at any moment, but he kept it afloat through frequent gales.[45]

Its pumps running nonstop, the *Roosevelt* slowly worked its way south, dropping off the Inuits as it passed their villages, and then steamed sluggishly for New York, where it arrived on Christmas Eve, 1906, after over five months at sea and a few more groundings. Sailors who saw it in dry dock marveled that it had made it back at all. Perhaps no other ship could have survived. Yet throughout the anxious passage, Peary spoke of taking it back to the Arctic within a year.

"I should have thought he wouldn't have wanted ever to see that place again," Bartlett commented.[46]

THE *ROOSEVELT* REACHED ITS first port with a telegraph on November 2, and news of the expedition quickly spread. At first the press did not know what to make of Peary's farthest north—once again it fell short of the pole—but President Roosevelt declared it heroic, and that became the story. Echoing the accepted view, Henson later blamed the shortfall on the ice pack "disintegrating much too early that year to suit," and stressed the prospect of winning out in a normal year.[47] On November 24, upon reaching the first port with rail connections, Peary dashed ahead for New York, leaving Bartlett, Henson, and the crew to bring in the ship over the next four weeks.

Peary received a hero's reception in New York. For his first public address, thirty thousand people descended on Jesup's American Museum of Natural History only to find that the auditorium only sat fifteen hundred. "The crush was tremendous," one reporter noted. "Women had their clothing torn and men lost their hats" in the surge to greet Peary. "The Stars and Stripes have been placed in the forefront of that international endurance contest known as the race for the north pole," Peary declared. "Had it been a normal season and not a mild winter I firmly believe I would have brought back the pole."[48]

Four days later, he received the formal congratulations of the Peary Arctic Club and gave much the same address. Jesup introduced Peary both times and, after earlier voicing disappointment at Peary's failure to reach the pole, now fully endorsed him and his next effort. "We have come so near it that we are not going to give up the quest," Jesup proclaimed. "I am determined to stick to him."[49]

After New York, Peary rushed on to Washington, where he attended the annual cabinet dinner at the White House and received the National Geographic Society's highest award, the Hubbard Medal. Roosevelt personally presented the medal to Peary.

"Civilized people usually live in conditions of life so easy that there is a certain tendency to atrophy of the hardier virtues," the president said, in words expressing Gilded Age angst over a loss of physical vigor. "And it is a relief to pay signal honor to a man who by his achievements makes it evident that in some of the race at least there has been no loss of hardy virtue."[50]

Peary responded with a Rooseveltian testimonial to the adventurous life. "The true explorer does his work not for any hope of reward or honor, but because the thing he has set himself to do is a part of his being," Peary said. Applying this standard to his own endeavors, the fifty-year-old explorer observed that reaching the North Pole is "the thing I must do." And as to its greater value, he added, "Should an American first of all men place the Stars and Stripes at that coveted spot, there is not an American citizen at home or abroad, and there are millions of us, but what would feel a little better and a little prouder of being an American."[51] Roosevelt could not have been more pleased.

A month later, Peary expanded on this theme in comments to an alumni meeting of his college fraternity, Delta Kappa Epsilon, of which Roosevelt was also a member. Alluding to Roosevelt's ongoing program to cut an American-controlled shipping passage through Panama, Peary affirmed, "I believe it is as much the duty of this country to own not only the north, but the south pole, as to build the Panama Canal and control the Pacific."[52]

Yet there was nothing at the North Pole to own or control. Reaching it first had fundamentally the same worth as a first ascent of the Matterhorn or K2: extraordinary human feats, to be sure, but ones that gained value by the meaning that people attached to them. For himself, Peary staked everything on the pole. This was both a strength and a weakness. His detractors and his deifiers agree that Peary was obsessed. They disagree on whether his obsession was rooted in reaching his goal, serving his country, or glorifying himself. These varying views of Peary mark the difference between seeing him as a fanatic, a patriot, or a mountebank. No one doubts his devotion. "I believe that this is the work that God Almighty intended for me," Peary wrote to Roosevelt.[53]

PEARY CAME BACK FROM his 1905–06 expedition claiming that damage to the *Roosevelt* was minor and easily repaired. He would be off again for the pole by June, he vowed.[54] Bartlett knew better, and with a short window open each summer for navigating north through Smith Sound and beyond, leaving in 1907 proved impossible. Costs mounted too. When Jesup died early in 1908 without providing for the Peary Arctic Club in his will, Peary was thrown back on public appeals for funds. With the president's blessing, the navy granted Peary another three-year-long paid leave. And eventually enough money came in, much of it in small donations, such that by spring 1908, the expedition was just $4,000 shy of its projected budget.[55]

Given his age and physical condition, what would surely be Peary's final expedition left New York on July 6, 1908. This departure date pushed the earliest possible assault on the pole back to spring 1909. Peary vowed to use much the same methods on this expedition as he had on the last one, though he hoped to have his support parties advance as a unit that would fall back in stages rather than to shuttle supplies separately.[56]

By the time of his departure, Peary had the added worry of Frederick Cook. After claiming the first ascent of Denali in 1906, Cook agreed to guide a hunting trip to Greenland's Smith Sound region aboard a gleaming white, gold-trimmed yacht for casino mogul John Bradley during the summer of 1907. The mogul and his guide had a private understanding that Cook could remain north over the ensuing winter to embark on a trek to the North Pole in 1908 (with support from local Inuits) should conditions warrant. They did. "I find that I now have a good opportunity to try for the North Pole," Cook wrote in a letter sent back with Bradley in October. "My plan," Cook reported, "is to cross Ellesmere Land and reach the Polar Sea by Nansen Strait."[57]

Bradley's yacht had taken along supplies for this purpose, and the ship's twenty-nine-year-old German steward and cook, Rudolph Franke, volunteered to remain with Cook. They built a hut from packing crates on Greenland's Smith Sound coast 15 miles north of Etah, gathered the local Inuits around them, and settled in for the winter. News of Cook's planned assault on the North Pole spread rapidly. Newspapers reprinted Cook's letter and hailed the prospect of an American race to the pole between him and Peary.

Peary was livid. He did not think that Cook, who had little

sledging experience and none whatsoever on the polar ice pack, could reach the pole. Peary's fear was that Cook might claim it nonetheless.

At the urging of the Peary Arctic Club, Columbia University professor Herschel Parker, who had joined Cook on his second Denali expedition until convinced that it was futile, now denounced Cook's claim to have climbed North America's highest mountain. "He might have ascended one of the peaks in the range," Parker said, "but I do not believe that he made the ascent of Mount McKinley."[58] Peary then agreed to succeed Cook as president of the Explorers Club on the condition that it would question any claim that Cook reached the pole. Peary also published warnings that, in the event Cook returned before him claiming the pole, no one should believe him, and sent letters to supporters urging them to denounce any such claims by Cook.[59]

In the developing media battle, the *New York Times* (which held exclusive newspaper rights to Peary's own story nationally through syndication) became Peary's mouthpiece while the larger *New York Herald* favored Cook and bought his story. "That Cook had got the start of Peary does not count for so much," the *Times* commented in October 1907. "Peary will be in the race."[60] Its editors clearly hoped so because they paid Peary a $4,000 advance for exclusive first rights to his story of reaching the pole.

Matters stood on the precipice, with the public divided and popular interest mounting as Peary's ship made its courtesy call at Oyster Bay on July 7, 1908, for inspection by the president before steaming north toward the Arctic. "Decks of the 'Roosevelt' must be cleared absolutely," Peary wrote to Captain Bartlett in anticipation of the presidential visit, "even if some of the stuff has to be pulled out of the hold again later."[61] After Peary and his wife lunched with the first family at Roosevelt's summer home, the entire party toured the ship, with the president showing keen interest. "Nothing escaped his attention," Bartlett noted. "He went into the lower hold and into the engine room. He inspected Peary's quarters and the living spaces of the sailors."[62] The president insisted on personally greeting everyone aboard. "It's ninety or nothing; 'the North Pole or bust' this time, Mr. President," Bartlett declared.

"We'll reach the pole, Mr. President, if it is possible for human beings to get there," Peary added.

"Yes," Roosevelt replied with a toothy grin, "I believe in you, Peary."[63]

CHAPTER 6

Beyond the Screaming Sixties

MIDSUMMER DAYLIGHT IN THE Arctic coincides with midwinter darkness in the Antarctic. Thus, by the time Peary's expedition left New York in July 1908, Shackleton's men were tucked into their winter quarters on Antarctica's Ross Island. When full daylight returned in October, they could focus their undivided effort on their polar sledge trips. After what these men had already endured, they had to wonder, how much worse could it get? Bonded by shared adversity, boyish enthusiasm, and Shackleton's charismatic leadership, they were prepared for virtually anything. Adventure was in the air, and with Shackleton in charge, it infused the entire enterprise.

THE EXPEDITION HAD STARTED royally. King Edward VII, who then reigned over the largest empire in history, Queen Alexandra, two of their adult children, including the Prince of Wales, the future King George V, and George's twelve-year old son, the future King Edward VIII, personally inspected Shackleton's diminutive ship, the *Nimrod*, on August 5, 1907, two days before its departure from England. It was a grubby little barkentine: a forty-year-old, 136-foot-long, oak-hulled, steam-and-sail-propelled Newfoundland sealer that had suffered more than its fair share of hard use and heavy seas over the years. But it was solidly built and, at £5,000, within Shackleton's limited budget. Even at that price, title was held by expedition patron William Beardmore, who had made a fortune manufacturing armor plate and heavy guns for Royal Navy vessels before diversifying into building the ships themselves. Beardmore, who went to the same private school as Shackleton, had hired the explorer as something of a roving company spokesperson after he returned from the *Discovery* Expedition without suitable job prospects.

For its royal inspection, the *Nimrod* anchored in Cowes Harbor on the Isle of Wight, near the newly commissioned HMS *Dreadnought*, the largest ship in the British navy and first in a new class of big-gun battleships that would revolutionize naval warfare for a generation. Many reports commented on the contrast. Both ships were there as part of Cowes Week, an annual regatta and naval show that, in 1906, featured nearly two hundred battleships, cruisers, destroyers, gunboats, and submarines of the Royal Navy's newly formed home fleet, which was created to counter the growing threat of German naval expansion. By extending Britain's claims in the Antarctic and perhaps establishing them all the way to the South Pole, the *Nimrod* was serving somewhat similar imperial purposes as the *Dreadnought*. The little ship had been summoned to Cowes Week by royal command, delaying its departure from England for several days.

Boarding the *Nimrod* by steam pinnace from the royal yacht *Victoria and Albert* must have come as something of a shock for the royals, who were dressed in the finest yachting attire. By some accounts, the ship's smell was pungent and its deck crowded to the point of cluttered. "The King expressed a desire to see the equipment of the vessel, and he and the Queen and the rest of the distinguished company were shown the sledges, sleeping-bags, tents, and a vast variety of preserved foods," one report noted. "Heaps of fur-lined clothing also attracted the attention of their Majesties. In respect to one stout blue suit the King, with a smile, remarked to the lieutenant, 'Do you think you will find this warm enough?'" Having rejected Fridtjof Nansen's advice that the explorers wear outer garments made from the skins of Arctic animals and instead opted to manufacture them from donated, British-made Burberry gabardine, Shackleton could at best reply, "It should do."[1]

After the queen presented Shackleton with a Union Jack to plant at the South Pole and the king conferred on him the Royal Victorian Order for service to the empire, Edward VII concluded, "There is nothing left for me to do except to wish you a very safe and prosperous voyage in connection with your important and difficult enterprise."[2] Few British explorers had ever received such a royal send-off.

WITH ONLY ITS CREW aboard, the *Nimrod* sailed from England on August 7, 1907, bound for New Zealand by way of Cape Town and a long, slow crossing of the Indian Ocean. Oval shaped with a broad, ironclad bow and wide beam, the ship bobbed through the ocean like a toy boat, pitching and rolling excessively but always righting itself.

"The ship is good, but dirty when deep," Captain Rupert English reported to Shackleton after the *Nimrod* reached New Zealand on November 23, following a three-and-a-half-month passage.[3] One Australian newspaper described it as "the smallest craft that has ever tried to reach the South Pole."[4] Nevertheless, over two thousand people had turned out to see it off from England, and twenty-five times that number did the same from its final port of call in New Zealand. Thinking better of taking the long voyage, Shackleton and the entire shore crew traveled by fast steamers, some leaving as late as November 7 but still catching up with the *Nimrod* in Lyttelton.

Added time in London followed by a series of stops in Australia gave Shackleton a chance to complete preparations and raise funds for an expedition that he had organized on the fly and financed on a shoestring. He had told his wife, Emily, about the expedition only in mid-February 1907, less than six months before the *Nimrod* sailed and barely six weeks after she had given birth to their first child.

"It will only be one year and I shall come back with honour and with money and never never part from you again," he promised her in a letter that he closed with the words "Your Boy, Ernest, Your lover and husband."[5]

Emily knew it was a promise Ernest could not keep. "It was his own spirit 'a soul whipped on by the wander fire' that would keep him going back," Emily later commented.[6]

Indeed, without tipping his hand, seven weeks before telling his wife about the trip, Shackleton had said to Royal Geographical Society librarian Hugh Robert Mill about the lure of Antarctica, "What would I not give to be out there again doing the job, and this time really on the way to the Pole."[7] At the time, Mill could not reveal that Robert Scott was planning a second polar expedition for 1910, and it came as a shock to Scott when Shackleton publicly announced his own strikingly similar plans at one of the society's dinner meetings in February 1907.

"It is held that the southern sledge party of the *Discovery* would have reached a much higher altitude if they had been more adequately equipped," Shackleton then said of his own failed polar dash with Scott in 1902. "In the new expedition, in addition to dogs, Siberian ponies will be taken, as the surface of the land or ice over which they will have to travel will be eminently suited for this mode of sledge travelling." He also announced that he would take along an Arrol-Johnston automobile modified for driving on ice, without mentioning that Beardmore, the automaker's largest stockholder, brokered the arrangement as a publicity stunt.[8] Neither the ponies nor the car worked well in Antarctic conditions.

Pointing out that dogs performed admirably for Peary and the Duke of the Abruzzi in their polar quests, Nansen had urged Shackleton to rely on them. The British explorer could not forget his bad experience with dog-sledging during the *Discovery* Expedition, however, and would not admit that poor handling had caused it. The only dogs he took along were those left in New Zealand after Borchgrevink's 1898–1900 expedition, and he would never give them a chance to show their stuff. If the ponies and car failed, which they did, Shackleton vowed to fall back on old-fashioned British man-hauling, which he did. He even rejected Nansen's plea to try skis, which the Norwegian had so successfully used in Greenland.

In his initial public announcement and an earlier private circular, Shackleton identified reaching the south geographic and magnetic poles as his new expedition's twin objectives, with primacy for the former. The *Discovery* Expedition's old Ross Island base would be his winter quarters. "The expedition has the support of many influential men who wish British prestige in exploration to maintain its premier place," Shackleton boasted.[9]

Upon learning of Shackleton's plans, Scott was livid. Fearing a British competitor for the pole, Scott asserted a proprietary right to the Ross Island route toward the South Pole, much as Peary claimed the Smith Sound route toward the North Pole. Both claims had little basis even under strict Victorian standards of rectitude, but Shackleton relented under pressure from the Royal Geographical Society. He agreed to establish his winter quarters where Borchgrevink's expedition had briefly landed near the ice barrier's eastern end and to sledge south across the ice shelf where it abutted King Edward VII Land in the east. The route had its advantages: the distance from the barrier's edge to the geographic pole was 60 miles less starting from there rather than from Ross Island. But the route south was utterly unexplored, and the magnetic pole most likely would be beyond reach.

DURING THE FINAL WEEKS of 1907, the *Nimrod* with twenty-two officers and crewmen; Shackleton and eleven members of the shore party from Britain; Edgeworth David, Douglas Mawson, and two others that Shackleton had recruited in Australia; and fifteen ponies from Manchuria converged on Lyttelton, New Zealand. They were ready to sail south on January 1, 1908. The small ship was so chock-full of supplies and equipment that five ponies had to be left behind. As their common cabin, fifteen members of the shore party shared a 24-by-6-foot aft hold, reached by climbing down a hatch from the foredeck and packed with the shore parties' luggage and equipment, which one occupant described as "more like my idea of Hell than anything I have ever imagined."[10] Even the ever-optimistic Shackleton termed it a "twentieth-century Black Hole."[11] Six-foot-three-inch-tall Mawson called it "an awful hole" and opted instead to sleep in a lifeboat on deck, even during raging storms.[12] Shackleton billeted with two others in the captain's cabin.

Worse yet, with everything else aboard, the ship could not carry enough coal to make the round trip safely. To conserve fuel, Shackleton persuaded a local steamship company and the New Zealand government to provide a ship to tow the *Nimrod* as far as the ice pack—or over 1,600 miles through the world's most notorious seas. Even with this aid, the *Nimrod* sailed with its waterline 2 feet below the safe maximum draft, virtually assuring that water would spill over the deck in even moderately heavy seas. "We would have added at least another fifty tons to our two hundred and fifty; but the risk was too great," Shackleton said of the stores.[13] Towing aggravated the situation by pulling the ship's bow down, into oncoming waves.

Nevertheless, the *Nimrod* received a resounding send-off from Lyttelton Harbour on New Year's Day, a midsummer holiday and the date of the harbor's annual regatta. "Quays, piers, shipping were just a swaying, shouting mass of humanity," David wrote of the throng that gathered there.[14] "Tremendous crowds everywhere on hills, special steamers, [and a] fleet of 4 warships, including flagship" of the Royal Navy's Australian fleet, Mawson noted. Estimates placed the number of spectators at fifty thousand.[15] Shackleton put the figure at thirty thousand for the harbor entrance alone, with another six or seven thousand on the special steamers. "The air trembled with the crash of guns, the piercing steam whistles and sirens of every steamship in the port, and a roar of cheering," he wrote. "Then we drew abreast of the flagship and from the throats of the nine hundred odd bluejackets aboard her we got a ringing farewell, and across the water came the sound of her band playing 'Hearts of oak are our ships,' followed by 'Auld Lang Syne.'"[16] Shackleton's bare-bones expedition had become a grand voyage of empire.

WITH THE *NIMROD* PERILOUSLY overloaded and in tow, those aboard it hoped for a smooth passage. They did not get one. Three separate gales pounded the ship as it passed through the so-called Furious Fifties and Screaming Sixties. "The little *Nimrod* pitched about like a cork on the ocean," Shackleton wrote on the second day. "The seas began to break over her, and we were soon wet through." Two days later he added, "As evening wore on the weather became worse, and we shipped huge quantities of water." Calling it a "struggle against nature in its sternest mood," Shackleton reported that "the *Nimrod* rolled over fifty degrees from perpendicular to each side; how much more than that I cannot say, for the indicator recording the roll of the ship was only marked up to fifty degrees, and the pointer hand passed that mark."[17] Rolls of this magnitude repeatedly put the ship more than halfway onto its side in raging seas. Water rushed through the deck-level wardroom and poured into the shore party's below-deck cabin.

Every living thing on board suffered. "We were nearly all more or less horribly sea-sick," David wrote, speaking for the nonsailors aboard. "Many even of the officers were distinctly off-colour." With each sharp roll, the ponies were thrown headlong or hind-first into the ends of their stalls and struggled to remain standing.[18] "On going aft," chief surgeon Eric Marshall noted on January 9, "a huge sea came on deck & left me hanging on to a life line with a seething mass of water up to my waist. It was goodbye to anyone who let go."[19]

Without fear of understatement, Mawson commented on the voyage a day later, "Up to date life has been hideous." Surveying the damage so far, he added, "The bulwarks and some deck houses are broken, one dog and a pony are dead."[20] Marshall admitted to being "sick as hell."[21] One officer declared, "I have never seen such large seas in the whole of my seagoing career."[22]

The *Nimrod* survived its harrowing voyage with no loss of human life. On January 15, after two weeks at sea, a white line of ice appeared on the southern horizon. After a brief exchange of letters, supplies, and one passenger, the tow ship cut its cable and turned north, leaving the *Nimrod* to sail south through the ice and into the Ross Sea. The exchanged passenger, Maclean Buckley, was a wealthy English yachtsman with landholdings in New Zealand who, scarcely an hour before the *Nimrod* left Lyttelton, joined it on a lark with nothing but the summer suit on his back and an overnight bag from his club in Christchurch. A £500 donation secured his passage as far as the ice pack. He joined "for sheer love of adventure," Shackleton said of Buckley, who previously had sailed his yacht around the world.[23] According to David, Buckley stood on deck shouting "Splendid!" and "Well done, old girl!" as the *Nimrod* crashed through the storm-tossed sea.[24] With the ice in sight, Buckley returned north with the tow ship and more thrilling tales of survival at sea.

The letters sent back with the tow ship included one from David saying that he would stay with the expedition through 1909 rather than return with the *Nimrod* as first agreed. Shackleton made the offer on the voyage, David claimed, and he accepted.[25] David's wife, Cara, expected something of this sort all along. Interviewed when the expedition left, she had said about David, "I believe he is praying that the *Nimrod* will be iced in, so that he will have some excuse to stay."[26] The love of adventure that had carried him from Oxford to a geologic survey post in colonial Australia, repeated expeditions into the bush, and research on Funafuti was not extinguished when he reached age fifty. For a geologist of his stature, Antarctica was *the* destination of a lifetime. For an expedition leader with Shackleton's ambitions, David's presence offered the promise of scientific credibility beyond even what Scott had gained with his big-budget *Discovery* Expedition. If the deal was sealed on the voyage south after each of these larger-than-life figures had fully sized each other up, rather than before departure as some historians suspect, it was a match made amid conditions that gave both men fair warning of the challenges ahead. Neither would have been deterred by them.

In addition to David, the fourteen-member shore party included five persons charged mainly with conducting scientific work in the Antarctic and two surgeons. To distract them from storms and seasickness during the roughest part of the voyage south, Shackleton abruptly put all fourteen to work tending the distressed ponies, making hourly meteorological records, and operating hand pumps. David suspected that Shackleton did it to build morale. If so, it worked. "There can be no doubt that regular duties are healthful and chastening," David wrote home from the voyage, and added about Shackleton, "He is certainly fulfilling the high expectations that had been formed of him as a leader."[27] For his part, Buckley returned to New Zealand praising Shackleton as a leader "under whose discipline and magnetic influence every member of the expedition will put forth his heartiest efforts."[28]

And as for David, calling him as "hard as nails," Shackleton wrote back from the *Nimrod*, "He will prove invaluable to me."[29] Shackleton and David may have made a heavenly match, but they consummated it in hellish conditions.

UNDER ITS OWN STEAM at last, the *Nimrod* headed south roughly along the 180th meridian until the morning of January 16, when it reached a broken wall of tabular icebergs drifting north. "Tongue and pen fail in attempting to describe the magic of such a scene," Shackleton wrote. "As far as the eye could see from the crow's-nest of the *Nimrod*, the great, white, wall-sided bergs stretched east, west and south, making a striking contrast with the lanes of blue-black water between them." David compared it to sailing through Venice, but with buildings of pure alabaster and on a far vaster scale. "With full steam and all sail we hurried along, now down the wide water-ways between burgs, now along narrow lanes, with a wall of ice to starboard and a wall of ice to port," he wrote. "It was the most wonderful and fascinating sight, in the way of natural scenery, that had ever met our gaze." The maze stretched for over 80 miles, north and south, and had untold breadth, east to west. After twelve hours passing through the bergs, Shackleton wrote, "A few more turnings and twistings through the devious water lanes, and we entered the ice free Ross Sea."[30]

Once exiting the "silent city of the Snow King," as David called the belt of icebergs, it was six days of smooth sailing south-by-southeast to the Great Ice Barrier.[31] "We were now reveling in the indescribable freshness of the Antarctic that seems to permeate one's being, and which must be responsible for that longing to go again which assails each returned explorer from polar regions," Shackleton said of this part of the voyage.[32] He loved being back, and the others delighted in discovering it for the first time.

Then another wonder: the barrier rose before them, a vertical wall of glacial ice reaching 200 or more feet above the waterline and extending up to 2,000 feet below it, the front of a floating ice shelf extending more than 500 miles south to the mainland. "It is hard again to convey in words what this wonderful ice barrier, which may fairly rank as the eighth wonder of the world, is really like," David noted. "It seemed too mystic and wonderful for this earth, and fitter rather for those 'crystal battlements of Heaven' that Milton pictured." Shackleton commented on the "exclamations of wonder and astonishment at the stupendous bulk of the Barrier" from everyone on board who had not seen it before.[33] In an age of high adventure, the Antarctic was working its magic.

Upon reaching the barrier, Shackleton sailed east along its front looking for the twin inlets that Borchgrevink's *Southern Cross* Expedition and Scott's *Discovery* Expedition had charted earlier in the decade. In these inlets, those expeditions had landed parties that sledged for a few miles southward over the ice shelf. Shackleton planned to winter here, but the ice front had broken off, leaving one large bay, which he named the Bay of Whales, where two inlets had been. That raised concerns about the safety of wintering on the ice shelf. Further, a thick skin of sea ice blocked the ship from entering far enough into the bay to find moorage. Shackleton looked farther east for landing sites, but sea ice again barred the way, leaving him with the apparent alternatives of returning west toward Ross Island or going north to New Zealand. But for his promise not to use Scott's route toward the pole, Ross Island was the obvious pick. As he put it in a letter to his wife, Shackleton had to choose between either the duty owed his men and country to carry on or the honor of keeping his word to Scott. "Of course, for a moment the second alternative could not be entertained," David declared. "So with a heavy heart I gave the order for turning back" to Ross Island, Shackleton explained to his wife. "My conscience is clear but my heart is sore."[34]

Arriving at Ross Island on January 28, Shackleton spent a week exploring landing sites before settling on Cape Royds, a rocky promontory jutting from the island's west coast into McMurdo Sound. He had hoped to reach the *Discovery*'s old anchorage, where Scott's expedition had left a cabin, or "hut," on shore, but the sea ice had not yet gone out that far south. Cape Royds, 23 miles north of Scott's Hut Point base, was as far as the *Nimrod* could sail in 1908. The chosen site boasted an Adélie penguin rookery for eggs and meat, a shallow lake for freshwater, and an easy slope from the shore to a level site for buildings. Work began at once unloading the tons of supplies, equipment, ponies, car, and other materials needed for the expedition. Racing to get the ship unpacked before the weather turned, the men labored long hours for two weeks until the *Nimrod* departed on February 22, leaving them to face winter on their own. They erected a 19-by-33-foot prefabricated wooden hut for themselves, makeshift stables for the ponies, and a shed for the automobile. The hut's door opened to a stunning view of the Western Mountains rising across McMurdo Sound on the Victoria Land coast. Mount Erebus, the active volcano then assumed to be Antarctica's highest peak, rose dramatically behind them.

WHILE IN SOME WAYS Cape Royds offered a good setting for Shackleton's winter quarters, and a more scenic one than either Scott's Hut Point or Borchgrevink's base at Cape Adare, it had one major drawback as the starting point for a trek to the South Pole. Unlike Hut Point, which had ready access onto the Ross Ice Shelf, Cape Royds was cut off by bays, glaciers, and ice falls in the south. The only practical way by foot, sledge, or motorcar from Cape Royds toward the South Pole lay over the sea ice to Hut Point and from there onto the ice shelf. Once that sea ice broke apart, shortly after the expedition's arrival in February, the explorers could not travel south until the ice reformed during the winter, by which time it was too dark for anyone to venture far from the base until spring. The south magnetic pole was equally problematic on foot from Cape Royds. It lay across McMurdo Sound, which was open water when the expedition arrived and only froze over in winter.

The location of his expedition's winter quarters left Shackleton with a dilemma. During March and April, before the full onset of winter, he planned to lay advance supply depots along the route south in preparation for his dash to the pole, which he hoped to begin in October of the following spring. Not only would these depots measurably assist the southern sledge journey, laying them would give his restless men something constructive to do. As Cook and

Amundsen had discovered during the 1897–98 Belgian expedition, and Borchgrevink's men had learned during the 1899–1900 *Southern Cross* Expedition, idleness and lack of purpose among persons cooped together through a long Antarctic winter leads to bitterness, backbiting, and both mental and physical illness. On both expeditions, members died over the winter and collegiality was lost forever.

A natural leader, Shackleton knew his men should not remain idle during the winter and planned various activities for them. To help keep his men occupied and working together during the *Discovery* Expedition, Scott had them write and print a newspaper, which Shackleton edited. Besting Scott, Shackleton took along equipment so that his men could publish a book, *Aurora Australis*, with many of them contributing articles, short stories, poems, or illustrations. Like Scott, he also planned to have the men keep regular meteorological and other scientific records, celebrate birthdays and holidays, engage in sports, and maintain a daily regimen of work, meals, leisure, and sleep. Further, his men had ponies to tend, which included regular feedings and exercise. Perhaps as important as anything, Shackleton brought along an acetylene gas lighting system to keep the hut bright during the midwinter darkness. But he struggled to come up with a meaningful replacement for laying depots in the south until he looked more closely at the mountain rising behind Cape Royds. Some speculate that David gave him the idea.

Mount Erebus, though well known since James Clark Ross's day as the world's most southerly active volcano, had never been climbed. "From a geological point of view the mountain ought to reveal some interesting facts," Shackleton wrote. "Apart from scientific considerations, the ascent of a mountain over 13,000 ft. in height, situated so far south, would be a matter of pleasurable excitement both to those who were selected as climbers and to the rest of us who wished for our companions' success."[35] Though no one in the group had training or equipment for mountaineering, Shackleton felt that climbing Erebus in the fall would give his men a sense of shared achievement to savor over the winter. Further, it could provide material for the expedition's book, and, at a time when interest in mountain climbing was ascendant and first ascents hailed, it would represent a noteworthy feat for the expedition, different from anything that Scott's *Discovery* Expedition accomplished. Shackleton was all for firsts and farthests, especially if they involved beating Scott.

The enterprise came together quickly. "No sooner was it decided to make the ascent, which was arranged for, finally, on March 4, than the winter quarters became busy with the bustle of preparation," Shackleton wrote, "yet such was the energy thrown into this work that the men were ready for the road and made a start at 8.30 a.m. on the 5th."[36] They jury-rigged three pairs of crampons by driving spikes through strips of leather, which were then looped with straps so they could be attached, nail-points down, onto the bottom of the climbers' finnesko boots. In place of backpacks, which the expedition did not carry, the climbers strapped their sleeping bags over their backs and shoulders as a sort of makeshift knapsack. They also hauled an 11-foot sledge loaded with a quarter ton of supplies as far as possible up the mountain, which proved to be about a third of the way.

Attuned to the potential geologic significance of the climb, Shackleton tapped David, Mawson, and the expedition's Scottish assistant surgeon, Forbes Mackay, for the main party assigned to summit. Shackleton would remain behind. The expedition's second-in-command, Jameson Adams; its assistant geologist, the young, adventure-loving English baronet Philip Brocklehurst; and chief surgeon Eric Marshall went along to help pull the sledge as far as it would go up the mountain, with authority to continue on to the summit should conditions warrant. Shackleton was considering all three members of this supporting party for the polar trek and saw the climb as a chance to test their mettle. Given their enthusiasm and ambition, the men naturally found conditions warranting all six to attempt the summit.

———

ALTHOUGH CAPE ROYDS SITS on the flanks of Mount Erebus only 17 miles from the summit, the climb was complicated by a steeply rising grade, bitter cold, inadequate preparations, and a blizzard. "At one spot," Shackleton wrote, "the party had a hard struggle, mostly on their hands and knees, in their effort to drag the sledge up the surface of smooth blue ice thinly coated with loose snow."[37] At others, deep sastrugi, or wind furrows in the crusted snow, made pulling uphill almost impossible. "Frequently," David wrote, "these 'sastrugi' caused our sledge to capsize, and several times it had not only to be righted, but repacked."[38]

On day three, at an altitude that David estimated as 5,630 feet, or less than halfway up the mountain, the climbers exchanged their 560-pound sledge for 40-pound improvised knapsacks and proceeded with only essentials. "Some of us with our sleeping bags hanging down our backs, with the foot of the bag curled upwards and outwards, resemble the scorpion men of the Assyrian sculpture," David wrote; "others marched with their household goods done up in the form of huge sausages."[39] Beginning that night, gale-force southeast winds pinned them in two collapsed tents for thirty-two hours at 8,750 feet above sea level. "There was nothing for it, while the blizzard lasted, but to lie low in our sleeping-bags," David noted.[40]

The storm passed after a full day and two nights, and the combined party resumed its ascent. Nearing the rim of the volcano's old, dormant crater, which lay about 2,000 feet below the new, active one, the slope became so steep that the climbers had to cut steps in the hard-packed snow with an ice ax or resort to rocky arêtes where possible. Climbing was difficult even for those with crampons and nearly impossible for those without them. Unaccustomed to the altitude and burdened with heavy loads, the climbers gasped for air.

Reaching the rim after noon on March 9, the men made camp with the intention of spending the rest of the day exploring the old crater. Climbing on his twenty-first birthday in badly fitting ski shoes that pinched off circulation to his toes, Brocklehurst had developed frostbite in both feet that he only now admitted. It later cost him a big toe and a place in the polar sledge party; for now, it cost him the summit. He stayed in camp as the others entered the crater. Here, crossing a snow plain, the men found a fairyland of whimsically shaped, hollow ice mounds, formed when hot steam rising from volcanic vents hits the frigid Antarctic air. No one had seen such a sight; it took David to explain it.

Starting the next morning at 6 A.M., the party (minus Brocklehurst) made for the mountain's summit at the active crater's rim. "Our progress was now painfully slow, as the altitude and cold combined to make respiration difficult," David reported. "The cone was built up chiefly of blocks of pumice, from a few inches up to three feet in diameter." The top was reached after four hours of hard climbing. "The scene that now suddenly burst upon us was magnificent and awe-inspiring," David wrote. "We stood on the verge of a vast abyss, and at first could neither see to the bottom, nor across it, on account of the huge mass of steam filling the crater." After a northerly breeze cleared the air, David added, "Mawson's measurements made the depth 900 feet, and the greatest width about half a mile."[41] Using a combination of methods, the party placed its altitude at 13,370 feet above sea level, which was nearly 600 feet too high but stood for generations as the mountain's accepted elevation.

With their injured companion waiting at the last campsite, the climbers quickly headed back down once they took photographs and measurements. Reaching Brocklehurst after noon, the party pushed on past one more prior campsite in a single afternoon. "Finding an almost endless succession of snow slopes below us, we let ourselves go again and again, in a series of wild rushes towards the foot of the main cone," David recalled.[42] Tossing their packs ahead and using ice axes like rudders, they had slid well over halfway down the mountain by 10 P.M., to where they had left the sledge. Marshall described the plunge: "Pushing bag, glissading, following up, recovering it, dragging, shoving, soaked through." After one more night out, all six climbers stumbled into winter quarters before noon on the next day. "Bruised all over," Marshall wrote, "nearly dead."[43] They were greeted with champagne and Quaker Oats. Along with its two polar treks, this first ascent of Mount Erebus became one of the expedition's three best-known feats. "Fierce was the fight to gain that height," Shackleton wrote in a poem commemorating the event.[44]

EVEN AS THE EXPLORERS celebrated the Erebus party's success, they had growing concerns about their main mission. The car, they found, would not operate on snow, which made it useless for the South Pole trek. The drive wheels spun in place, one of the mechanics noted, "Burying themselves to such an extent that the car moved not an inch."[45] Shackleton had never placed much faith in motor transport, however. He was relying on ponies to pull the sledges across the snow-covered ice shelf toward the pole and thought that six were needed for the job. Two ponies had died due to the rough voyage, leaving eight. Another succumbed during the unloading process after eating wood shavings used to pack chemicals. A fourth pony, unfortunately named Sandy, died at winter quarters while the Erebus party was away. Seeking the cause, a postmortem found Sandy's stomach full of sand. Upon landing, the ponies had been picketed on sandy ground that sea spray had coated with salt, leading the pony to eat the sand. "All the ponies seem to have done this, but some were more addicted to the habit than the others," Shackleton reported. "We shifted them at once from the place where they were picketed, so that they could get no more sand, and gave them what remedial treatment lay in our power, but two more died in spite of all our efforts."[46] By the onset of winter, only four ponies survived: Socks, Quan, Grisi, and Chinaman.

With the deepening darkness and worsening weather limiting

outings to Cape Royds and its environs from May through August, Shackleton and his party settled into a winter routine that lasted for four months. David and Raymond Priestley, a novice British geologist who had signed on to the expedition before anyone knew that a scientist of David's stature would join it, ventured as far afield as conditions permitted collecting rock specimens and then sorted and studied them over the long Antarctic night. Priestley later credited his work with David as the inspiration for his own distinguished career in science.

David's restless energy did not stop with collecting rocks. Drawing on his youthful experience charting the retreat of Ice Age glaciers by the placement of erratic boulders left behind in his native Wales, David, aided by Priestley and Mawson, used this technique to study the history of glacier movement in the McMurdo Sound basin. Although David and Mawson said they joined the *Nimrod* Expedition to study an "ice age in being," by their examination of erratic boulders, they became the first to find that glaciers were retreating even in the Antarctic.[47] For his individual research, stretching his official role as the expedition's physicist to include work in his favored field of glaciology, while taking the obligatory magnetic readings of the southern lights, Mawson studied the structure of ice and snow crystals at low temperatures.

Beyond the specific tasks given to the scientists and the added ones given to others, all members of the shore party followed an enforced routine of meals and sleep. Breakfast began at 9:00 A.M. sharp followed by a morning smoke. Lunch was catch-as-catch-can depending on one's daily duties. Dinner came at 6:30 P.M. followed by tea, tobacco, and conversation until 7:30. Even though it was dark outside for twenty-four hours each day, the party followed the clock in keeping a set pattern of sleeping from around midnight to about 8:30 A.M. Everyone took turns both as "messman," cleaning up after meals, and in standing the night watch. This included the fifty-year-old David—a Fellow of the Royal Society, or F.R.S.—who never sought or received special treatment. "It was a sight for the gods," Priestley noted, "to see a well-known F.R.S., drying a wet plate with a wetter cloth, and looking ruefully at the islands of grease remaining, after he has spent five minutes hard at work on it."[48] By his willing attitude, David set an example for others.

Each pair of men had a six-by-seven-foot designated cubicle for sleeping and storage. David and Mawson shared one that others called "The Old Curiosity Shop," owing to its odd array of scientific instruments and geological specimens. Only Shackleton had a private room, but he swapped bunks with Brocklehurst while the baronet was recuperating from the amputation of his big toe. He used the occasion to try to cheer up Brocklehurst's morose roommate, Bertram Armytage. To boost morale, Shackleton also visited the men as they worked, lending a hand or telling stories. It was his way to build esprit de corps.

"He had a facility for treating each member of the expedition as though he were valuable to it," Brocklehurst said of Shackleton. "He made us feel more important than we could have been."[49]

Despite later recollections that perfect harmony prevailed during the *Nimrod* Expedition, some dissension bubbled up from below. Armytage remained despondent despite Shackleton's best efforts. Marshall's diary overflowed with criticism of various members of the expedition, particularly Shackleton. Damning him as "a consummate liar & practiced hypocrite," Marshall at one point depicted Shackleton as "a coward, a cad, who was incapable of keeping his word."[50] Shackleton's broken vow to Scott about not wintering on Ross Island touched off Marshall's venom, though it seemed rooted in the clash between the superior's glib-tongued style and the subordinate's judgmental religiosity. Then there was the prickly Mackay, who could overreact to perceived slights or indiscretions, as when a roommate stepped on his locker or when expedition artist George Marston, who sometimes dressed as a woman to lighten the mood, greeted him flirtatiously. These were exceptions to the rule, however.

Robert Peary as he portrayed himself in his 1910 book, *The North Pole*.

Peary with President Theodore Roosevelt in Oyster Bay, New York, before departing for the North Pole expedition, 1908.

Matthew Henson in polar garb, 1910.

George Borup of Yale at age 22, Peary's youngest sledge-party leader, 1908.

Robert Bartlett of Newfoundland, captain of the *Roosevelt* and a senior sledge-party leader, 1908.

Peary on the *Roosevelt*, trading goods for services with the Inuit, 1908.

On the *Windward* in Smith Sound, 1901. (*From left to right:*) Peary's Inuit mistress, Allakasingwah; her son with Peary, Anaukak; and Marie, Peary's daughter with his wife, Josephine.

Ootah, Peary's most highly acclaimed Inuit sledge driver on the North Pole expedition, 1909.

An Inuit sledge with dogs, 1909.

One of Peary's sledge teams on the trail, 1909.

A double team of sledge dogs at the North Pole camp, 1909.

Sledge and dogs ferrying across an open lead on a floating cake of ice, 1909.

Sledging over a pressure ridge, 1909.

Peary shown calculating the latitude at the North Pole camp, 1909.

Igloo used by Peary and his sledge party at the North Pole camp, 1909.

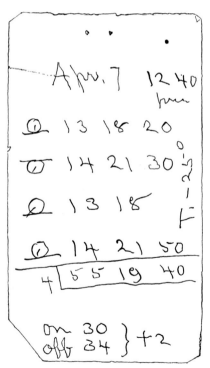

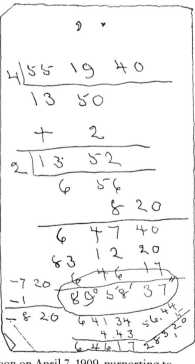

Peary's calculation of the sun's altitude at noon on April 7, 1909, purporting to find a latitude of 89°50'37" north, putting the party virtually at the North Pole.

Peary's ceremonial photograph at the North Pole camp, April 7, 1909. (*From left to right:*) Ooqueah, Ootah, Matthew Henson, Egingwah, and Sigloo.

Four members of Peary's North Pole expedition aboard the *Roosevelt* posing for a photograph on one of the sledges from the North Pole, 1909. (*From left to right:*) Donald MacMillan, George Borup, *Roosevelt* first mate Thomas Gushue, and Matthew Hensen.

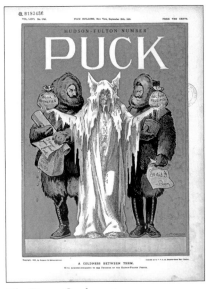

The Peary-Cook controversy as portrayed on the cover of a New York humor magazine, highlighting the unseemly lure of lecture receipts and book royalties, 1909.

An editorial cartoon showing Peary and Frederick Cook as vultures racing back from the North Pole, 1909.

Above: The gold metal awarded to Peary by the National Geographic Society in recognition of reaching the North Pole, 1909.

Left: The author's photograph of Peary's Eagle Island, Maine, summer home and retirement retreat following the polar controversy.

Due largely to Shackleton's ability to pick and lead people, the shore party survived the long, dark Antarctic winter of 1908 in shape for a record-setting summer in 1909.[51]

THE EXPLORERS NEEDED ALL the mental and physical reserves they had built up over the winter because in other respects they faced greater challenges than they had anticipated at the outset. Due to the orientation of the Ross Ice Shelf, starting the southern sledge journey at the west rather than the east end of the ice barrier added 120 miles to the distance from winter quarters to the south geographic pole and back. Losses had cut the number of ponies from ten to four, which was two less than Shackleton thought necessary for the southern sledge journey and left none for the northern sledge journey toward the south magnetic pole. Situating winter quarters at Cape Royds rather than Hut Point cut off the shore party from the route south during the critical months before midwinter darkness stopped all travel. As a result, the men could not lay advance supply depots for the southern sledge journey until spring. And of course the car proved useless for hauling supplies on the ice shelf. Each of these factors added to the man-hauling. Together, the combined effect was staggering.

Fully aware of the expedition's situation, Shackleton tried to right it as much as possible with the coming of first light. Although the sun would not rise above the horizon at Cape Royds until August 22, a distinct midday twilight began brightening the icescape earlier in the month. On August 12, Shackleton set out with David and Armytage to test conditions in the south with an eye toward beginning the movement of supplies well before the actual southern sledge journey could start, with the return of long days and warmer temperatures in late October. Anticipating extreme cold and bitter conditions on an August outing, rather than risk any of the remaining ponies, they man-hauled a single sledge the 20-some miles south to Hut Point. There, they spent one night in the *Discovery* Expedition's drafty old shelter before proceeding another 12 miles south onto the ice shelf.

"The surface generally was hard, but there were very marked sastrugi, and at time patches of soft snow," Shackleton noted about travel on the ice shelf in late winter. "At 6 p.m. the thermometer showed fifty-six degrees below zero" and fell still lower before dawn. The party shared a single three-person sleeping bag in a lone tent. "Everything we touched was appallingly cold, and we got no sleep at all," Shackleton wrote.[52]

Turning back toward Hut Point in the morning, the men arrived at the shelter just before a blizzard struck. It kept them inside for five days. At these extreme temperatures, individual snow crystals become like glass shards. Propelled by gale-force winds across the glacial surface, they can penetrate layers of clothing and flash-freeze exposed flesh. It was hard to stand against the wind, and not much easier to crawl. With no hope of reaching Cape Royds until the weather cleared, they used the time to clean and reconfigure Scott's shelter for use as a storage depot for the southern sledge party. Although not much farther south than Cape Royds, Hut Point offered direct access onto the ice shelf without fear of being cut off should the sea ice break out in McMurdo Sound.

SO THE HAULING BEGAN, as the men took turns pulling sledges loaded with supplies from Cape Royds to Hut Point for the coming polar trek. "Sledging work in the spring, when the temperature is very low, the light bad, and the weather uncertain, is a rather severe strain on man and beast," Shackleton wrote. And since by this point ponies were in shorter supply than people, he added, "Man-hauling was the order for the first journeys."[53] One party left each week for what was typically a four-day trek, two days out and two days back. Each hauled about a quarter ton of gear and provisions, half of which it left at Hut Point for use on the southern sledge journey with the remainder used or consumed on the trip. "Each party came back with adventures to relate, experiences to compare, and its own views on various matters of detail connected with sledge-travelling," Shackleton observed. "Every one of the parties encountered bad weather."[54] By mid-September, enough equipment and supplies were stored at Hut Point for the polar trek. The focus shifted onto getting some of it farther south before the main journey commenced a month later.

On September 22, Shackleton and five others began what they called the "southern depot journey"—a three-week, 320-mile march to move supplies onto the ice shelf. Much of this backbreaking man-hauling was in service of the ponies, which were not used in this trek. Dogs can eat what people eat. When they run out of food, they can eat each other. In short, as Peary, Amundsen, and the Duke of the Abruzzi learned, dogs pull their own weight even as they pull for the party, and when they reach the end of the line, they become food for each other and their handlers. Not so ponies. During a trip as long as the southern sledge journey, they eat more maize and compact fodder than they can haul, and will not eat one another. Men can eat ponies as well as dogs, of course, but there are more of the latter, allowing them to be culled selectively as needed for food. To accommodate the peculiar needs of a polar trek with ponies, the southern depot journey carried nothing but maize to stock a depot on the ice shelf over 100 miles south of Hut Point. By doing so, as Shackleton noted, "our load would be lightened considerably for the first portion of the journey when we started south."[55] In the meantime, however, everyone slated for the southern ledge journey had a brutal workout because all were among those participating in the maize-hauling depot journey. As a result, they started the main mission already somewhat spent.

In addition to himself, Shackleton chose Marshall, Adams, and Frank Wild for the polar party. Marshall knew cartography as well as medicine, so he was essential for the mission. Once Shackleton opted to send Mawson with David toward the magnetic pole and Brocklehurst became incapacitated, the choice of Adams and Wild for the southern sledge journey became all but obvious. Raised to the Royal Navy's officer corps from positions in the merchant marine before leaving it to join the *Nimrod* Expedition, both were strong, smart, and self-reliant. "We only had four ponies left," Adams later explained about the choice and number of men, "so it was the four fellows most likely to stay the course."[56]

The weak link was Shackleton, Marshall worried. Ever since his health problems on the *Discovery* Expedition's southern journey, Shackleton had feared he had a weak heart. The palpitations that sometimes followed asthma attacks deepened his anxiety. He never had it checked out prior to the *Nimrod* Expedition for fear of what the doctor might find, but during an otherwise routine medical examination at Cape Royds, Marshall found that Shackleton had a heart murmur, though neither man knew its severity. The Boss (as Shackleton soon became known) still insisted on going south, and so he did.

Each participant received a baptism in ice during the depot-laying trek. "The journey was a severe one, for the temperature got down to fifty-nine degrees below zero Fahr., with blizzard winds," Shackleton reported. "Most of us had the experience at one time or other of dropping into a crevasse to the length of our harness."[57] The harnesses were one advantage of man-hauling sledges over glacial ice. When anyone broke through a snow lid and dropped into a deep crevasse, which was likely to happen without warning, the traces would arrest the fall with a stiff jerk on the upper torso, leaving one's feet dangling in thin air and hands grasping for the ice walls on either side. The bottom could lie hundreds of feet below, resulting in certain death if nothing stopped the descent. No one was immune to the risk or became hardened to the danger. The more it happened, the more unnerving it became. It was worse for the ponies, though, because there was no lifting them back to the surface and an ever-present worry that any sledges in tow would follow them down the abyss. In this respect as well, dogs were a safer option because they pull in a pack rather than one to a sledge, tread lightly over snow lids, hang secure in their harnesses when they fall, and are easily pulled back up to the surface.

For the southern depot party, after duly stocking the so-called Depot A with 167 pounds of maize, the return trip proved even worse than the outbound march. The temperature remained low and blizzards increased. "We could not see more than ten or fifteen yards ahead," Shackleton noted at one point. "Then we found we were amongst crevasses, for first one man and then another put his foot through a snow lid."[58] Badly frostbitten on their faces from the bitter wind and blowing snow, the party camped in a hastily erected tent for thirty hours only a few miles from the Hut Point shelter. In all, the men had been able to march only about two out of every three days and lived on reduced rations by the end, which did not bode well for the polar journey. The six men finally reached Cape Royds hungry and tired on October 13, by which time David, Mawson, and Mackay had already left winter quarters for their thousand-mile round-trip trek to the south magnetic pole. Two weeks later, with the promise of perpetual daylight for the next four months, Shackleton, Marshall, Adams, and Wild headed back out, retracing their route for 150 miles to Depot A before beginning the added 700 miles to the geographic pole.

The stage was set. With boundless faith in their cause, the *Nimrod* Expedition's two polar parties, one heading northwest and another due south, hoped to reach their respective poles early in 1909. And as the Antarctic day extended to continuous light, the Arctic night descended into perpetual dark at the *Roosevelt*'s winter anchorage off Ellesmere Island, where Peary's eighth and presumably last expedition waited for dawn to launch its final assault on the North Pole. Like Shackleton, Peary planned to reach his goal early in 1909. Meanwhile, as these parties struggled toward their goals, the Duke of the Abruzzi planned his expedition to reach a Pole of Altitude in the greater Himalayas.

After decades of relentless striving by multiple parties toward those marks, 1909 was shaping up to become the year of their conquest. Adventure was in the air and on countless minds. The era's omnipresent press fixated on these stories. To accommodate the burgeoning new media of silent film, Shackleton and the Duke of the Abruzzi took along motion-picture cameras to complement their battery of still cameras. With boundless resources, the duke also recruited the world's premier mountain photographer, Vittorio Sella. Like Peary, they had visions of lasting glory to follow on the heels of reaching a pole. Claiming them, all three reasoned, would bring a symbolic close to the age of exploration and open one of limitless human attainment.

CHAPTER 7

The Savage North

EVEN INTO THE EARLY twentieth century, ocean voyages severed communication with the mainland. Expeditions departed, navies dispatched, or ships sailed, and contact ended for months or more. Returning vessels might bring back reports, and letters could come from distant ports, but before the telegraph, once an overseas expedition sailed, no matter how newsworthy it was, the news largely stopped until it came back. Transcontinental and transoceanic telegraph wires and cables began bridging the gap during the 1800s, but these did not reach to the polar regions or, for that matter, the central Himalayas and Karakoram. Communicating with such places required wireless radio technology. The expeditions of 1909 were among the last to travel without transmitters. Just two years later, in 1911, Antarctic parties would take along wireless equipment that allowed them to talk directly with radio operators in Australia. In contrast, despite the widespread attention on Robert Peary when his expedition left New York in July 1908, and the growing interest in the race to the North Pole between him and Frederick Cook, the public knew virtually nothing about their exploits until they returned over a year later. The same, of course, was true of Shackleton's British Antarctic Expedition.

In the case of Peary's expedition, the news largely dried up soon after his ship left Theodore Roosevelt's Oyster Bay summer home. Skipping the slow voyage, Peary remained behind after his ship sailed and traveled instead with his family and some major donors by train to Sydney, Nova Scotia, the northernmost port with a rail connection, by way of his summer house at Eagle Island, Maine. Peary met the ship at Eagle Island, where it took on a spare rudder, and then boarded it at Sydney, where it loaded coal and supplies. A few more stops in Labrador followed to add whale meat for the dogs, pick up fur boots, and rendezvous with Peary's old ship, the *Erik*, which was going along as far as Smith Sound with extra coal and whale meat.

"When may your friends expect to hear from you again?" Peary was asked upon departure.

"Late next Summer or early next Fall," he replied.[1]

While he made a few changes to improve on his last effort, such as planning to start farther east to counter sea-ice drift, to travel with his support parties as a group until those parties fell back, and to move his resupply base to a more northerly position, Peary vowed to take much the same approach as before. It was "the Peary System" or way.[2] Captain Bob Bartlett was back from Peary's last voyage, as was Ross Marvin, who in the meantime had become an engineering instructor at Cornell and whom Peary now listed as his "secretary," and Matt Henson, who had been with Peary since 1887. "He is about forty years old," Peary wrote at this time of Henson, "and can handle a sledge better, and is probably a better dog-driver, than any other man living, except some of the best of the Eskimo hunters."[3] Henson also knew the local language, and could communicate with the Inuit drivers and hunters. Like Peary, Henson had fathered at least one Inuit child and was well accepted in the Smith Sound community.

Counting the ship's crew, the *Roosevelt* sailed from Sydney with twenty-two men, all of whom would winter in the Arctic. This number included John Goodsell, a solidly built Pennsylvania physician who served as the expedition's surgeon, and two former New England varsity athletes, thirty-four-year-old fitness instructor Donald Mac-Millan of Peary's Bowdoin College and twenty-one-year-old championship runner George Borup from Yale, each of whom idolized Peary as a model explorer and traveled as his "assistant."[4] Borup had rich parents, and, although Peary invited him to join the expedition "unconditionally" on June 14, within two days Peary asked him, and then his father, to contribute toward its unpaid expenses.[5] Peary referred to Goodsell, MacMillan, and Borup as "my Arctic 'tenderfeet'" and sought to toughen them for the grueling sledging ahead.[6] At first Henson dismissed Borup, who had a ready smile and boyish face atop a strapping frame, as "the kid" but grew to admire his cheerfulness and pluck.[7]

The expedition had a masculine cast. Of course, all prior polar expeditions had only taken men, except for the two times Peary took along his wife, Jo. Since those 1891 and 1893 trips, however, the Spanish-American War had occurred, Theodore Roosevelt had risen to prominence, and a cult of manliness had taken hold in America. Indeed, upon departing for his 1898–1902 expedition, this is how Peary explained his project to the American people: "I am after the Pole because it *is* the Pole; because it has a value as a test of intelligence, persistence, endurance, determined will, and perhaps, courage, qualities characteristic of the highest type of manhood."[8] In so saying, he spoke for the age.

Thereafter, Peary increasingly depicted polar exploration as a savage, almost primeval experience that tested an explorer's manhood. In his 1904 presidential address to the International Geographical Congress, for example, Peary portrayed Arctic exploration as "man's work" and assured his audience that the attainment of the pole by him or anyone "would move the man and the geographer in every one of you."[9] So there could be no mistaking his meaning, at a dinner for the mostly male foreign delegates to that congress, Peary added about his race to the pole, "If I win, you will . . . be proud because we are of one blood—the man blood."[10] Peary expanded on this theme in his *Hampton's Magazine* account of his 1908–09 expedition: "One may know a man better after six months with him beyond the Arctic Circle than after a lifetime of acquaintance in cities," he wrote. "There is something—I know not what to call it—in those frozen spaces, that brings a man face to face with himself and with his companions; if he is a man, the man comes out."[11] Peary, like Roosevelt, feared that modern consumer culture was emasculating Western society and saw exploration as a cure.

In line with this theme, except for the state-of-the-art ship designed to take his party north, Peary eschewed modern technology in his quest for the pole and repeatedly declared that no one could get there without relying on the "barbarian" and "uncivilized" ways of the Inuit people and their dogs.[12] Stressing the masculinity of Arctic life, he noted, "Among the Eskimos the woman is as much a part of a man's property as his dog."[13] Peary even cast his one concession to technology, the *Roosevelt*, in sexually suggestive terms by describing it as "black, slow, heavy, almost as solid as a rock" and observing that it "bored and twisted through the ice."[14] When wealthy white "ladies" came on board from a passing yacht, he wrote that "the dainty dresses of our guests further accentuated the blackness, the strength, and the not overcleanly condition of our ship."[15] And when Inuit women joined the expedition as part of the families carried from their homes in Greenland's Smith Sound region to the *Roosevelt*'s winter anchorage on Ellesmere Island's northern coast, they were assigned domestic roles cooking, cleaning, sewing, and caring for their families while their husbands served as hunters and sledge drivers. "The life is a dog's life," Peary said of polar exploration, "but the work is a man's work."[16]

In his narratives of the expedition, when Peary wrote about Jo and their daughter, Marie, it was in strictly domestic terms. The fragrant pillow of soft Maine pine needles that Marie gave him for the voyage became a much-noted source of comfort and he depicted Jo as that "brave, noble little woman" who bore the brunt of his Arctic work.[17] Jo's last trip north was in 1900, when she went with the relief ship for Peary's 1898–1902 expedition only to spend the winter icebound in Smith Sound with Peary's Inuit mistress, Allakasingwah, and her son with Peary, Anaukak, while Peary wintered at Fort Conger. Jo bore the brunt of that Arctic discovery with resignation and dignity.

Peary had a second son with Allakasingwah on his 1905–06 expedition. Henson fathered a son during the same expedition. "The presence of women," Peary had said, was "an absolute necessity to keep men contented," and he predicted that by joining "the hardiness of the mothers with the intelligence of the fathers," the descendants of Inuit women and white men "would surely reach the Pole if their fathers had not succeeded in doing it."[18] As it turned out, two of Peary's Inuit grandsons, Peter and Talilanguaq, reached the North Pole by dogsled in 1971 along with one of Henson's Inuit grandsons, Avatak, in a team led by Italian adventurer Guido Monzino, who repeated many of the Duke of the Abruzzi's feats. Despite the general knowledge of Peary's Inuit relations among those on his expeditions, word of them stayed out of the press and never reached his chief benefactor, Morris Jesup, a devout Presbyterian who would have been outraged. A nominal Protestant, Peary opposed converting the Inuits to Christianity or otherwise "civilizing" them. He gave rifles, knives, and utensils to them in return for services and taught them basic principles of health and sanitation. "But there I think their civilization should stop," Peary wrote. Anything more "would only soften and corrupt them."[19]

A SEMINOMADIC PEOPLE, THE Smith Sound Inuits lived along a 200-mile stretch of Greenland's west coast running from Cape York in the south, at about 76° north latitude, to Etah in the north, at over 78° north latitude. The *Roosevelt* had smooth sailing from Sydney to

Cape York—"a pleasant summer cruise," Peary called it—arriving on August 1 to find only four or five families encamped there.[20] Peary picked up those he wanted and sailed on looking for others. At the time, the region's native population stood at about two hundred thirty, and Peary hoped to transport nearly a quarter of them to his winter anchorage near Cape Sheridan, some 350 miles beyond Etah. From past experience, Peary knew each of these Inuits personally and knew which ones he wanted for the expedition: the best hunters and sledge handlers with their families. "I had studied their individual characters," Peary explained, "until I knew just which ones to select for a quick, courageous dash, and just which dogged, unswerving ones would, if necessary, walk straight through hell for the object I had placed before them."[21]

Peary also sought about two hundred fifty of their best dogs, and bartered for them even from the Inuits that he did not take along, inevitably giving items of little cost to him but great value to them. Henson did much of the bartering. "I should be ashamed to take such an advantage of them," he wrote in self-justification, "but if I should stop to consider the freight-rates to this part of the world, no doubt a hatchet or a knife is worth just what it can be traded for."[22] "On the whole, these people are much like children, and should be treated as such," Peary noted. Yet he also acknowledged, "These Eskimos are one of the most important tools in all my programme of Arctic work."[23]

At the *Roosevelt*'s next stop, Peary and Henson transferred to the *Eric* to scour the region for more recruits while the *Roosevelt* went to Etah, where the two ships would meet before the *Eric* returned south. Although as far north as Shackleton's Cape Royds winter quarters was south, due to the peculiarities of currents and climate the coastline here is green in summer. With temperatures that can exceed 40°F in July and August, flowers bloom, grasses grow, and land mammals from reindeer and musk oxen to foxes and hare abound in a bright, treeless oasis that turns forebodingly dark, cold, and snowy by

November. At every settlement, Peary picked up more Inuit families and dogs. He reached Etah on August 11, where he found that those aboard the *Roosevelt* had disturbing news about Cook.

Looking and acting much like a half-starved inmate of Bedlam, Cook's sole white companion, Rudolph Franke, had approached the ship shortly after it arrived at Etah. Having spent five months alone in Cook's deteriorating hut near Etah and wearing tattered, lice-infested fur clothes, Franke came begging for food but was turned away by the ship's steward. At the urging of Goodsell, the expedition's doctor, Captain Bartlett intervened a day later to bring Franke aboard, feed him, and hear his story.

After a winter together in their packing-crate hut, Franke explained, he set off for the pole with Cook, nine Inuits, over a hundred dogs, and eleven heavily loaded sledges in February 1908. Cook planned to go west over Ellesmere Island to Nansen Sound, then turn north to the pole, perhaps traversing the never-explored Crocker Land that Peary had reported sighting on his last expedition. After five days, however, Cook ordered Franke to return to the hut with two of the Inuits and guard the goods and supplies while he proceeded west. "I stood as if I had been struck by lightning," Franke later wrote. "I was crushed."[24] He never understood the reason, though over the winter Cook had traded for valuable blue fox skins and narwhal tusks that perhaps needed guarding. Some also speculate that Cook may not have wanted a credible witness along if he anticipated claiming the pole regardless of whether he reached it.

Franke remained at the hut in growing desperation until May, when more of Cook's Inuits returned to Etah with a long letter from Cook dated March 17. The party had gotten as far as Cape Hubbard on the Arctic coast, the letter stated. "To the present we have seen nothing of Crocker Land, and I am taking a strait [sic] course to the pole," Cook wrote. "I hope to succeed." To conserve food, Cook would proceed with only two Inuits, Ahwelah and Etukishuk, and their dogs. If he did not return by the end of May, the letter directed Franke to go south with the furs and tusks to North Star Bay and hitch a ride home with the whalers that stop there in June. "These must be our money on the return trip," Cook said of the furs and tusks.[25] When Cook did not appear in May, Franke departed for North Star Bay as directed, but bad weather and a leg injury slowed his progress so much that the whalers had sailed before he arrived. Leaving word of his plight at the village of Oomanui, Franke returned to Etah, resigned to enduring another winter. Then he spied the *Roosevelt*. Half crazed, he clambered aboard to a decidedly mixed welcome.

Franke's situation scarcely improved when Peary and Henson arrived on the *Eric*. They had learned some of the story at Oomanui but not the full account. "At Etah," Henson wrote about Franke, "we were met by the most hopelessly dirty, unkempt, filth-littered human being any of us had ever seen, or could ever imagine; a white man with long matted hair and beard, who could speak very little English and that only between cries, whimperings, and whines."[26] Peary interrogated Franke regarding Cook and only let him return on the *Eric* in exchange for Cook's supplies, furs, and tusks. Peary then unloaded more supplies so that, along with Cook's, Etah could serve as a supply base should he lose the *Roosevelt*.[27] He left two crewmen from the *Roosevelt* to guard the supplies and deal with Cook should he return. Although Peary posted a sign on Cook's storehouse stating that Cook was dead and the contents belonged to him, he sent a message back with the *Eric* assuring Cook's wife that her husband was most likely holed up on some island "where game is plentiful."[28] Of course, Peary never thought that Cook could actually reach the pole with two Inuits and a few dogs, but he did worry about what Cook might later claim.[29] A wealthy sportsman, Harry Whitney, who had traveled with the *Eric* to hunt Arctic animals, also decided to winter near Etah and try for more Arctic game. He rebuilt Cook's hut as his lodgings and was entrusted by Franke with letters for Cook.

———

THESE DEVELOPMENTS CREATED PROBLEMS for Peary. The *Eric* would carry back the last news from his expedition to reach the public for nearly a year, and now Cook would dominate the headlines.[30] The fate of an explorer lost in the Arctic and maybe heading for the pole created more compelling copy than a story about Peary's uneventful cruise to Etah. Cook's letter to Franke was sensational in itself, but worse still, Franke would be in New York to expand on it, tell of his own ordeal, and put Peary's actions in a bad light. "I imagine the affair will create newspaper talk when *Erik* returns," Ross Marvin predicted in a letter from Etah.[31] Peary knew it would and sent his own batch of letters home to his wife, Jo, and his supporters, telling his side of the story and urging them to dispute any claims made by Cook or on Cook's behalf. They had their hands full when Franke told his story to Bradley Osbon, secretary of the Arctic Club, the pro-Cook rival to the Peary Arctic Club, and a former reporter for the pro-Cook *New York Herald*. According to Franke, not only had Peary coerced him to relinquish Cook's supplies, but he had sent the furs and tusks south on the *Eric*.

Osbon promptly denounced Peary for stealing Cook's property and charged that the furs and tusks had been distributed as gifts to Peary's wife and supporters. President Roosevelt allegedly received a narwhal tusk. Jo responded by giving out copies of letters that Peary had wrung out of Franke, consenting to the arrangement. "Please Mr. Peary, let me now go home with your other vessel," one of them pitifully concluded. She also released a letter from Peary denying any intention of sending back the furs and tusks, but going on to state that "the skins were wet, mildewed and rotting, and the horns broken." For their part in the matter, members of the Peary Arctic Club denied any knowledge of furs or tusks on the *Eric* and, to add injury to insult, billed John Bradley, the casino mogul, $100 for bringing back Franke, even though the transfer of Cook's supplies had supposedly covered the cost.[32] Cook's wife sent $50 to the club to repay a cash advance that Peary had given Franke to cover travel expenses.

Caught in the tug-of-war among newspapers over the two explorers, Peary's reputation suffered.

In a further blow to Peary's reputation, while the *Roosevelt* was still in Etah, word reached Copenhagen, and from there the public, that Ludvig Mylius-Erichsen, the leader of a Danish expedition, and his three-man sledge party had died in northeast Greenland. The expedition had sought to map the last uncharted portion of the island's coastline, from the northernmost point accessible by ship on its east coast to the westernmost point on its north coast attained by Peary in his 1898–1902 expedition. In 1892, during a prior expedition, Peary had crossed Greenland from the west, claimed to reach its northeast corner at a place he called Independence Bay, and asserted that from a high cliff above the bay he had seen the coastline turning west, which established Greenland as an island. This discovery was Peary's first claim to fame as an explorer. Records retrieved from Mylius-Erichsen's party suggested that the coastline turned east here, not west, and whatever Peary had claimed to see did not exist. Greenland extended north, and any attempt to round its northeastern corner would take far longer than expected under Peary's reports. Whether or not Peary's faulty claim contributed to the loss of Mylius-Erichsen's party, which perished after exhausting its supplies, the error raised questions about Peary's work and undercut his assertion that he had proved the insularity of Greenland. Even if the finer points were lost on the general public, geographers took note.[33]

The public, however, could readily follow the growing scandal surrounding Minik (or Mene), the youngest of the six Inuits that Peary had brought to New York ten years earlier at the request of researchers at the American Museum of Natural History. "Lieut. Peary asked if some of us wouldn't like to go back with him," Minik said in a 1907 full-page article in Joseph Pulitzer's muckraking *New York World*, the nation's bestselling newspaper. "They promised us nice warm homes in the sunshine land." Minik's father accepted Peary's offer and took his son, then seven or eight years old. Studied like laboratory animals and housed in the museum's basement, all six Inuits contracted tuberculosis, four died, and one returned home. An orphan, Minik remained behind as the ward of an increasingly disgruntled and later disgraced museum employee. To assuage Minik's grief over his father's death, the museum had staged a faux funeral of the father, using a coffin without a corpse. By 1906, Minik had learned the truth. Researchers had dissected his father's body and preserved the bones in a museum collection that included other Inuit remains supplied by Peary. "Just because I am a poor Esquimau boy why can't I bury my father in a grave the way he would want to be buried?" Minik plaintively asked in the article. Peary, it noted, "was notified of the death of his four Esquimau protégés, but he paid no attention to it."[34]

When museum officials refused to relinquish the bones, the story fed on itself. More articles appeared, especially after Peary rejected a request from Minik to return him to Greenland on the *Roosevelt* in 1908. Apparently, Peary feared that Minik's story might turn other Inuits against him. "I have lost hope. I lost it when Peary refused to take me with him on this last trip," Minik lamented in a feature article in William Randolph Hearst's *San Francisco Examiner*, the flagship daily in one of the world's largest media empires. "I would shoot Mr. Peary and the Museum director, only I want them to see how much more just a savage Eskimo is than their enlightened white selves." The article was illustrated by a quarter-page drawing of Minik recoiling from the skeleton of his father in a museum exhibit with the caption "What would Mr. Peary do if he was walking through the museum and suddenly came face to face with the skeleton of his father staring at him from a glass case?"[35]

Jo Peary now sought to be rid of Minik, even if it meant returning him to Greenland. "I am enclosing some [newspaper] clippings just to give you an idea of things and hope you will take Mene over your knee & lick him until he begs for mercy," she wrote in growing frustration to her husband in the Arctic.[36]

Long a national hero but always ruthless in pursuit of his goals, Peary had been in the limelight for two decades and his popularity suffered from overexposure. Cook, in contrast, had been a bit player in enough expeditions to be a credible contender in any polar race but remained little known to the general public. By 1908, some Americans were openly pulling for the plucky upstart Cook to beat the establishment-backed Peary to the pole.

WITH THE PROBLEM OF Cook dealt with as much as possible and the *Eric* soon to sail south with Franke aboard, the *Roosevelt* steamed north on August 18 into the Nares Strait.[37] From south to north beginning at Etah, the 310-mile-long Nares Strait includes Smith Sound, Kane Basin, Kennedy Channel, Hall Basin, and Robeson Channel before opening out into the Arctic Ocean's Lincoln Sea, where Peary was headed. Frozen over in winter, the strait is clogged in summer with glacial-fringe and Arctic pack ice driven south on strong currents and flood tides. Particular bottlenecks form at the channels, which narrow to little more than 10 miles across and where surging tides can raise the sea level 12 feet or more. "Looking across the channel, there seems to be no water—nothing but uneven and tortured ice," Peary noted at one point on the voyage. Only five ships had previously made it through Nares Strait. The *Roosevelt* was the most recent, in 1906, but it was heavily battered during the passage. "When the tide is at the ebb, the ship follows the narrow crack of water between the shore and the moving pack," Peary explained; "then, when the flood tide begins to rush violently southward, the ship must hurry to shelter in some niche of the shore ice, or behind some point of rock, to save herself from destruction, or being driven south again."[38]

Ultimately, in 1908, the *Roosevelt* took eighteen days to transit the 350 miles from Etah through the strait and around the coast to Cape Sheridan on the Arctic Ocean. The ship had a reinforced steel prow and bypass engines that could more than double their power for short spurts. Without these features, Peary declared, it never would have passed through the strait that year. The *Roosevelt* could slice through light sea ice, pry open leads, and push aside small bergs. "Its passage means constant butting of the smaller ice, and constant dodging of larger pieces," Peary explained. "When the ice is not so heavy as to be utterly impenetrable, the ship under full steam moves back and forth continually, butting and charging the flows. Sometimes a charge will send the ship forward half a length, sometimes her whole length— sometimes not an inch."[39] It was held up by heavy pack ice for days at some points, and once the crew had to dynamite a large floe that had pushed the *Roosevelt* on shore and partially grounded it. Even with the floe shattered, it took high tide, full steam astern, and pulling on a cable made fast to a grounded berg to free the ship.

The *Roosevelt* reached Peary's former winter quarters at Cape Sheridan on September 5, the same date that it had arrived there in 1905. Since Peary planned to start across the pack ice farther west this time, he tried to push the ship on toward a sheltered bay about 30 miles beyond his old anchorage. "But after two miles," he wrote, "we came to another impassable barrier of ice, and it was decided that it was Cape Sheridan again for this year's winter quarters." Those 2 miles, Peary boasted, gave him a new "farthest north" by a ship sailing under its own steam.[40] Bartlett burrowed the ship into the ice foot closer to shore this time. The dogs and most of the supplies went ashore, three packing-crate huts went up, and the party settled in for the winter. All told, the encampment consisted of sixty-nine people, forty-nine of them Inuits, and two hundred forty-six dogs. "I had the dogs, the men, the experience," Peary wrote at this point in his narrative, "and the end lay with that Destiny which favors the man who follows his faith and his dream to the last breath."[41] It was as close as Peary ever came to a religious declaration.[42]

Once settled in, Peary spent the remaining weeks of waning autumnal daylight moving supplies 90 miles northwest along the Arctic Ocean coast from his winter quarters to Cape Columbia, where he planned to depart from land for the pole. "The tractive force was, of course, the Eskimo dogs," Peary wrote, "and sledges were the means of transportation."[43] Any supplies moved to Cape Columbia in the fall would not have to be taken there in the spring. Peary set up a relay system with six roughly spaced camps. Sledge teams moved back and forth among the camps until everything needed for the polar trek was deposited at Cape Columbia. The first team left Cape Sheridan on September 16 and the last one returned from Cape Columbia on November 5. By then, full winter darkness had descended and would continue until late February.

During the fall, Peary also dispatched hunting parties for fresh meat, with musk oxen being their easiest prey. Herds of the large, cowlike animals lived in the region and stood out sharply against the white landscape. "For myself," Peary wrote, "I never associate the idea of sport with musk oxen," but others got in the spirit and felled them by the dozens.[44] Some reindeer and polar bears were also shot, as well as small game. For his part, Peary remained at the ship throughout the fall and winter except for one eight-day sledge journey in October with three Inuits and thirty dogs to explore and map Ellesmere Island's largest fjord, Clements Markham Inlet. Although he had not gone to hunt, Peary returned with more than a ton of fresh meat after his party felled fifteen musk oxen, a deer, and, following a spirited chase, one massive polar bear.

"If there is anything that starts the blood lust in an Eskimo's heart more wildly than the sight of a polar bear, I have yet to discover it," Peary wrote. "I was thrilled myself." All set off in rapid pursuit of the bear, but finding that his feet (or "stumps," as he termed them) could not tolerate the pounding, Peary fell back and let the Inuits have the kill.[45]

LIKE SHACKLETON, PEARY RECOGNIZED the importance of keeping members of his expedition meaningfully occupied over the long polar night, even if that meant inventing meaning. The sledging and hunting trips served this purpose during the fall. After the sun set for the last time in late October, except for hunting trips during the full moons, the explorers kept mainly to the ship. "Much material in the rough had been carried along in order to keep everybody busy working it into shape for use," Peary noted. Throughout the winter, "every member of the expedition was almost constantly engaged in work that had for its object the completing of preparations for the final sledge journey in the spring."[46] The Inuits were kept especially busy, with the women sewing new fur clothing for the men and the men building sledges and caring for the dogs.

Living arrangements reinforced working conditions. The Inuits resided communally in family groups on the ship's curtained forward deck and ate separately from the non-Inuits. Seen as a distinct race, they were treated as an inferior one suited for particular tasks. Even Henson viewed them as doomed for extinction in the modern world.[47] For the expedition's twenty non-Inuit members, Peary imposed a light routine with two set meals each day and two ship's bells, one at 10 P.M. for all quiet and one at midnight for lights out. "Commander Peary was an officer in the United States Navy," Henson noted, "but there never was the slightest military aspect to any of his expeditions."[48] Yet he was all about work. It was the main topic of conversation when Peary was present. Holidays were celebrated, including Thanksgiving, the winter solstice, and Christmas. MacMillan kept regular tide records, sometimes aided by Marvin and Borup. Goodsell charted the temperature. By far the oldest person on board, at fifty-two, and over twice the age of some, Peary spent most of his time alone in his large, private cabin when not giving directions and dined there on Sundays. He had a more aloof leadership style than Shackleton, but like his British counterpart, he pushed himself harder than he did anyone else on his expeditions.

In mid-November, violent onshore winds coupled with a flood tide drove a tumbled mass of ice blocks and floe bergs against the ice foot at the *Roosevelt*'s anchorage, tilting the ship toward shore and threatening to lay it on its side. The tide turned in time to prevent the worst outcome, but the *Roosevelt* remained akilter until spring. The fiercest winds came from shore, however. "Falling off the highland of the coast with almost the impact of a wall of water, [they] are un-equalled, I believe, anywhere else in the arctic regions," Peary wrote. "On deck it is impossible to stand or move, except in the shelter of the rail; and so blinding is the cataract of snow that the lamps, pow-erful as are their reflectors, are absolutely indistinguishable ten feet away."[49]

Much like the 1905–06 venture, this expedition suffered a con-tinual and unexplained loss of dogs at winter quarters. Over a fifth of the original two hundred forty-six had died by early November and another fifth by the end of that month. "It looked for a time as if we should lose the whole pack," Henson reported, "but constant care and attention permitted us to save most of them, and the fittest survived."[50] Beyond seeing the Darwinian process at work, Peary again attributed the losses to diet and found that switching to walrus meat helped. "Had an epidemic deprived us of these animals, we might just as well have remained comfortably at home," Peary wrote. No one could reach the pole without them, he believed.[51] Drawing on experience, Peary had taken twice the number needed, and that proved adequate. He never mentioned the reactions of the Inuits to the losses, but given their attachment to their dogs and their expec-tations of getting their surviving ones back after the expedition, it must have been severe. "Dogs are a valuable asset to this people," Henson noted. They depended on them.[52]

ON FEBRUARY 15, 1909, with a faint glow of daylight beginning to brighten the southern horizon at midday, the first sledge party left winter quarters for Cape Columbia. "It was still so dark that we had been obliged to use a lantern in order to follow the trail northward along the ice foot," Peary noted.[53] "The route to Cape Columbia is through a region of somber magnificence," Henson added. "Huge beetling cliffs overlook the pathway; dark savage headlands, around which we had to travel, project out into the ice-covered waters of the ocean; and vast stretches of wind-swept plains meet the eye."[54] Bartlett led the first party; Goodsell the next. The trail had been cut over the fall and winter by supply and hunting parties. By February it was a well-established route. A party led by Henson departed on the 18th, as did one led by MacMillan. Each included three Inuits, four sledges, and twenty-four dogs. Peary had it nearly down to a science: small parties composed of three or four men, with most men driving a sledge pulled by six or more dogs and each party led by "a member of the expedition," as Peary termed the non-Inuits who had sailed north with the *Roosevelt*.[55] Parties led by Marvin and Borup followed over the next days, with one led by Peary drawing up the rear on February 22. Peary's party included only two Inuits and two sledges. Presumably Peary rode much of the way, though he never said so in his accounts of the trip.

The seven parties rendezvoused at Cape Columbia, with Peary's reaching there on February 26. Because the trip from winter quarters took each party four or five days, the others arrived before Peary. Henson enjoyed this interlude in a snug igloo with few chores beyond moving supplies from their depot on the cape to the shore. Although the temperature dipped to 57°F below zero, the sun, while not yet rising above the horizon, gave sufficient light to see from late morning to early afternoon. "With the coming of the daylight a man gets more cheerful," Henson noted. "The snows covering the peaks show all the colors, variations, and tones of the artist's palette." It was not the sort of observation that Peary would make, and the spell was quickly broken when he arrived and began issuing orders. "From now on we must be indifferent to comfort," Henson wrote; "we must always be moving on."[56] Each member of the expedition received new fur clothing to replace the furs worn previously. Since the so-called Peary

System of Arctic travel involved close contact with dogs and having all persons in each sledge party sleep huddled together fully dressed, the old furs had become infested with lice and bugs. At least everyone started for the pole clean. As an added precaution, each member had his hair shaved before leaving the ship.

Bartlett and Peary mounted the bluff at Cape Columbia on the morning of February 28, 1909, to survey the way north. The sun would not rise for another week, but there was a waxing quarter moon, and the full moon was only six days away. This was the date that Peary had chosen to begin his final push north. Bartlett's party would go first, breaking the trail. Borup's party would follow that day and the other five at intervals on March 1, with Peary's party again leaving last. Six more dogs had died since arriving at Cape Columbia, leaving one hundred thirty-three, and two Inuits had become incapacitated, leaving seventeen. The expedition departed the Cape with twenty-four men and nineteen sledges traveling in seven separate parties. From the bluff, Bartlett and Peary saw a ragged jumble of broken shore ice as far ahead as they could see, but no open water. That encouraged Peary. The temperature stood at minus 50°F. A vicious wind was blowing from the east, kicking up snow from the surface. Given his age, Peary knew it would be his last chance to reach the pole. He felt ready, and had crossed the glacial fringe onto the Arctic Ocean sea ice by midday.

CHAPTER 8

Poles Apart

THE TURN OF THE season that brought winter darkness to Peary's expedition at Cape Columbia in October 1908 bestowed summer daylight on Shackleton's men at Cape Royds. Focused in purpose and eager to begin, they had two poles in sight. By September, Shackleton had settled on who would go on each journey. He would lead a party of four men with four ponies and four sledges south over the Ross Ice Shelf toward the south geographic pole. Shackleton still believed his pole lay on that flat, stable shelf some 850 miles away—a brutal but achievable pony march. In contrast, David would lead a party of three men hauling two sledges west over the Ross Sea's frozen surface, then north along Victoria Land's icebound coast, and finally over the Western Mountains and Great Ice Plateau to the south magnetic pole. Six decades earlier, James Clark Ross had determined that the magnetic pole lay beyond those mountains, which Scott's *Discovery* Expedition found to front a 2-mile-high ice sheet.

Beyond these rough outlines, no one knew what lay ahead for either party. Among the few certainties was that both destinations, though storied, were but unmarked abstractions on featureless ice fields. Reaching them had no practical value: at the time, Shackleton depicted them as "ungilded by aught but adventure."[1] Adventure, however, mattered and gilded them beyond measure for the Gilded Age.

Shackleton planned for both teams to start in October, with David's so-called northern party leaving on October 1 and his own southern party about four weeks later. Because of weather conditions, neither party could safely start sooner. Both groups were to return by March 1909 for the voyage home. The *Nimrod* could not remain in the Antarctic beyond that month without the risk of being frozen in for the winter. Anyone not returning by then would be left behind.

Before setting off in mid-September with five others to lay advance depots for his southern sledge journey, Shackleton gave his final written instructions to David for the northern party, which included Mawson and Forbes Mackay. Somewhat muddled and wildly over-ambitious, these orders set forth three tasks. Paragraph (1) directed the party to take observations to determine the location of the magnetic pole and, "if time permits," to reach it. Second, the party was to survey the Victoria Land coast running north, collecting geological specimens as it went, but not at the cost of "time that might be needed to carry out the work noted in paragraph (1)."[2] Logically, the party would do this work on the way to the pole, before turning inland, and the instructions seemed to permit skimping on it. They knew the rough distances: sledging from Cape Royds across McMurdo Sound and north along the coast on sea ice would cover about 250 miles, with another 250 miles inland from the coast to the pole, most of it uphill. To this point, the orders were clear, though Shackleton probably did not anticipate just how much resolve the Victorian-minded David would bring to the task of reaching the pole at the expense of all else, even the party's safety. But there was more.

Shackleton's third instruction showed that he did not yet appreciate either the challenge posed by man-hauling sledges in polar conditions or the vast distances involved. On its return journey, he directed David's party to stop at Victoria Land's ice-free Dry Valley, located roughly across McMurdo Sound from Cape Royds, and look for gold or other valuable minerals. David and Mawson had a well-earned reputation for finding coal and mineral deposits in Australia. Before leaving, David had hinted of the prospect of finding another Klondike in the Antarctic, which piqued widespread interest in the immediate aftermath of a gold rush that had drawn a hundred thousand prospectors to the Arctic. Shackleton bet on there being valuable rocks in Antarctica too.

Here, Shackleton's instructions became confusing. On the one hand, they authorized the party to delay returning to the Dry Valley if lengthening the northern journey would allow it to reach the pole. On the other hand, they stated that a *"thorough* investigation of the Dry Valley is of supreme importance."[3] Further, Shackleton knew that the sea ice might break up before the northern party could return to Cape Royds, because his instructions speak of the *Nimrod* retrieving it at some undetermined point on the coast around February 1. If the sea ice was out when the men arrived back at the coast from the pole, they could not get to the Dry Valley. Cliffs and coastal glaciers rendered the shoreline itself impassable. When time proved too short for both reaching the pole and prospecting in the Dry Valley, the orders gave David grounds for pushing on toward the pole over the initial objections of Mawson, who wanted to prospect in the Dry Valley, and the later pleas of Mackay, who lost all faith that they could reach the pole.

The magnetic poles held a strong attraction for scientists and explorers during the Victorian era, though this had weakened by the turn of the twentieth century. Shackleton and Mawson were men of a new era; David was not. During the nineteenth century, scientific organizations and governments across Europe and in the European colonies had launched a global crusade to map the curved lines and shifting patterns of terrestrial magnetism to their convergences at the magnetic poles. It became the largest shared scientific enterprise to date, with three magnetic observatories erected with British funds in Australia alone. Navigation by compass had always required knowledge of the variation between the magnetic and geographic poles, but the discovery in the early 1800s of a relationship between current electricity and magnetic fields added to the interest in terrestrial magnetism. Physicists thought that it might affect electrical transmission. Early in the 1830s, James Clark Ross became a British national hero for leading the first party to reach the north magnetic pole; a decade later, he sailed in search of the southern one. It was his Antarctic expedition that first navigated through the pack ice to discover the Ross Sea, Victoria Land, and the Great Ice Barrier, but determined that the magnetic pole was out of reach beyond Victoria Land's Western Mountains.

In Ross's day, because of their supposed scientific and economic importance, the magnetic poles attracted more attention than the geographic poles. By 1900, however, with the press feeding popular interest in the geographic poles as the last two great unreached destinations on earth, goals shifted. Although the official instructions for Scott's 1901–04 Antarctic expedition stressed magnetic research over geographic discovery, for example, Scott reversed the emphasis and received the most acclaim for his farthest south. Yet many in Britain and its colonies remembered the mystique surrounding the magnetic poles, and so, at the outset, Shackleton named the south magnetic pole as his expedition's second objective. When pressed by Scott to shift his intended winter quarters from the ice barrier's western to its eastern sea edge, the magnetic pole seemed beyond reach, and Shackleton dropped it from his plans. With David and Mawson joining the expedition in Australia and Shackleton opting to winter on Ross Island after all, the magnetic pole was back in play. Hastily organized, the northern party took up where Ross left off.

David was delighted. Leading the first party to the south magnetic pole was a Victorian explorer-scientist's dream, and for a glaciologist like David, it had the added appeal of a long trek over the world's largest ice sheet. Yet he faced a peculiar problem: no one knew the pole's precise location. Unlike their geographic counterparts, magnetic poles are not fixed points. Indeed, they are not even points. The south pole of any magnet (and the rotating earth with its molten iron core acts like a huge magnet) is where its lines of induction converge. An explorer reaching the earth's south magnetic pole does not see or feel anything special except that the southern end of a magnetic dip needle points directly down toward the earth's center. Further, the pole's location migrates over time in an unpredictable manner due in part to the earth's fluid core. Ross used nearby readings to fix the south magnetic pole's location in 1841, only to have Scott's team determine that it had moved east by 1902. Mawson would find that it had migrated northwest since 1902, increasing its distance from the coast.

Notwithstanding the transitory nature of "discovering" the south magnetic pole, David knew that it would attract the sort of professional and popular attention that he cultivated. In addition to his many academic publications and presentations, David crafted a public image by writing newspaper articles, giving lyceum lectures, and leading field trips. While others battled seasickness on the voyage to Antarctica, for example, he penned a series of thirteen popular articles about the trip that he sent back with the *Nimrod* for publication in Sydney's leading paper. At winter quarters and on the polar journey, despite his senior-scientist status, David did his share of the menial tasks, but in a laborious, conspicuous way that some saw as designed to attract attention and approbation. Polite to a fault and seemingly deferential but actually strong-willed and opinionated, David typically got his own way while appearing to accede to others. On the northern sledge journey, David's deliberate manner grated on Mawson and exasperated Mackay.[4]

WITH THE FOUR REMAINING ponies needed for the southern sledge journey and no dogs trained to pull sledges, Shackleton offered David the motor car. Already proved to be useless on snow, it did drive on smooth ice, and the first part of the northern sledge journey was over the Ross Sea's still-frozen surface. Only the expedition's motor expert, an Arrol-Johnston engineer named Bernard Day, could keep the temperamental vehicle running, so he played a bit part in the initial polar push, which was delayed by early spring blizzards.

"On September 25 we were up at 5:30 a.m., and found that the blizzard had subsided," David wrote. "Day and I started in the motorcar, dragging behind us two sledges over the sea ice." They planned to lay an advance depot for the northern party, which was to depart a week later. They did not get far. First, the engine overheated, forcing one delay; then, a cylinder stopped firing, causing another; finally, 10 miles out, slight but steep sastrugi stopped the vehicle's forward progress. "A little low drift," David called it, "brought up by a gentle blizzard." The sastrugi were too much for the automobile's frail motor drive to handle. The party left one fully loaded sledge behind and raced back to winter quarters in the car before the storm worsened. David hoped to try again the next day with another load, but the car's piston rings needed fixing after the last effort, causing more delay. Then Day injured his foot tobogganing, and another storm hit, pushing the next outing with the car back to October 3. This time, it traveled 15 miles before depositing its load. David ripped the flesh from his finger pushing the car, and Mackay broke his wrist cranking the starter. They hobbled back to winter quarters at 10 P.M., David noted, "All thoroughly exhausted, all wounded and bandaged."[5]

The northern party set its departure for October 5. With 500-odd miles man-hauling sledges over some of the roughest terrain on earth just to reach the south magnetic pole, David, Mawson, and Mackay faced a Herculean task, and they knew it. After supper on October 4, they gathered with those at winter quarters for an emotional farewell. The gramophone began with the aptly titled "We Parted On the Shore," a new recording by Scottish vaudevillian Harry Lauder, then the world's highest-paid entertainer and the first to sell a million records. "It's a terrible thing being hundreds and hundreds of miles away," Lauder ad-libbed on the cylinder. "Of course, there is one consolation; you're away back from anyone you owe money to." Then the music became more serious with "Loch Lomond": "'Twas then that we parted, in yon shady glen / . . . But me and my true love will ne'er meet again." Last of all came the John Henry Newman hymn "Lead, kindly Light, amid the encircling gloom," which would be sung by doomed passengers on the *Titanic* as it sank and imperiled British soldiers in the trenches during World War I: "The night is dark, and I am far from home." No one knew what lay ahead for the northern party, but everyone took it seriously. David could not sleep that night.

THE PARTY LEFT EARLY the next morning. "Day was there with the motor-car," David reported, but the snow was blowing so heavily that the car went only 2 miles before the men left it behind. From there they took up their harnesses and "with a one, two, three, and away, pulled off into the thickly falling snow." They reached their 10-mile depot at 7 P.M. and set up camp. "We slept that night on the floe-ice, with about three hundred fathoms of water under our pillow," David noted.[6]

Adding the sledge from this depot, the men now pulled two overloaded sledges with a combined weight of 900 pounds. They could not manage both at the same time, so they left the one behind and hauled the other half a mile forward, then returned for the first and repeated this backbreaking relay throughout the day. The men covered only 4 net miles but marched 12, with Mawson reporting that David, or "Prof" as he called him, was "dog tired all day."[7] Picking up their 15-mile depot early on October 7 raised the total drag-weight to 1,100 pounds, or about 370 pounds per person. It was a mark of their desperation that they took their biscuits out of tins, repackaged them in bags to save 8 pounds, and used some of the tins for other purposes.

The ensuing days proved much the same, or worse. The men rarely covered more than 4 net miles each day, and often much less. The sledges would bog down in snow and capsize on sastrugi. At times the men had to chop a way through pressure ridges with axes, navigate around or over cracks in the ice, or camp during storms. Sometimes a stiff breeze would enable them to hoist sails on the sledges to propel both along, but the wind could freshen into storms that cost more time than the sails saved. During this part of the trip, temperatures often dipped far below zero, and the unrelenting sunlight reflecting off the surface caused snow blindness.

Moreover, the party could never go faster than its slowest member: David. "The Prof is certainly a fine example of a man for his age," Mawson confided in his diary, "but he is a great drag on our progress. He certainly and admittedly does not pull as much as a younger man." It was worse during breaks, when David was painfully slow at cooking and making or breaking camp. "The more we bustle to get a move on the more he dawdles," Mawson wrote. He "takes double the time do to a thing than any ordinary person would." The men shared a three-person sleeping bag that David typically entered long after the others. "God only knows what he does" before turning in, Mawson complained. "Finally, when we have the chill off the bag, he struggles in all cold and bedaubed with snow. Of course he has the warm middle berth and occupies certainly more than $1/2$ the bag as he wears innumerable clothes."[8]

David had his own complaints about the sleeping arrangements. "A three-man sleeping bag," he observed, "where all snore and shin one another and each feels on waking that he is more shinned against than shinning, is not conducive to real rest."[9]

Both David and Mawson realized by the end of October that they could not make it to the pole and back in one season at their current rate. The slender David suggested proceeding on half rations with one sledge and without relaying. Mawson wanted to skip the pole in favor of prospecting in the Dry Valley. Mackay sided with David about the pole but seemed dubious about the half rations. "I cannot do anything but agree," Mawson conceded in his diary. Yet he added that "the Prof's idea of $1/2$ ration scheme for $2^1/2$ months with same amount of work is ridiculous," so Mawson ultimately countered with a plan of his own that the others accepted. "We must give up all else this summer," he proposed, "preserve about a full ration of sledge food for 480 m[ile] journey inland, [and] in order to make this possible we must live on seal flesh and local food cooked by local means as much as possible."[10] It was the pole or bust for the northern party without as much as a nod to the Dry Valley.

Mawson's plan allowed the party to discard immediately everything not needed for the polar trek and travel with a single sledge once they headed inland, but in the meantime it meant surviving on seals and penguins cooked over a makeshift seal-blubber stove made from a surviving biscuit tin. The men had not planned to hunt such food, did not know how to prepare it, and had not brought along the proper cooking equipment. They knew that Peary lived off the land in the Arctic, but he ate familiar game like bear, deer, and musk oxen.

Further, given their new schedule, the sea ice would be gone by the time they returned from the pole, so they had to hope that the *Nimrod* could retrieve them from the shore farther north than planned. The party left messages in marked depots along the coast announcing the changed plans, but could not be sure anyone would find them. "At tea this evening," Mawson wrote on October 29, "the Prof began to talk of the importance of our journey [to the pole] and asked that we should give up all else for it."[11]

HUNGER STALKED THE MEN. "About 18 days out I had a food dream," Mawson wrote, "dreamt that we came upon a depot containing all sorts of choice delicacies." Instead, their overland sledging rations consisted mainly of dried-meat-and-fruit pemmican and hardtack biscuits, which they boiled with melted snow or glacial ice to make a hoosh stew. While on the sea ice, they lived mostly on freshly butchered seals, which were easily killed as those large, lumbering mammals lounged on the shore or ice near holes and open-water leads, coupled with a much-reduced ration of hardtack. Seal meat was an ongoing experiment for the men. "Young bull seal is always good—steak from loins, liver and blubber," Mawson reported. "The latter melts in the mouth and appears and cuts like bacon about 1¹/₂" thick." The kidneys, he noted, were rubbery, and "cow seal in breeding season is to be avoided." Mawson liked penguin better than seal, with Emperor penguin liver "best of all," but it proved difficult to get in sufficient quantity.[12]

The new diet had drawbacks. Though calorie-rich, no amount of seal meat ever seemed to fill the men up, and the unbalanced diet quickly caught up with their digestive systems. "I am now ravenous and delight in blubber though it does not agree with me," Mawson noted only days after starting the new regimen. "When feeding on seal meat," he later added euphemistically, "we opened out every hour at least."[13] While sledging, they planned diverse menus for future feasts back home. A Scotsman, Mackay spoke of haggis, "to be played round the table by a piper," and bramble jam roly-poly.[14] English by birth and upbringing, David craved jugged hare with mashed potatoes. Mawson focused on rich foods and sweets. "We don't intend to let a meal pass in after life without more fully appreciating it," he vowed.[15]

While still traveling with two sledges, the party crawled north at roughly 4 miles per day along the coast and over two glacial ice tongues that protruded so far into the Ross Sea that the men could not feasibly go around them. At one point, they ran so low on food that Mackay walked back 7 miles for seals from a place they had sledged past five days earlier. It took him a full day going and coming, which offers some measure of the difference between walking and sledging. "I got lots of seal-meat, and one Adelie penguin," Mackay reported in his diary about this venture. "The bag which I carried back must have weighed 40 or 50 lbs."[16]

This first part of the journey, covering some 250 of the estimated 500 miles to the pole, took over two months, with the crossing of the 20-mile-wide Drygalski Ice Tongue consuming nearly one-quarter of that period. There the men encountered walls of ice running perpendicular to their path and hidden crevasses that could swallow them whole. Their initial attempt to cross the ice tongue failed. "For half a day we struggled over high sastrugi, hummocky ice ridges, steep undulations of bare blue ice with frequent chasms impassable for a sledge, unless it was unloaded and lowered by alpine ropes," David wrote, before retreating and trying again at another point farther east on the ice tongue. Even there, David noted, "the surface still bristled with huge ice undulations as far as the eye could see." He likened it to a storm-tossed seascape and noted, "It was obvious, too, that the glacier ice over which we would have to travel, was still very heavily crevassed."[17]

One day in camp, while Mackay was away and Mawson was changing light-sensitive photographic plates in the sleeping bag, David fell through a snow-covered crevasse. He saved himself by throwing his arms onto the surrounding snow lid, but the surface was so weak that he feared to move. "Mawson, Mawson," he cried. When Mawson did not come without some explanation of his dire situation, David politely inquired, "Oh, you're in the bag changing plates, are you?" and waited, again without further explaining his predicament. Gradually losing his grip, he called again with the same result before finally explaining, "I am really hanging on by my finger tips to the edge of a crevasse, and I don't think I can hold on much longer. I shall have to trouble you to come out and assist me."[18] It became the two Australians' favorite story of the trip and acquired legendary status down under.

Before the northern party reached the Drygalski Ice Tongue—

their last obstacle along the coast—midday temperatures rose to the freezing point, making the salty sea-ice surface soft and sticky. "It gripped the runners of the sledges like glue, and we were only able with our greatest efforts to drag the sledges over this at a snail's pace," David complained. With twenty-four hours of sunlight daily, the men began sleeping in the afternoon and traveling during the early morning hours when the sun was lower and the footing firmer than later in the day. Still, they worried that the ice would break up around them, leaving them unable to proceed north.

After crossing the Drygalski Ice Tongue, the men spied a smooth-looking glacier with a steep snout flowing from the interior around the south side of Mount Larsen to the coast. They had originally planned to travel farther north along the coast before turning inland but, from the ice tongue, they could see the sea ice broken up ahead. The shoreline looked impassable. Larsen Glacier, as the men called it, became the party's path through the Western Mountains. "Looks good going, icy, and not very rough," Mackay wrote. His spirits rose. From the day before on the ice tongue, when he had despaired in his diary, "I feel as if we have very little chance of the pole," now he exulted: "Really a joyful day."[19]

With the ice tongue behind them and a seemingly manageable glacier rising from the sea through the mountains toward their goal, the men gained hope. In anticipation of returning here after their dash to the pole, they looked for a conspicuous site near the Drygalski Ice Tongue's base to cache excess supplies under a well-marked mound of snow. Should all go well, they counted on the *Nimrod* finding this depot and retrieving them here in early February. Mawson took note of the occasion by starting a new diary, leaving his old one in the depot with a sledge, spare equipment, the geologic specimens collected so far, and letters from all three men.

"These are last adieus, so they ought to be tragic," Mackay wrote in his diary about the letters, "but I cannot make mine so, as I feel we have such a good chance of reaching the pole."[20] It was mid-December, however, and time was running short.

BY THIS TIME, SHACKLETON and his southern party were on the way to the geographic pole and, in comparison to the northern party, all but flying over the ice. After returning to Cape Royds from his depot-laying journey and giving instruction to those remaining behind on what they should do while he was away and if he did not return, Shackleton set off for the pole on October 29. His party took provisions for ninety-one days, knowing that it was entering a barren land with no alternative sources of supply. Biscuits, pemmican, oatmeal, cheese, and chocolate were virtually the only foods that it carried, except feed for the ponies and, of course, the ponies themselves, which would become food for the men. Tea and tobacco rounded out the consumables.

Shackleton left behind a letter for his wife, to be delivered if he did not return. "Think kindly of me and remember that if I did wrong in going away from you and our children that it was not just selfishness," he wrote. "Your husband will have died in one of the few great things left to be done."[21] Peary, of course, expressed similar sentiments to his wife, but about reaching a different pole. Again sounding like Peary, in his sledging diary Shackleton depicted the pole, in his case the South Pole, as "the last spot of the world that counts as worth the striving for."[22] And strive he would with a determination that matched Peary's stride for stride.

A support party man-hauling one sledge accompanied the southern party for nine days, which included three spent at Scott's Hut Point shelter and another in camp during a blizzard. This initial 50-mile stretch took the men onto the ice shelf at the place where it presses against Ross Island to the north and Victoria Land to the west. When the support party fell back on November 7, the four ponies took up the full load, hauling nearly a ton of supplies and equipment. Beginning at this point, Shackleton, Eric Marshall, Jameson Adams, and Frank Wild each led one pony and sledge south over a featureless expanse of snow-covered ice. Hidden crevasses and whiteout conditions slowed their progress for the first few days as they pulled away from land, but gave way to better sledging terrain and weather as they moved deeper onto the shelf. Temperatures dipped well below zero at the outset but reached into the low 20s by late November.

The Ross Ice Shelf, which is about the size of France, has a smooth or undulating surface except where it abuts land and the resulting friction upturns hummocks and opens crevasses. Fed by glaciers from the East and West Antarctic Ice Sheets, it varies from about 1,000 to over 2,000 feet in thickness and contains over 50,000 cubic miles of frozen freshwater, making it the largest flowing body of ice in the world and the source of enormous tabular icebergs. In 1902, when Shackleton traversed some 300 miles of it with Scott and Edward Wilson, they hugged the Victoria Land coast, where the disrupted surface slowed their progress. This time, Shackleton led his party along a line running parallel to the coast but sufficiently east of it to gain a better surface. At some points, he likened it to "a billiard table, with no sign of any undulation"; at others, he spoke of "long undulations, the width from crest to crest being about one and a half miles, and the rise about 1 in 100." Sometimes the surface was icy firm; sometimes soft with snow; and sometimes covered with a hard crust that the ponies broke through but dogs could have walked across easily.[23]

"We have never seen the surface alike for two consecutive days," Shackleton noted on November 14. It is "as wayward and as changeful as the sea." The direction stayed fixed, however: "We are going straight as a die to the south," he wrote.[24]

As it turned out, this route also provided a more dramatic view of the Western Mountains than Scott's close-in perspective. "Each mile shows us new land, and most of it consists of lofty mountains whose heights at present we cannot estimate," Shackleton wrote on

November 24 about the view toward the southwest. "There is an impression of limitless solitude about it all that makes us feel so small as we trudge along, a few dark spots on the snowy plain, and watch the new land appear."[25]

So far as Shackleton knew at the time, those mountains could remain to the west as his party marched south. If so, the ice shelf might extend all the way to the South Pole, which by this point was (as he noted) about "750 miles as the crow flies."[26] In that event, he had the men and means to get there and back in time to meet the ship by March and return home in June. Of course, crows do not fly to the pole. As Shackleton soon learned, neither would his party. The pole did not lie on the ice shelf, as he hoped, but over those lofty mountains, which slowly swung from his right to dead ahead as the party pushed farther south.

Through late November, however, the party sped along over the ice shelf at a clip in excess of 15 miles per day, with ponies doing most of the hauling. The oldest pony, Chinaman, was put down on November 21 and butchered on the spot. He "was the least fit," Wild noted matter-of-factly.[27] Shackleton added about Chinaman, "He cannot keep up with the others, and the bad surface has played him out."[28] By then the load had diminished through the laying of depots for the return trip and the consumption of food to where it could fit on three sledges. Further, the men gained fresh meat for their diet, which Marshall viewed as essential to preventing scurvy.

"The killing of the ponies was not pleasant work," Shackleton conceded. "Marshall and Wild would skin the carcass, and we took the meat off the legs, shoulders and back. In the case of Chinaman the carcass was opened and the liver and undercut secured, but the job was such a lengthy one that we did not repeat it in the case of the other animals."[29] Shackleton could not bring himself to do the killing. That duty fell to Wild, who used Marshall's pistol. "We got about 150 lbs of good beef off him, which will be a welcome addition to our bill of fare," Wild noted in his diary.[30]

Shackleton consoled readers at this point in his published narrative with a comment that the ponies were "well treated to the last, and that they suffered no pain."[31] If he believed this, then it evidenced a remarkable blindness. Marshall noted near the outset of the march that the ponies "seem very unhappy" and were "off their feeds," eating little.[32] Shackleton later observed that, when marching over the ice shelf, "the poor ponies are having a most trying time. They break through the crust on the surface and flounder up to their hocks."[33] Often they sank to their bellies in soft snow, he added.[34] "Cruel work for the ponies," Wild called it.[35] Sweating through their hides doing heavy hauling in freezing weather, they also suffered miserably from the cold and wind, especially when tethered overnight.

"A DAY TO REMEMBER," Shackleton wrote of November 26, 1908. His party had surpassed Scott's farthest south and done so in half the time. "We celebrated," Shackleton reported, "with a four-ounce bottle of Curaçao." He felt exonerated of the charge of unfitness that Scott had leveled against him after the *Discovery* Expedition's disappointing polar trek. He also expressed a sense of "awe" at viewing "land not previously seen by human eyes." Of those never-before-seen mountains appearing in "the south-south-east," however, Shackleton added ominously, "I trust that no land will block our path."[36] For the pole to lie at or near sea level on the ice shelf, as Shackleton hoped, those mountains should remain to the west or southwest. If, however, the range swung around to the east or southeast, the peaks would stand astride their path to the pole and make reaching it fearfully more difficult. The men veered reluctantly to the southeast to avoid the mountains, and hoped for the best.

The southern party had gone so far so fast in November because of the ponies, but the animals could not pull heavy sledges through deep snow day after day, only to stand outside in the cold wind each night. Unlike Peary's Inuit dogs, no one bred Manchurian ponies for such work. Wild put down Grisi one week after Chinaman and shot Quan three days later, leaving a depot of horsemeat at each spot. Three ponies gone; only Socks remained. He missed his mates and whinnied dolefully for them at night.

So long as two survived, the ponies could still do all the heavy hauling by consolidating the shrinking load onto two sledges weighing 630 pounds each. With only Socks, however, the men had to haul the second sledge. Then bitterness began bubbling over, with Wild in his diary scorning Marshall and Adams for not pulling their weight and Marshall privately faulting Shackleton's leadership. "Following Sh[ackleton] to pole is like following an old woman," Marshall wrote in his diary. "Always pausing."[37]

One such delay began on December 2, as Shackleton looked for a way forward. Mountains curved across the southern horizon from northwest to southeast, leading him to suspect that his party had nearly reached the ice shelf's end while still 450 miles from the pole. Worse, the inflow of an enormous glacier from the Western Mountains horribly disrupted the surface ahead. Unable to proceed on the Ross Ice Shelf, the party veered back to the south toward those mountains, which ran in a decidedly southeast direction. The pole, Shackleton worried, lay on the other side, across the mountains, on the snow-covered high-altitude East Antarctic Ice Sheet: the coldest, driest, windiest place on earth. Scott named it "the Great Ice Plateau." For Shackleton, it became "the Polar Plateau."

Approaching the mountain range, the men saw a 3,500-foot-high rock outcrop 7 miles away, with a low, snowy pass on its western side that Marshall hailed as "the Golden Gateway to the S[outh]."[38] In their optimism, they dubbed this dome-shaped hill "Mount Hope." Leaving Socks and the sledges behind, the men maneuvered through a deeply crevassed belt between the ice shelf and the coast, and then struggled up Mount Hope to survey what lay ahead. "There stretched before us a great glacier running almost south and north between two great mountain ranges," Shackleton wrote.[39] "It is at least thirty miles in width and we can see over one hundred miles of its length, beyond that must be the Great Plateau. Our Gateway is only a very small side entrance" to it, Wild added.[40] Yet only this pass appeared navigable with sledges. On the next day, December 4, the party headed through it to the glacial highway that Shackleton named the Beardmore Glacier for the expedition's sponsor. "The Almighty has indeed been good to us," Marshall proclaimed in his diary about this broad pathway to the plateau and the pole beyond.[41]

With the men already stressed by a month of marching 300 miles over the ice shelf, now their real work began. They faced a 9,000-foot rise in altitude while traversing 120 miles of some of the most diffi- cult glacial terrain on earth, ranging from sheer blue ice to deep snow and hidden crevasses. Believing that the pole lay on the ice shelf, they did not carry crampons and climbing gear. One day in and struggling for every inch, they cached excess supplies at a lower glacier depot. Stripped to their shirts for the ordeal, the men became badly sun- burned. Shackleton also suffered snow blindness after searching for a way through the broken ice without goggles. "Thirty-six days' food supply had been exhausted of the ninety days' total supply," Marshall noted, "so drastic cuts lay ahead if we were to achieve our object."[42] Lacking sufficient nutrition for man-hauling at high altitude, the men fantasized about what they would order if they were let loose in a good restaurant.[43]

Then, disaster. Socks broke through a snow-capped crevasse on the second day, nearly taking Wild and a sledge with him. "We lay down on our stomachs and looked over the gulf, but no sound or sign came to us," Shackleton wrote.[44] The pony had disappeared into the crevasse. Only a snapped whiffletree, the crossbar in the pony's har- ness, saved the sledge, and with it half the party's supplies and rations. "This accident left us with two sledges and a weight of about 250 lbs. per man to haul."[45] Like the northern party, the southern party began relaying. "Often it became necessary to cut steps with our ice-axes, and haul the sledges after us with the Alpine rope," Shackleton noted of the party's ascent up Beardmore Glacier.[46] "On December 6 the surface was so crevassed that it took a whole day to fight our way 600 yards," he wrote.[47] Further, with Socks went the meat he would have provided at some point along the way. "The loss of Socks," Shackleton commented, "was a severe blow to us."[48] Yet Wild's first thought was "Thank God I won't have to shoot Socks."[49] The pony was his favorite. "There never was a more clever horse," Wild wrote. "Socks must have been killed instantly."[50]

The party pushed on, about ten hours each day. The weather remained mostly clear on the glacier, but the temperature steadily dropped from 20°F at the base to minus 20°F near the top. "Sometimes we were able to pull both sledges & were able to do as much as 16 miles in a day," Wild reported, "but there were many days of relay work when 5 miles was considered good work."[51] On December 12, he called it damn hard work "over the most awful stuff ever sledges were pulled on."[52] If their private writings revealed their faith, then on this punishing march, Marshall trusted in God, Shackleton trusted in Providence, Wild trusted in Shackleton, and Adams trusted in Empire.

Sharp blue ice was the worst for sledging, shredding runners and bruising men, but hidden crevasses spawned the greatest dread. "To find oneself suddenly standing on nothing, then to be brought up with a painful jerk & looking down into a pitch black nothing is distinctly disturbing, & there is the additional fear that the rope may break," Wild wrote of the sensation. He got used to it after a few dozen falls, he said, but Adams never overcame the horror.[53] "Marshall went through one and was only saved by his harness," Shackleton noted on December 9. "Soon after, Adams went through, then I did."[54]

Having gained a mile in altitude by December 14, the men gained in hope as they neared the top. "One more crevassed slope, and we will be on the plateau, please God," Shackleton wrote on the 16th. "Almost up!" he noted two days later. "Not yet up, but nearly so," he added on the 20th. Even on the 23rd, at 8,820 feet, Shackleton reported, "Still steering upward amid great waves of pressure and ice-falls, for our plateau."[55]

They had passed beyond the glacier's head but not yet attained the Polar Plateau. Winds increased as they neared the top, cutting their faces and causing frostbite. "We have only the clothes we stand up in now, as we have depoted everything else," Shackleton wrote on December 24, "and this continued rise means lower temperatures than I had anticipated."[56] Thinking themselves finally on the plateau, they left a sledge and some supplies behind early that day in what they called the "upper glacier depot" and proceeded with one tent, one sledge, and reduced rations. Having rejected Peary's example and Nansen's advice to wear hooded fur parkas, Shackleton and his men shivered in threadbare gabardine. They did not carry a change of clothes, and spent much of their time in camp mending what they had without ever making it fully satisfactory.

The next day was Christmas. After hauling their remaining sledge for eleven hours up to 9,500 feet, they stopped for their first full meal since starting their ascent, complete with plum pudding, medicinal brandy, and cigars. "May my worst enemies never spend their Xmas in such a dreary God forgotten spot as this," Wild wrote.[57] "Up here the biting wind is always in our faces," Marshall added.[58] That night, they all discussed how to proceed. Still 280 miles from the pole and over 1,000 miles from getting there and back to Cape Royds, Shackleton reported his men deciding, "We are going to make each week's food last ten days. We will have one biscuit in the morning, three at mid-day, and two at night. It is the only thing to do. Tomorrow we will throw away everything except the most absolute necessities."[59] Reduced to similarly dire straits as the northern party, the southern party was equally resolved to reach its pole. It would not enjoy another full meal for two months. "It is now or never," Marshall wrote in his diary, "and we must average 14 miles per day."[60]

WHILE THE SOUTHERN PARTY shared Christmas dinner atop its glacial highway to the Polar Plateau, their counterparts heading to the south magnetic pole still faced most of their climb from sea level to the plateau and barely acknowledged the holiday. "No Christmas luxuries at all," Mackay noted in his diary.[61] After leaving one of its two sledges along with supplies and equipment at a depot on the north side of the Drygalski Ice Tongue on December 12, the men had spent the next two weeks navigating the badly faulted surface of the tongue's northern rim to the coast and then looking for some way up the steep snout of a broad glacier flowing around the south side of Mount Larsen to the plateau.

With the summer solstice, temperatures at the glacier's base hovered around the freezing point and everything was wet. Pools formed on the surface; meltwater rushed beneath the ice and opened chasms in it; avalanches thundered down the nearby mountains. Successive blizzards buried the tent in wet snow and shredded its worn-out shell nearly beyond repair. The 670-pound sledge sank deep into drifts. "Crevasses found by falling in them," Mawson noted on December 20.[62] About one such fall, David wrote of Mawson, "He seemed to disappear as certain characters do through trap doors in the stage."[63]

At first they tried to lift their lone sledge directly up the steep snout of the Larsen Glacier. When this failed, they found a side outlet to the main glacier running around a rock outcropping to the north. They named it Backstairs Passage because it rose in steps to the glacier's more manageable middle. Relaying their load up this passage and onto the glacier, the men reached 2,000 feet above sea level by the 25th. This was their Christmas. Like the southern party on this day, they were roughly 280 miles from their goal.

Time became the limiting factor. Hauling two sledges, the men had covered 210 net miles from Cape Royds to the glacier in eighty days. Now, to get to the pole and back with any chance of the *Nimrod* retrieving them, they would have to go over twice as far in half the time. After leaving climbing gear, some food, and added geologic specimens in a small depot on the south side of Mount Larsen, they hauled seven weeks of rations and camping gear on a single sledge. From this point on, the way would be over the Polar Plateau with no opportunity for further geologic field work.

Mackay gave up hope of success, and at times even of survival, but was duty bound to follow. "He would make a good soldier but no general," Mawson said of Mackay in a late-December diary entry.[64] Mawson reasoned that 10 miles per day going out and 15 miles per day coming back should do it; such figures struck Mackay as utterly unreasonable.

To complicate matters, David showed signs of severe stress. "Prof very doggo," Mawson noted on Christmas. "He has of late appeared to have lost all interest in the journey."[65] Yet he never declined to go on, and seemed intent on doing so. Mackay called him "very nearly crocked," and feared that he could not continue much longer.[66] On New Year's Eve, Mawson wrote of David, "Something has gone very wrong with him of late as he is almost always morose," and on January 3 Mawson added, "How much better though would we get along had we a third younger man."[67]

From their Christmas Day perch above the glacier's snout, the way opened out onto a smooth incline with remarkably few obstructions. The men made their 10 miles per day, gaining roughly 600 feet in altitude daily through January 3, and then somewhat less in altitude but often more in distance until the way leveled out at 9,000 feet atop the plateau on January 9. The work was grueling, but they kept to it, even in stiff winds that frosted exposed flesh and peeled the skin off lips. "Feeling the exhaustion and hunger awfully," Mackay wrote on December 29, adding a day later about repairing the tent in a blizzard, "It was intense torture."[68] To lighten their load, they carried reduced rations from the coast, consisting mainly of seal meat, which continued to cause diarrhea. Once on the plateau, the surface became undulating, with mixed sastrugi and patches of snow, which made it almost as difficult as the glacier incline for sledging. Moreover, it foretold a harder than expected return trip.

Mackay recorded the miles since the coast and to the pole in daily diary entries that reflected his growing anxiety about returning alive. Then a bombshell. "Last night Mawson made the astounding announcement that the pole is probably 40 miles farther off than we had ever thought," Mackey wrote on January 13. "I, of course, agreed to go if the others were decided, but I said plainly, as I think now, that we have not more than a 50 per cent chance of getting back."[69] They settled on racing some 50 extra miles over the next four days, which Mawson thought would put them within the region of the magnetic pole. He would not have time to make precise observations.

After three days and 39 miles, the magnetic dip circle registered 89°48', or 12' shy of vertical. "Mawson considered that we were now practically at the Magnetic Pole, and that if we waited for twenty-four hours taking constant observations at the spot the pole would, probably, during that time, come vertically beneath us," David noted.[70] They decided to rush 13 more miles to reach the place where Mawson thought the pole's mean position should lie.

Departing at 6 A.M. on January 16, the men sledged 2 miles before dropping their heavy gear, and another 6 to where they ate lunch and left the tent and sledge. Then, without instruments to guide them, they marched northwest for 5 more miles: their "pole by acclamation." "Mawson placed his camera so as to focus the whole group, and arranged a trigger which could be released by a string," David wrote. "Meanwhile, Mackay and I fixed up the flag-pole. We then bared our heads and hoisted the Union Jack at 3:30 p.m. with the words uttered by myself, in conformity with Lieutenant Shackleton's instructions, 'I hereby take possession of this area now containing the Magnetic Pole for the British Empire.' At the same time I fired the trigger of the camera." At the suggestion of Mackay, a Scot, they gave three cheers for the king. "The temperature at the time we hoisted the flag was exactly 0° Fahr.," David reported.[71]

The party began marching back within minutes and reached its heavy gear by 10 P.M. As Mackay repeatedly reminded the others, they had a long way to go and only a few weeks to get there.

ALTHOUGH THE *NIMROD* EXPEDITION'S two polar parties each stood about 280 miles from their respective goals on Christmas, the southern party would face at least 450 more miles getting back from its pole than the northern party. Both treks tested the limits for human endurance in 1909, but once they lost their ponies, Shackleton's men confronted the stiffer test. It showed. When Marshall took their temperatures on Christmas, every man was 2° below normal, and that was after their only full meal in weeks. Four days later, all had dropped at least 2° more. By January 4, their temperatures no longer registered on Marshall's clinical thermometer, which started at 94.2°.

After losing Socks, the northern party lacked fresh meat to supplement its sledging rations. As the trip stretched on, the men further reduced even these scant rations so that, by the first of January, they survived on 20 ounces per man per day, mostly in the form of a few biscuits and some pemmican, which was scarcely more than half of the planned daily total. The ponies' maize, which they ground with a stone for human consumption, ran out on December 28. Although marching over the largest frozen reservoir of freshwater in the world, they also suffered dehydration due to a lack of sufficient fuel to melt enough snow and ice to satisfy their thirst. Shackleton and Adams endured throbbing headaches from the high altitude.

"The sensation is as though the nerves were being twisted up with a corkscrew and then pulled out," Shackleton wrote on December 29. "The others have bled through the nose, and that must relieve them."[72]

From the descriptions of the plateau in reports from the *Discovery* Expedition, Shackleton expected the surface to level out at 9,000 feet once his party crossed the mountains. These reports came from two inland treks made across from Ross Island, and roughly fit what the northern party found. The plateau proved higher in the south. The men reached the head of Beardmore Glacier by Christmas at around 9,000 feet, but the surface kept rising long after the mountains disappeared behind them. It was not the same sort of continuous steep rise as on the glacier, but rather long flat stretches of snow separated by ridges of deeply crevassed pressure ice that Shackleton called icefalls. "Every time we reach the top of a ridge we say to ourselves: 'Perhaps this is the last,' but it never is the last," he complained on December 26. Shackleton compared the topography to a series of terraces and wrote of "the waste[land] of snow all around."[73] To keep from all falling into the same crevasse at once, the men attached ropes to the sledge and pulled from scattered places.

After passing the last ridge, instead of a firm, level surface, the men found soft snow and hard sastrugi. "Still further south we keep breaking through a hard crust that underlay the soft surface snow, and we then sank in about eight inches," Shackleton noted.[74] Each surface posed new challenges for men pulling a sledge on foot without skis, and the sledge had become so badly bent that it did not pull straight.

"The most awful day we have yet had," Wild wrote on December 29. He found the next two days even worse.[75] "Eleven miles only on the 31st in the face of a heavy southeast drift and 46 degrees of frost," Marshall explained.[76] Nevertheless, on New Year's Day 1909, they crossed 87°6' south latitude and claimed another record by passing closer to a pole than Peary, the previous record holder from his 1906 effort. Every first or farthest mattered greatly, and each man took note of this one.

"THE MAIN THING WE have against us is the altitude of 11,200 ft. and the biting wind," Shackleton wrote on January 4. By repeatedly leaving behind small depots with anything not needed for going forward, they dropped their sledge weight to under 300 pounds but could not push their pace much past 1 mile per hour. That was not enough to get to the pole and back with the food available. To make the pole seem closer, the men had switched from using customary statute miles to 20 percent longer geographical miles, but that did not shorten the actual distance.

"The end is in sight," Shackleton added on the 4th. "We can only go for three more days at the most."[77] This would not be enough, they now realized. At most, it would pad their record farthest south. "Although mid summer, the temperature was seldom higher than 20° below zero," Wild wrote, "& all the time whilst we were on the plateau we had to contend with a strong head wind which froze our breath into masses of ice around our mouths, & our faces were so frequently frostbitten they were covered with blackened skin & blisters." They could have reached the pole, he claimed, "but our records would all have been lost with us."[78] They could not have returned, and most likely no one would ever have found their remains. Shackleton later summed up the situation: "We were weakening from the combined effects of short food, low temperature, high altitude, and heavy work."[79]

They had, however, established the pole on the world's highest plateau and seen what it must look like. "But all this is not the Pole," Shackleton acknowledged.[80] The men dropped the sledge just past 88° south latitude after marching over 15 miles on January 6, which put them roughly 115 geographical miles from the pole.

"Tomorrow we make our last dash without the sledge," Marshall wrote.[81] That might take them to within 100 (geographical) miles of the pole—a made-up goal to be sure, but something to shoot for nonetheless. "I would fail to explain my feelings if I tried to write them down," Shackleton noted. "There is only one thing that lightens the disappointment, and that is the feeling that we have done all we could. It is the forces of nature that have prevented us from going right through. I cannot write more."[82]

As if to punctuate Shackleton's point, a blinding blizzard with hurricane-force winds kept them in camp for the next two days, the first such delay in two months. "During this period the temperature fell to minus 40 degrees Fahr., and the feet of two men froze in their sleeping bags and had to be restored," Marshall reported.[83] "The wind cuts through our thin tent, and even the drift is finding its way in," Shackleton added.[84] The men passed the time by reading Shakespeare aloud from a small volume Shackleton carried. "We cannot smoke as our supply of tobacco has run out," Wild complained on behalf of the group, all of whom were smokers, particularly Shackleton, who picked up the habit during Scott's *Discovery* Expedition.[85]

The men began their final march south in the early hours of January 9, 1909. "We covered 18 miles without sledges, carrying only a small supply of biscuits, chocolate and sugar," Marshall reported.[86] "At 9 a.m. we were in 88°23' South, half running and half walking over a surface much hardened by the recent blizzard," Shackleton wrote.[87] There they raised the British flag given to them by Queen Alexandra and proclaimed dominion over the region in the name of King Edward VII.

"We have shot our bolt," Shackleton declared.[88]

With this territorial claim, Shackleton pushed the British Empire—the largest empire in human history—to its greatest extent, a pinnacle it would maintain only briefly before it began unraveling with World War I. "The highest, coldest, bleakest, windiest plateau in the world, the 'great King Ed[ward] VII Plateau,'" Marshall wrote in his diary that night with a faintly mocking tone.[89]

"While the Union Jack blew out stiffly in the icy gale that cut us to the bone, we looked south with our powerful glasses, but could see nothing but the dead white snow plain," Shackleton wrote. This was their "pole of consolation." "We stayed only a few minutes, and then, taking the Queen's flag and eating our scanty meal as we went, we hurried back and reached our camp about 3 p.m."[90] Wild smoked a cigar he had saved for the occasion; they all had extra pemmican and a drop of sloe gin. The stated latitude of their farthest south put them 97 geographical miles from the pole, but it rested on dead reckoning. They did not take a reading from the sun, and the distance meter on their sledge had broken. All four men swore by the mileage covered, however, and few besides an embittered Scott questioned it as too much for the final day. "It did give us pleasure to get within one hundred miles" of the pole, Adams later commented.[91]

"Homeward bound at last," Shackleton wrote at the end of his diary entry for that climactic day. "Whatever regrets may be we have done our best. Beaten the South Record by 366 miles and the North Record by 77 miles. Amen."[92] He later asked his wife, "A live donkey is better than a dead lion, isn't it?" She answered, "Yes darling, as far as I am concerned."[93]

Assessing their situation at the time, Marshall wrote, "We were satisfied that we had strained our resources to the limit of achievement, but unless we maintained our effort . . . we stood a good risk of not returning to tell the tale."[94]

Adams said of the harrowing dash back, "It was as close as [anything] ever was." Close in every sense. Close to reaching each depot even as they seemed to recede before them; close to running out of food and fuel altogether. Close to dropping into the ever-present bottomless crevasses; close to treading lightly over them. Close to being trapped in the sort of endless blizzard that would kill Scott and his men three years later; close to skating by on fair weather. Close to falling just short; and close to returning with the greatest story of the young century. The days ahead would inspire Adams to hail Shackleton as the "king of leaders and adventurers."[95]

CHAPTER 9

On Top of the World

TWO MONTHS TO THE day after Shackleton's southern party claimed Robert Peary's record for reaching nearest a geographical pole, the American, without knowing of the British team's stunning achievement, set off from Cape Columbia to recover that title and more. Traveling with all deliberate speed, Peary's northern party was sledging toward its goal even before Shackleton returned to Cape Royds. Unlike the *Nimrod* teams, Peary (after three failed attempts to reach his pole) knew precisely what to expect and was prepared to face it.

"The only variation in the monotony being that it occasionally gets worse," he warned his men at the outset of the journey.[1] At age fifty-two, this surely would be Peary's last attempt to reach the pole. The wind blew strongly from the east—an unusual direction for the region and seen as a bad omen by Peary's Inuit drivers. The temperature hovered around 50 degrees below zero.

"Sunday, February 28, I left the land with three Eskimos and dogs," Captain Bob Bartlett wrote. "We were the pioneer party. Our work was to set the course, break the trail, and gauge the distance for the main party."[2] As Peary explained, "The pioneer party was the pace-setter of the expedition, and whatever distance it made was the measure of accomplishment for the main party."[3]

The leader of the pioneer party often marched ahead on snow-shoes charting the course. His party's three lightly loaded sledges followed close behind, breaking a rough trail in the snow and ice. Borup's more heavy-laden party departed from Cape Columbia later on the 28th, deepening and widening the trail.

The remaining five parties, or "divisions," as Peary called them, left the land in rapid succession on March 1, with Peary's departing last. Sometimes bunching together, sometimes traveling apart, the divisions remained fundamentally separate during this portion of the expedition. Rough ice and pressure ridges occasionally required pickaxes to cut through, but the old floes were mostly level. Each succeeding party improved the trail by use so that it was generally clear by the time the last one passed, carrying Peary. Prior parties also built igloos at their camps that later arrivals used. By going last, Peary explained, he could monitor movements ahead, address delays, and remain fresh for the final burst after the support parties fell back. To start, he directed Bartlett to set a pace of 10 miles per day.

During this first day, each party crossed the rough, upturned surface of the tidal crack, which could shred wooden sledges. Riding on his 12-foot-long sledge, Peary passed Inuits from prior parties repairing their 9-foot-long broken ones or running back to land for replacements. "It had been a trying day for the sledges," Peary noted after the first march. "The new 'Peary' type, by reason of its shape and greater length, had come off best." Each division traveled with one longer and two or more shorter sledges, but only the "old Eskimo type," as Peary called the 9-foot-long ones, broke down that first day.[4] Each division also carried a "repairing outfit" and spare parts for fixing broken sledges, plus all the essential equipment and supplies for traveling on the Arctic ice pack, including a small oil stove for drying clothes and an alcohol-fueled one for heating tea. At the outset, each fully loaded sledge weighed about 450 pounds.[5]

Peary reached the first major open-water lead at 3:30 P.M. on the second day. It ran east to west directly across his path like an enormous moat, and he estimated it at one-quarter mile wide. The parties led by Bartlett and Borup had gotten over before it opened, but those led by Henson, Goodsell, MacMillan, and Marvin were backed up when Peary arrived. "If a lead is full of floating ice," Henson noted, "we can use a large cake as a ferryboat and paddle across with our snowshoes."[6] This fresh lead was ice-free except for a thin skin of new ice forming over it. The parties had no choice but to wait for an opportunity to cross.

THE LEAD CLOSED OVERNIGHT with a grinding crush of collapsing, or rafting, young ice, and the parties pushed on without further delay. "Imagine crossing a river on a succession of gigantic shingles, one, two, or three deep, and all afloat and moving, he will perhaps form an idea of the uncertain surface over which we crossed this lead," Peary would explain. "Such a passage is distinctly trying, as any moment may lose a sledge and its team, or plunge a member of the party into the icy water."[7] Much later, Goodsell vividly recalled the thin ice "crackling, buckling and rafting under our feet."[8]

On the second day after resuming his northward march, Peary lost a friend in the White House. "Mr. Taft becomes President today," Peary noted in his diary on March 4 as if it were a matter of consequence for the expedition.[9] It was. Having Roosevelt in office assured Peary of a hero's reception in Washington and a prompt promotion to rear admiral should he reach the pole. Retired and most likely on a yearlong expedition of his own to Africa, Roosevelt could do little on Peary's behalf during the balance of 1909.

ON THE SAME DAY that Peary wrote this note, his division reached the so-called Big Lead between the coastal ice and the oceanic pack. Bartlett's pioneer party had stalled here a day earlier, and the other divisions had backed up here as well except for the two led by Borup and Marvin, which Peary had sent back 45 miles to Cape Columbia for fuel. "Our alcohol and petroleum tins had sprung leaks in the rough going of the last few days, and I wanted an additional supply to make up for present and possible future loss," Peary explained.[10] Borup blamed the problem on poor soldering of the tins by Henson.

The wind shifted to the west and then dropped as they waited, the temperature rose to the minus single digits before falling back into the double numerals, and the late-winter sun finally rose above the horizon, but forward progress stopped for six days at the Big Lead. "I paced back and forth, deploring the luck which, when everything else was favorable—weather, ice, dogs, men, and equipment—should thus impede our way with open water," Peary complained. "I think that more of mental wear and tear was crowded into those six days than into all the rest of the fifteen months we were absent from civilization."[11]

Bartlett called the six-day delay "Hell on Earth."[12]

The Inuits felt it too, and three cried to go back, citing sickness. Convinced that their illnesses were feigned, Peary persuaded one to stay but let the others go, including Panikpah, who was with him at his farthest north in 1906. "Am done with those two," Peary scrawled in his diary.[13] He sent them with a note directing the mate on the *Roosevelt* to give them enough provisions to depart immediately with their families on the 600-mile trek to Etah. They received nothing more for their efforts, Henson noted, while Peary promised the one who stayed "nearly everything that was on the ship."[14] Exiling the two men and their families over land to Etah, Goodsell wrote, should "impress the other Eskimos of the consequences of malingering and disobedience."[15] It was Peary's way. Although the departure of two senior Inuits disturbed the rest, Bartlett wrote, "Peary managed to keep them in line, one minute by being fatherly and the next minute being firm."[16] MacMillan helped by organizing athletic contests to divert attention from the delay.

In camp and on the trail, the divisions were functionally independent. They had separate igloos, which they constructed in about an hour from blocks of hard snow. The men slept fully clothed atop animal skins laid on snow and used food tins for pillows. "After two or three hours of sleep, a man usually wakes up cold, and he must then get up and beat his feet together and slap himself to start the circulation," Henson noted.[17] The men suffered worst at the coldest camps. "Each of us would sleep or doze for a few minutes and then awaken chilled with the cold," expedition surgeon John Goodsell wrote about one minus 59°F night. "Had we not heeded the warning chill our feet and legs would have frosted, and then we probably would have felt the fatal drowsiness that is so frequently claimed to be the first symptom of freezing."[18]

Each division cooked over an alcohol stove in its own igloo. "There is no variation in the bill of fare—pemmican and biscuits and tea make up a menu as unvarying as that of a boarding house," Henson added.[19] Breakfast and supper consisted of a half pound of cold pemmican and eight hardtack biscuits plus tea made with condensed milk. Lunch was three biscuits and tea. To lighten the load by carrying less fuel, there was no warm hoosh for Peary's divisions, unlike for Shackleton's polar parties. Only the tea was hot, and the men savored it. "There is nothing like hot tea," Borup later recalled. "It will warm you down to your very cold toes."[20]

Everyone on Peary's polar push received the same daily ration regardless of race or status. Consumed at this spartan rate, supplies remained sufficient. Peary planned exactly: "A total of 2 lbs. 4½ oz. of solids per man, per day," he wrote. "On this ration a man can work hard and keep in good condition in the lowest temperatures for a very long time."[21] On this trip, the men never had to resort to killing, cooking, and eating their dogs, though the Inuits occasionally supplemented their rations with worn-out dogs that could no longer pull in harness.

During the six days that the parties waited on the south side of the Big Lead, the temperature slowly dropped and the wind calmed. "It was dark, ominous, and deep," Goodsell said of this lead. "The opposite side, which we judged to be nearly a mile away, could be seen faintly through the rising vapor and falling frost mist."[22] Much as happened during Peary's return across the Big Lead in 1906, a thin skin of new ice formed over the lead as the surface became colder and stiller. By March 8, Peary thought the new ice was perhaps thick enough to cross. He remembered the anxious crossing in 1906, however, when the men spread wide to distribute their weight and shuffled breathlessly over the translucent surface. This time, going north, the sledges would be heavier and more numerous than on the return trip in 1906.

Even more troubling for Peary, the parties led by Borup and Marvin had not yet returned from Cape Columbia with the much-needed fuel. Peary waited two more days for the ice to thicken and the fuel to arrive, shifting the focus of his frustration from the open lead to Borup and Marvin. "God Damn Kid to Hell," Peary wrote in his diary, apparently about Borup, using only initials to encode his words but underlining them twice for emphasis. "When the party arrives we shall have a storm," Peary added without encoding.[23]

Borup and Marvin were as anxious as Peary about their delayed arrival. They knew the commander's wrath. Halted three days by a different lead, Borup wrote, "Besides knowing the success or failure of the Expedition might depend on our catching the others, we also thoroughly comprehended that, if we did not get out, we could never explain it, and at home there would always be the question of someone having lost his nerve."[24]

When Borup and Marvin still had not arrived by March 11, Peary pushed on without them, despite the lack of fuel. He would not wait any longer. Peary thought that open leads might be delaying them, which was in fact the case, but began to fear that they might never arrive. "Even if they did not come," he vowed, "I shall not turn back here." Such was the extent of Peary's desperation that, while nervously waiting for Borup and Marvin, he contemplated the prospect of melting ice for water and making tea by burning pieces of the wooden sledges. "By the time the wood of the sledges was exhausted," he reasoned, "it would have become warm enough for us to suck ice or snow to assuage our thirst, and get along with pemmican and raw dog without tea."[25] Proceeding without sufficient fuel after weighing such extreme options showed Peary's iron determination to proceed at all costs. He would not give up 45 miles from shore. "The delay had become unendurable, and I decided to take the chance of Marvin's overtaking us with the oil and alcohol," Peary wrote. He left a note behind. "Can wait no longer. We are short of fuel. Push on with all possible speed to overtake us," it said. "Do not camp here. Cross the lead."[26]

Peary's gamble paid off. Traveling as a single group, the five divisions chalked up three successive marches of at least 12 miles per day, despite a succession of frozen leads and zones of rough ice. The temperature dropped steadily from minus 40°F at the outset to minus 59°F at the end. Peary called it "Distinctly crisp," but there was less wind and more sun than before.[27]

On the evening of March 13, an advance sledge from Borup's division sped into camp with news that the resupply parties were a day behind and moving fast with full loads of fuel. "That night I slept like a child without care," Peary wrote.[28] He had crossed the 84th parallel and stood roughly 385 miles from the pole. Rushing ahead alone across the sea ice in minus 50°F weather for 60 miles with no supplies, the Inuit driver of the advance sledge, Sigloo, earned a place on Peary's final polar party. Borup hailed Sigloo's dash as "one of the finest displays of nerve I have ever known."[29]

———

WITH THE BIG LEAD behind him and the prospect of ample supplies, Peary took this opportunity to reorganize the expedition. He
sent Goodsell back to the ship with two Inuits and one sledge. "I was
disappointed to go back," the surgeon wrote, "but I knew it was part
of the Commander's plan."[30] Dogsleds could not carry enough food
for a party to reach the pole; only by using support parties that fell
back in stages could some succeed. At this point, Peary also sent Henson ahead with three Inuits and three sledges to pioneer the route,
relieving Bartlett's party from this demanding role. Henson had the
most experience at sledging of any division leader, and Peary viewed
him as completely loyal if somewhat lacking in resourcefulness. Henson started on March 14, while Peary and the others remained in
camp awaiting the resupply parties, which arrived that evening.

MacMillan now admitted to Peary that he had a severely frostbitten heel. It had happened three days earlier but MacMillan had
not realized it until a day later, and by the 14th the heel was badly
festered. Peary had no choice but to send him back to the ship, along
with two Inuits and two sledges, only one day after Goodsell left.
MacMillan was heartbroken over his early departure, as were Marvin
and Borup. The three young college graduates—Yale, Bowdoin, and
Cornell—had bonded during their shared ordeal, often gathering
to sing their college songs. "It's been a Marathon race and a damn
long one," Marvin commented at the time. "How we hated to see
him go off limping," Borup wrote about MacMillan.[31] Peary, in contrast, remained characteristically reserved. "It was a disappointment
to me to lose MacMillan so early," he conceded, "but his disability
did not affect the main proposition. I had ample personnel, as well
as provisions, sledges, and dogs; and the men, like the equipment,
were interchangeable."[32] Considering himself indispensable to the
enterprise, Peary never applied such a crude calculation of worth to
himself.

The heaviest work now fell on Henson, who by his own admission had a devil of a time with it. Soon his pioneer party encountered

soft, deep snow, which the sledges plowed through to the depth of their crossbars. "The dogs became demons; at one time, sullen and stubborn; then wildly excited and savage," Henson reported. After struggling through snow-filled fissures, the dogs finally refused to pull against the added strain even when whipped. "To break them of this stubbornness, and to prevent further trouble, I took the leader or king dog of one team and, in the presence of the rest of the pack, I clubbed him severely," Henson wrote.[33] The Inuit drivers used a different approach on recalcitrant dogs, Borup explained. "They get on top of a lazy dog, get a back hammer lock, and proceed to chew his ear."[34] Though he later regretted his brutality, Henson claimed that his method worked.

After plowing through the deep snow, Henson's pioneer party hit jagged, rough ice mixed with steep pressure ridges. The men used pickaxes to get through the former and lifted and lowered their heavily loaded sledges bodily over the latter. Henson remembered this day as the hardest march of the trip. "Two of the sledges had split their entire length and had to be repaired," Henson noted, "and the going had been such that we could not cover any distance."[35] The second day was scarcely better, and the third featured the deafening roar of moving ice and an open lead that the party crossed on broken floes hardly large enough to support a sledge. After this, it encountered such rough rubble ice that Henson halted his division at midday to rebuild two sledges from the wrecks of three. Then Peary appeared with a scold and a scowl.

Peary charged the pioneer party with staying ahead of the rest and gave it a full day's head start, yet, following the same route, the other parties caught up in two. They too had plowed through heavy snow, crossed rough ice, and ferried over leads with only the rough outline of a broken trail to follow. At one dramatic moment, when dogs in one team slipped into the water between cakes of floating ice, Borup stopped the sledge from following them down with his one arm while hauling them up to the surface with his other. "You had to fight for every yard-gain here as you'd do on the football field," the exuberant former collegiate athlete observed.[36] Borup's spirit and strength impressed Peary.

In contrast to his praise for Borup, Peary disparaged "Henson's 3 short marches," as he referred to them in his diary, and published a scathing account of them in his narrative.[37] "I knew, from past experience, that yesterday's movement of the ice and the formation of leads all about us would take all the spirit out of Henson's party until the main party should overtake them again," he wrote in that published narrative.[38] For Peary, success in the Arctic was all about spirit—human spirit. Henson's short marches confirmed Peary's view of Henson as a loyal follower but not an inspired leader. Following these three marches, Peary relieved Henson of command over the pioneer party. It must have humiliated Henson.

The next day, March 17, Peary put Marvin in charge of the pioneer party with directions to pick up the pace even if it meant marching for more hours each day. Bartlett, Borup, and Henson followed on the 18th, using pickaxes on the broken, upturned floes. As usual, Peary brought up the rear. "Marvin gave us a good march of not less than seventeen miles, at first over very rough ice, then over larger and more level flows," Peary reported approvingly.[39] This left him near 85° north latitude. At the end of that twelve-hour march, the fourth after Goodsell and MacMillan left, Peary gave the order for the remaining three support parties to fall back at five-march intervals. Borup would return first with three Inuits after one more daylong march; Marvin next, with two Inuits, five daily marches later; and Bartlett last, with two Inuits, at the end of another five.

An engineer by training, Peary planned in such a fashion that, assuming a pace of 14 miles per march, this schedule had each successive division falling back with each degree of latitude gained, leaving 3°, or about 200 miles, for the final polar party. "At the end of each five-march period I would send back the poorest dogs, the least effective Eskimos, and the worst damaged sledges," Peary explained.[40]

Henson would go with him to the pole along with four Inuit sledge drivers and a total of five sledges.

At this point in the narrative, Peary's critics typically begin noting that the plan of advance left Peary with the only division leader incapable of using a sextant to verify Peary's measurement of the party's latitude should they reach the pole. In short, no one else in the polar party could credibly prove or disprove whatever Peary might claim. Peary repeatedly hailed Henson as the best sledge driver of the lot, however, which offered a plausible reason for keeping him. With the pole almost within reach, Borup, Marvin, and Bartlett desperately wanted to go all the way. Peary knew their disappointment at turning back short of the pole, but held firm. "He wasn't heartless; he was just businesslike," Bartlett explained. "He was always that way."[41]

MARCH 20 BROUGHT A revised regimen. Borup headed back. "I would have given my immortal soul to go on," he wrote. "I never felt so bad in my life."[42] Bartlett resumed leadership of the pioneer party, with Henson's division slightly behind. Peary and Marvin started twelve hours later with their divisions traveling together. The continuous daylight allowed the four divisions to travel at any hour, with the first pair marching for twelve before making camp and the other pair doing the same. "When the main party had covered the march made by the advance party and arrived at their igloos," Peary explained, "the advance party broke out and started on while the main party occupied their igloos and turned in for sleep."[43] It offered a comfortable routine, at least for Peary, who enjoyed a prepared trail and ready-made igloo.

Each division now had three men—one leader and two Inuit drivers—whereas most divisions previously had four. Food remained the same for every man, but tea increased with each three-man party now sharing what four men received before. "Three men in an igloo were also more comfortable than four," Peary noted, "and the smaller igloos just about balanced in time and energy the lesser number of men that were left to build them."[44] Peary's division had two sledges; two of the others had three.

With continued fine weather, the remaining four divisions advanced north at an average rate of 14 miles per day through the last northward march of Marvin's party on the 25th. The surface alternated between rough ice and level floes, with an occasional open lead. "Some heavy going, small old floes, high rafters, & some young ice," Peary wrote on March 23, a day that he also reported ferrying one trailing sledge across an open lead on a cake of ice.[45] Marvin found a latitude of 86°38' north at the final camp before he turned south on March 26, which put Peary and his men past the farthest north of the Duke of the Abruzzi's team over a calendar month ahead of when the Italians had set their record in 1900. Peary was cautiously optimistic. His men were beating their daily targets, but not by much.

Now there were nine persons left. Bartlett's three-person division left camp late on the 25th, heading north. Henson's three-person division departed early on the 26th, following Bartlett. Before joining that procession, Peary and his two drivers remained behind until Marvin's party started south later that day. While noting Marvin's sorrow over turning back, Peary depicted him as "filled with exultation that with the exception of Bartlett and myself, he alone of all white men had entered that exclusive region which stretches beyond 86°34' north latitude."[46] If this passage paraphrased Marvin's last words to Peary, they were strange ones indeed, yet characteristic of his era. Despite their shared ordeal, by these words Marvin dismissed Henson and the Inuits traveling north with Peary to irrelevance in the epic struggle to explore. Only white men counted, and it did not matter if they were Italian, American, or British.

Peary claimed to have offered the following ominous final warning to Marvin: "Be careful of the leads, my boy!" A believer in signs and omens, Peary also later noted, "Soon after Marvin left us on his fatal journey back to land, the sun was obscured and a dull, lead-colored haze spread over all the sky."[47] In his diary, Peary called it "a dense lifeless pall of gray overhead."[48] He later saw it as foretelling his expedition mate's grim fate. Peary never saw Marvin again.

WITH BARTLETT'S DIVISION LEADING the way and roughly 230 miles remaining to the pole, the next five marches carried the parties over 70 miles farther north, or nearly a third of the way. They crossed a shifting array of surfaces in the teeth of a rising northerly wind and falling temperatures during this stretch. On March 28, the divisions led by Peary and Henson caught up with Bartlett's division at a widening lead. With the advance party already asleep in one igloo, the others built two igloos about a hundred yards away. Awakened by a shout, Peary looked out to see Bartlett's igloo floating on an ice raft broken from the main floe.

"The break in the ice had occurred within a foot of the fastening of one of my dog teams, the team being saved by just those few inches from being dragged into the water," Peary reported.[49]

Then he noticed that the other two igloos were also on a small floe at risk of breaking loose from the main one. Peary rushed the men, dogs, and sledges onto the main floe. Meanwhile, the swirling ice raft bearing the third igloo collided with the main floe, giving Bartlett and his party a chance to escape.

"He had scarcely set foot on the opposite floe when the floe on which he had been previously isolated swung off and rapidly disappeared," Henson wrote.[50] Still blocked by the lead from proceeding north, the men had no choice but to build new igloos and wait.

"That night we slept with our mittens on, ready for anything," Peary wrote.[51]

The lead remained open for another day, sometimes becoming so wide that the men could not see across it through the rising mist—"if, indeed, it had a northern shore," Peary added darkly.[52]

Their estimated position, calculated at 87°12' north latitude by dead reckoning based on prior marches, put them beyond Peary's 1906 farthest north, which gave them some satisfaction. The delay also extended the stay for Bartlett, because Peary linked his departure to marches, not days. One day spent in camp on March 29 rested his team for an all-out dash over its last two marches toward reaching the 88th parallel, which had become Bartlett's personal goal.

The previous three marches had taxed all three parties. Henson had lost one dog to thin ice. Deep, soft snow slowed the sledges at times. Sharp, jagged ice shredded their wooden runners at others. Henson compared the former snows to "granules of sugar, without their saccharine sweetness," while Peary wrote of the latter ice, it "seemed almost to cut through our sealskin kamiks and hareskin stockings, to pierce our feet."[53] Nevertheless, with Bartlett in the lead, the parties had averaged 13 miles per march, and now he aimed for more.

The lead closed during the early morning of March 30, and the parties were across within hours, now traveling together at their fastest rate yet. "During this march we had crossed a lake of young ice some six or seven miles wide—so thin in places that the ice buckled under us as we rushed on at full speed for the other shore," Peary wrote on March 30.[54] The next day was much the same, with a biting north wind blowing hard in their faces and the temperature below minus 30°F.

Peary estimated the average advance during these two marches at 20 miles per day, noting that this pace should put the parties "on or close to the 88th parallel" by the end of Bartlett's last march.[55] To ensure that he reached that mark, while waiting to find the latitude by a sun sight at noon on April 1, Bartlett walked 5 or 6 miles ahead of the camp as others resorted the supplies and rearranged the dogs for the final push. When he returned, however, he found a latitude of 87°47', which left him 10 miles shy of the mark even with his morning walk. Peary attributed this shortfall to the southward movement of the ice during the prior two days of strong northerly winds, but it could have come from not marching due north. "It was a tough blow to my pride, but made no real difference," Bartlett sighed.[56] His observation of the sun's altitude gave the expedition its last undisputed latitude reading. The men stood some 150 miles from the North Pole.

ALL THE SUPPORT DIVISIONS having departed, the polar party consisted of five sledges, forty dogs, and six men. Peary formed one division with Sigloo, Egingwah, and two sledges. Henson formed another with Ootah, Ooqueah, and three sledges. "It is the time for which I have reserved all my energies," Peary wrote in his diary on April 1, "and I feel tonight as if I was in trim & equal to the demands upon me of the next few days."

Peary estimated that it would take nine marches like the last eight, or six like the last two, to reach the pole. "Up to now I have intentionally kept in the extreme rear, to straighten out any little hitch, or encourage a man with a broken sledge," Peary added. "From here on I shall take my proper place in the lead."[57] Henson's accounts suggest that Peary did start off in front many days, marching on foot and leaving the others to break camp, but soon was overtaken and climbed aboard one of his division's sledges. Because of his damaged feet, Henson explained, Peary "was compelled to ride."[58] According to Henson, his division typically ran somewhat ahead of Peary's, at least in part to keep Peary from hitching a ride on one of its sledges. "He was very heavy for the dogs to haul," Henson later recalled. "We wanted him to remain with his own division."[59]

Peary has long been criticized for his decision to send Bartlett back, someone who could reliably use a sextant to verify the party's position at the pole and whose word as a captain everyone would trust. Peary offered three reasons in defense of choosing Henson.

First, Peary stated, "Henson was the best man I had with me for this kind of work, with the exception of the Eskimos."[60] On this expedition, however, Bartlett—and arguably Borup and Marvin as well—had distinguished themselves as march leaders, not to mention that independently confirming the party's position on a shifting polar landscape was a vital component of "this kind of work." With so much at stake, other polar explorers invariably took along someone who could serve as a creditable witness. Marshall served this role for Shackleton; Mawson for David.

Second, Peary noted, "I wished to give Henson some return for his many years of faithful service to me."[61] It was true that Henson had accompanied Peary on prior Arctic expeditions, yet even Peary's supporters acknowledge that ambitious explorers typically put success before sentiment and admit that Peary was more ambitious and less sentimental than most.

Third and most damning, Peary claimed that Henson could not safely lead a party back to land if he were to be sent back alone. "While faithful to me," Peary explained in terms that reflected the racial biases of his day, "and when *with me* more effective in covering distance with a sledge than any of the others, he had not as a racial inheritance the daring and initiative of my Anglo-Saxon friends."[62] Many of Peary's early critics used racist reasoning to condemn Peary for choosing Henson over Bartlett for the final dash; here Peary used similarly dubious racial reasoning to refute them. And even if true about Henson's personal abilities, this explanation offered added reason to take along someone capable of getting the polar party back to land should something happen to Peary rather than let the main party and its achievement be lost.

Once Bartlett left, the expedition record rested with some photographs taken at Peary's northernmost camp, Peary's disputed notations of the sun's altitude, and the sometimes-conflicting testimony of Peary and Henson. Part of the problem lay in that Peary, in stark contrast with virtually every other noted polar explorer of the era, inexplicably never checked his longitude en route, even though he was fully capable of doing so. From the outset, he vowed to march due north along the 70th meridian, which ran though Cape Columbia to the pole. With nationalistic pride, Peary called it his "Columbia meridian," and it virtually ran through his beloved Eagle Island, Maine, as well.

On drifting sea ice in perpetual daylight with countless obstacles in the way, Peary's pioneer party could not reliably maintain a beeline course in any direction, including due north, without checking its longitude. And riding in the rear, Peary simply followed the pioneer party for most of the way. Various members of the expedition later spoke of "the winding trail" north over shifting ice floes and around mountainous pressure ridges, in sharp contrast with Peary's depiction of a route "nearly, as the crow flies, due north, across floe after floe, pressure ridge after pressure ridge."[63]

Peary never offered a satisfactory explanation of how he maintained his course. A compass could not solve the problem because his parties were marching north of the magnetic pole without certain knowledge of the magnetic variation in the region. "As we got nearer to the Pole," Henson later confirmed, the compasses were not "much good."[64] Dead reckoning of the distance traveled gave Peary a fair idea of the latitude so long as his divisions stayed on course but could not reveal the longitude if they veered off it. Without any fixed markers on the moving ice pack or ever taking a longitude reading, Peary could only use imprecise methods to navigate northward, such as heading opposite to where the sun stood at noon. "Most of the time I judged direction from the ridges cut by the wind," Henson later reported about his means of navigation as a pioneer party leader. "Up there, the sastrugi, the ridges, run east and west. So the line due north would cut the sastrugi at right angles."[65] This was a rough gauge of direction at best.

HAVING FOOD AND FUEL for forty days, or fifty if the dogs were eaten, the two remaining divisions started north from Bartlett's last camp at 87°47' north latitude shortly after midnight on April 2. "The going was the best of any we had had since leaving land," Peary wrote. "The floes were large and old, hard and level." Although some pressure ridges between those floes reached 50 feet high, he noted that "they were not especially hard to negotiate, either through some gap, or up the gradual slope of some huge drift of snow."[66] Peary depicted his final party of five picked men as "an ideal which had now come to realization—as loyal and responsive to my will as the fingers of my right hand."[67] As for himself, he spoke at this point of taking up another hole in his belt, "the third since I left the land," and being "as lean and flat-bellied as a board, and as hard."[68]

With calm winds and clear skies, Peary claimed to cover an average of more than 25 miles per march over the next five days, or roughly twice the average mileage of prior marches. One east-west lead briefly slowed them, but Peary managed to cross the thin ice "bear style" by spreading his weight and sliding his feet, while two of the Inuits "came over on all fours."[69] The ice gave way, Peary reported, "as the last sledge left it."[70]

The men hurdled across another lead by "jumping from one [ice] cake to another," Peary wrote, all the while hoping that each "cake would not tilt under the weight of the dogs and sledge." A north-south lead sped their way for two hours by providing a runway of smooth young ice, with the dogs "galloping along and reeling off the miles in a way that delighted my heart," he added. "I had not dared to hope for such progress as we were making." Weaker dogs were shot and fed to stronger ones, further fueling the dash.[71]

AT NOON ON APRIL 5, after four remarkable ten-hour marches, Peary reported making the first observation of the sun's altitude by sextant since Bartlett's on April 1. "This indicated our position to be 89°25', or thirty-five miles from the Pole," he asserted.[72] These were nautical miles, however. In statute miles, the number stood nearer 40.

Peary began each of the prior four marches around midnight and ended them before noon. By starting earlier on April 6, he hoped to make a longer march and still end by noon for another sun sight. "I now felt that success was certain," he wrote.[73]

Indeed, Peary had anticipated his triumph for days and filled his diary with jottings about his just rewards. "Have 'Harpers,'" meaning Harper & Brothers publishers, "take entire matter, book, magazine articles, pictures & story (100). Kane got 75 from his book, Nansen 50 for his," Peary wrote in terms of the thousands of dollars that he should receive. "Senior Rear Admiral on retired list (with full pay?)," he mused about a promotion from the navy. "England promoted & knighted dozens," he noted, and "paid Parry $125,000, Phipps 25,000, etc., etc., for their Arctic work." Turning his attention to the lucrative lecture circuit, Peary wrote about New York's largest theater, "Look up Thompson Hippodrome proposition, modify perhaps, illustrated lecture with Hippodrome accessories, $15,000 (original amount), make society affair, auction boxes & seats." He contemplated marketing themed products, such as sleds, coats, and tents. The notes go on for pages, and include his design for a monumental mausoleum to hold his remains. It would have his figure on top, Arctic statuary, and a bronze tableau of the American flag at the North Pole. Dreams of fame and fortune possessed him.[74]

With such thoughts propelling him forward, Peary claimed a record distance on April 6. "Notwithstanding the physical exhaustion of the forced marches of the last five days," he wrote, "I went tirelessly on and on, the Eskimos following almost automatically." They made 15 nautical miles by lunch, and another 15 after lunch. "In twelve hours' actual traveling we covered thirty miles," Peary asserted. "There was no sign of a lead in this march."[75] These were straight-line distances from start to finish, not accounting for any added miles caused by detours. Critics seized on these distances as implausible for sledging in polar conditions, especially after Peary had struggled to make 10 to 15 statute miles per day earlier in the trek. "The story of the conquest of the Pole is what it is, not what someone thinks it ought to be," Peary countered. A small party of picked men and dogs can move faster than a large one, he stated.[76]

If Peary's latitude reading on April 5 was correct and if his party covered 30 nautical miles on the 6th, then Peary stood within 5 miles of the pole. "Can I wait to cover those other 5?" he asked himself in his diary.[77] The igloos built at this site served for the next two days as Peary's North Pole camp, which he named for his sponsor, Morris K. Jesup.

Henson would later present an alternative version of the events of April 6. "The trail was so easy that we made much more rapid progress than on any previous day," he agreed, but he made no mention of Peary taking a sun sight on April 5.[78] Relying on his own dead reckoning, Henson thought that the party had reached the pole on the 6th, and always maintained that belief.

"I stood there at the top of the world," Henson later crowed.[79] Since he was traveling ahead of Peary at the time, it would make *him* the first at the pole. Henson also reported that a hazy mist barred Peary from taking a sun sight on the 6th to confirm their achievement, and said that the men retired that day uncertain of their precise location.

ACCORDING TO HENSON, WITH "the Arctic sun shining brightly on the morning of April 7th," everyone eagerly waited for Peary to make his observations at noon. "The results of the first observations showed that we had figured out the distance very accurately," Henson wrote, "for when the Flag was hoisted over the geographical centre of the earth, it was located just behind our igloos."[80] This became Henson's pole of record, and he never wavered from that claim. The photograph of Henson and four Inuits with five flags taken by Peary at this site became the visual record of Peary's conquest of the pole even though Peary did not appear in it. Thus, as Henson reported it, they reached the pole on the 6th, but Peary did not confirm the position with a sextant reading until April 7.

Peary's own narrative differs from Henson's in key respects. Peary asserted that on April 6, "at approximately local noon, of the Columbia meridian, I made the first observation at our polar camp. It indicated our position as 89°57'," or 3 nautical miles from the pole—not 5, as he had written in his diary. At this point, Peary added, "I was too weary with the accumulated weariness of days of forced marches and nights of insufficient sleep to realize just yet that I had practically achieved my life's purpose." After dinner, he wrote, "I turned in for a few hours of absolutely fatigue-compelled sleep."[81] The written recollections of Peary and Henson differ on the date and results of these critical sun sights, and Peary's diary does not resolve the matter because it says nothing about making solar observations on either April 6 or 7 and only mentions Peary's April 5 sun sight in a marginal note added to the entry for April 6.

In his later-published narrative, Peary reported awaking sometime between noon and 6 P.M. on April 6 and writing in his diary the historic words he had wanted to utter for so long. "The Pole at last!!!" he exclaimed. "The prize of 3 centuries, my dream & ambition for 23 years. *Mine* at last."[82] Those words do not actually appear in his diary for April 6, however, but on an undated sheet inserted into his bound diary after the entry for April 6. The entry itself runs for three pages and includes a phrase suggesting that Peary wrote it in late afternoon. The next two entries in his diary, for April 7 and 8, are blank.

As he related the story in the published narrative in *Hampton's Magazine*, without the benefit of any diary notes, Peary rose by 6 P.M. on April 6 and, with Egingwah, Sigloo, a light sledge, and a double team of dogs, traveled along the 70th meridian for 10 miles. "I was able to get a satisfactory series of observations at Columbia meridian midnight, which observations indicated our position as being beyond the Pole," he wrote of his latitude readings.[83] So long as the sun is above the horizon, as it is in summer near the poles, a trained observer can use a sextant to find latitude just as readily at midnight as at noon. If Peary's party traveled along the 70th meridian on a straight line connecting the two points of latitude that Peary purportedly found on April 6, one at noon and one at midnight, then he passed directly over the North Pole.

This became Peary's "pole by affirmation," and he did not share it with Henson. "Going back along the trail, I tried to realize my position," Peary wrote. "That every direction was south; that every breeze which could blow upon me, no matter from what point of the horizon, was a south wind; that a day and a night were a year, and that a hundred days were a century."[84]

Hurt by his exclusion from this outing, Henson blamed it on the commander's anger at Henson's having hauled in ahead to the pole. Reasserting his claim to have gotten there first, Henson wrote in 1910, "For the crime of being present when the Pole was reached Commander Peary has ignored me ever since."[85]

Peary repeated this process of marking the pole on April 7. Although observers usually take sun sights at noon to determine latitude, with somewhat more effort and less precision they can make their observations at 6 A.M. or 6 P.M. Peary reported taking his next series of sights from camp at six o'clock in the morning of the 7th. Finding the camp to be 4 or 5 miles from the pole, he then traveled for 8 miles directly toward the sun, which would be due east of him at that time. Again leaving Henson behind, Peary took along Egingwah and Ootah to assist with the sledge and dogs.

Returning to camp by noon, Peary made another series of sights. "I had now taken thirteen single, or six and a half double, altitudes of the sun," he affirmed, "and to allow for possible errors in instruments and observations, had traversed in various directions an area of about eight to ten miles across. At some moment during these marches and countermarches, I had for all practical purposes passed over the point where north and south and east and west blend into one."[86] This remained Peary's defining claim. He never wavered from it.

"The objects of these various excursions being to cover the region in the vicinity over an area equal or greater than the probable error of my observations," he later declared in a certificate submitted to substantiate his claim.[87]

WHILE PEARY'S EFFORTS AND evidence satisfied his partisans then and ever after, they left his critics demanding more. From the outset, those critics homed in on Peary's asserted mileage to argue that the polar party could not have gone so far so fast after Bartlett's division turned back. Yet by his own reported sun sights, Peary reached the pole. The discrepancy left no plausible options other than that he made it all the way or knowingly lied. This left the controversy surrounding Peary's achievement entirely different from that over the claims to the south magnetic pole of Mawson and David, who readily admitted the various uncertainties of their record. During the 1980s, the National Geographic Society invited explorer Wally Herbert to reexamine Peary's claims with an eye toward reaffirming them, only to have Herbert conclude that, even if Peary went the distance, he still missed the mark by roughly 60 miles due to veering off course by not knowing his longitude and then deliberately falsifying the record to cover his error and claim the pole.[88] The society, Peary's steadiest institutional backer, vacillated in its stance even as the *New York Times*, an expedition sponsor, retracted its long-standing endorsement of Peary's claim.

Recorded sun sights rest on the credibility of those reporting them, and the texture of Peary's testimony left many doubters. A 1990 study by the pro-Peary Foundation for the Promotion of the Art of Navigation lent support to Peary's claim, particularly by its analysis of shadows in Peary's photographs, but found no hard evidence proving it and was criticized for relying too heavily on Peary's disputed records.[89] Adding to Peary's side of the ledger, a 2005 reenactment of the outbound journey by British adventurer Tom Avery matched Peary's overall time, though without achieving any sustained bursts as fast as Peary claimed near the pole or suffering as many delays due to open leads. In short, while comparable, the two expeditions were far from identical. Even Peary's fiercest critics—the ones accusing him of outright fraud—concede that, in a campaign that went far beyond any prior farthest north, Peary reached closer to one geographic pole than Shackleton did to the other. When coupled with the work of Mawson, David, and Mackay to reach the south magnetic pole, the remarkable efforts of Peary and Shackleton made 1909 the grandest year ever for polar discovery.

Once Peary completed his observations on April 7, his men hoisted the expedition's five flags on an ice hummock behind camp and, at Peary's direction, gave three spirited cheers for the American one.[90] Having long promised to "nail the Stars and Stripes to the Pole," Peary had carried this particular American flag on every expedition since 1894, and left a small fragment of it at each previous farthest north.[91] The team posed for the grainy photograph that was destined to appear in newspapers around the world. Although Peary could have posed it virtually anywhere on the Arctic ice pack, more than any sextant readings this iconic photograph became public proof that his party had reached the pole. Then, after trying without success to sleep for a few hours, the men left their North Pole camp about 4 P.M. on the 7th, heading south toward the last pair of igloos they had left on their trail coming north.

Cape Columbia lay 475 miles away. The window for sledge travel across the Arctic ice pack was closing fast with the approach of summer.

CHAPTER 10

The Third Pole

BY AN ODD COINCIDENCE, on the same day in March 1909 that Peary passed the Italian record north of 1900, Prince Luigi Amedeo, Duke of the Abruzzi, then age thirty-eight, after a rousing send-off from Turin, the historical capital of Savoy, boarded a commercial steamer in Marseilles for what some viewed as the boldest adventure in a year of adventures. Having made celebrated first ascents in Europe, Africa, and the Americas over the previous two decades, the duke now aimed to set a world altitude record and perhaps summit K2, the highest accessible mountain on earth and one of only three exceeding 28,000 feet. Due to K2's extreme height, notorious weather, and remote location, the Italian Alpine Club depicted this climb by the duke as "more difficult and perilous" than any of his previous attempts and hailed it on his departure as the "crowning of a brilliant career as a mountaineer and explorer."[1]

For the expedition, the duke recruited eleven crack Italian mountaineers to serve in staff or support positions. The former consisted of the duke's navy aide-de-camp Federico Negrotto as cartographer and two colleagues from his Saint Elias and Ruwenzori expeditions, the already renowned fifty-year-old photographer Vittorio Sella, who took along his assistant Erminio Botta, and Filippo De Filippi, the expedition's physician and chronicler. The latter included Joseph and Laurent Petigax, who went on the duke's African expedition, Alexis and Henri Brocherel, veterans of prior Himalayan climbs, and alpinists Emil Brocherel, Albert Savoie, and Ernest Bareux. The first four of these professional mountaineers officially served as guides and the last three as porters, but all seven performed guidelike functions at times and carry that designation here. Certainly as fine a team of Italian climbers as ever before assembled, it rivaled any other of its day.

AT THE TIME, SOME doubted if humans could survive for long at extreme altitudes. No one had yet climbed higher than 24,000 feet, with the reigning record recently set on Kabru, an Indian mountain near the easily accessible British hill station of Darjeeling in the eastern Himalayas. This allowed for short times at high altitude and rapid returns to low, long-inhabited levels. Climbing K2, in contrast, posed colossal physical and logistical challenges simply to begin the assault, much more to finish it. The mountain rose from a remote, uninhabited glacial valley, which itself stood higher than any peak in the Alps. Base camps would be higher than the summit of Mont Blanc. The cumulative effect of remaining at such high altitudes for long periods, some experts then thought, could prove fatal. Certainly they would test the known limits of human endurance. Nevertheless, on April 9, two days after Peary turned back south from his pole, the duke and his team disembarked with nearly 7 tons of climbing supplies and equipment in Mumbai, India. There they boarded a train bound north toward the Karakoram, which some geographers considered a northwestern extension of the Himalayas and others classified as a distinct range. Legendary British climber Bill Tilman later called the duke's effort "The original Himalayan expedition in the grand style."[2]

"The name Himalaya denotes no mere chain of mountains," De Filippi explained. "It denotes a complex system of ranges, of immense table-lands, of intricate valleys and of mighty rivers that has no rival upon the face of the earth." Running roughly 1,500 miles in length from the Afghan border in the northwest nearly to Myanmar in the southeast, and up to 500 miles in width, the Himalayas divided the subcontinent of India, then ruled by Britain, from Central Asia, then dominated by Russia. In 1909, the Karakoram was a remote and sparsely populated region of the wider Himalayas, which itself remained a place of mystery to Westerners. "Many of the valleys are nearly desert for hundreds of miles, with sparse and squalid villages, where a scanty population just contrives to wrest a bare living from the arid stony waste," De Filippi stated of the Karakoram.[3] Its high mountains and vast glaciers appeared as lifeless as the polar regions—even the locals avoided them. Yet by 1900, those very mountains and glaciers were attracting the sort of adventure-seeking, Gilded Age Westerner drawn to explore the unknown and climb the unclimbed. This was the Karakoram: like the poles, a virtual blank space on Western maps.

"It is separated from the Himalaya proper by the upper course of the Indus, and lies nearly 200 miles from the capital of Kashmir," De Filippi wrote about Karakoram and its isolation. "It is accessible only to expeditions organized for distant exploration, and on this account it has been seldom visited."[4] When the Great Trigonometrical Survey of British India reached the region in 1856, it measured many of the Karakoram's major peaks from a Himalayan observation post on Mount Harmukh, 130 miles south of K2. From this distance, Thomas Montgomerie first saw and sketched the mountain. Because of its location, K2 was not visible from settled areas and, at least so far as Montgomerie knew, was utterly unknown.

Reports of the unnamed mountain's staggering height and stunning beauty soon reached the world. The Trigonometrical Survey had a policy of labeling mountains by their local names, but K2 had none. It received the bureaucratic designation of Karakoram #2, or K2. By the century's end, geographers recognized K2 as second in height only to the central Himalayas' Mount Everest, which Nepal and Tibet had closed to foreigners.

Because it remained little explored and included many of the world's highest peaks, the Karakoram Range called to the duke. He knew it contained the largest glaciers outside the polar regions, some not fully mapped, and twenty-nine mountains over 24,000 feet, none yet climbed. His expedition could make major geographical discoveries and set climbing records even if it failed to summit on K2. The range, which runs southeast to northwest for over 300 miles at the intersection of modern-day Pakistan, India, and China, was typically approached from the south or west, whereas K2 rises in the east near the Chinese border. Several British expeditions had explored the western Karakoram around the Hispar, Chogo Lungma, and Biafo glaciers during the 1800s. In 1899 and 1902–03, the wealthy American climbing couple William and Fanny Bullock Workman, together with a small army of guides and porters, crisscrossed these glaciers and climbed their adjacent mountains, leading to a series of new altitude records for a female climber. From a 20,000-foot summit in 1899, Fanny Workman reportedly became the first Western woman to see K2, but neither she nor her husband ever ventured near it or into the eastern Karakoram. Returning to Kashmir in 1908, she set an altitude record for women of 22,735 feet that stood for nearly three decades.

Until the duke's expedition, only a small handful of Westerners had even seen, much less explored, the glaciers and mountains of the eastern Karakoram. Returning from a reconnaissance mission to China in 1887, the youthful British army lieutenant Francis Younghusband became the first European to cross the 18,000-foot-high Mustagh Pass near K2 and, by doing so, see the mountain's north face. Five years later, British mountaineer Martin Conway led the first expedition to traverse the entire length of the eastern Karakoram's Baltoro Glacier, which offers access to K2 from the south. Conway claimed first ascents of two lesser peaks on the glacier's flanks but never approached K2, which rises on the north side of a tributary glacier named for the Trigonometrical Survey leader Henry Godwin-Austen. Looking up the Godwin-Austen Glacier from its junction with the Baltoro to view K2 and its companion peaks for the first time from base to summit, Conway's Swiss guide Matthias Zurbriggen exclaimed, "They don't know what mountains are in Switzerland!"[5]

In 1902, Oscar Eckenstein, an original member of Conway's 1892 expedition, returned with four other Europeans to climb K2. Fearing espionage in the tense border region, British agents initially stopped Eckenstein from entering Kashmir. A socialist critic of imperialism and son of a Jewish immigrant to Britain, Eckenstein was a tempting target for security-conscious border officials, especially since he was traveling with Aleister Crowley, a Cambridge-educated hedonist and avowed Satanist. Eckenstein and Crowley were gifted climbers with elite connections, however, and ultimately pulled enough strings to gain entry. Their party established its base camp below K2's east face and made several unsuccessful attempts to scale the mountain before turning back due to a toxic mix of bad weather, altitude-related illnesses, and revolts against Eckenstein's authoritarian leadership. The expedition's Swiss physician, Jules Jacot-Guillarmod, returned proclaiming that K2's northeast ridge was climbable, while Crowley, the better mountaineer, came back touting the southeast ridge. These pronouncements caught the eye of the duke, who was looking for a worthy distraction from his failing romance with Katherine Elkins. Unlike Eckenstein, he traveled with the full support of India's British overlords and the blessings of King Edward VII.[6]

EVERY PRIOR EXPEDITION TO the eastern Karakoram had encountered bad weather. Climbing was only possible in the region during the summer, but even this season posed problems. July and

August, the best months for mountaineering in the Alps, brought the summer monsoon to India, the duke explained. By the time the weather improved in September, the days were cold and short. "I decided to start the exploration at the beginning of June," he stated. "This month, although the mountains can still be in unfavorable conditions, the days were long."[7] Eckenstein's party enjoyed its only brief spells of fair weather during June, though Conway found it as bad as other months. This timetable gave the duke less than two months to move men and supplies from Mumbai to the mountains and a month or so for climbing, depending on when the monsoon began. Once unimaginable given the distance, terrain, and political and cultural obstacles involved, British occupation made it possible. The duke took full advantage of his wealth and position.

Cleared through customs without the normal inspections, on April 9, the same day they arrived in Mumbai by steamship, the Italians departed the city with their tons of supplies by train, escorted by a British army officer. There began a royal cavalcade through British India from south to far north. A classic adventure of the Edwardian era ending in the deepest exploration to date of the eastern Karakoram, it captured the essence of the Raj as privileged Europeans saw it at its pre–World War I height.

Without exiting past the station at any stop, the Italians reached the railway's northern terminus at the garrison town of Rawalpindi in two days. "Temples and shrines, old forts and ruins, pass rapidly before our eyes," De Filippi wrote of the train trip. "Alas! We see nothing but the railway stations."[8] Arriving in Rawalpindi on the evening of April 11, by the next day their caravan began moving north by the new post road to Srinagar, the Kashmiri capital of the multiethnic protectorate of Jammu and Kashmir. A princely state within the British Empire in India, the protectorate had come into being a half century earlier through the forced union of Hindu Jammu with Sunni Muslim Kashmir and lesser realms. These included the

Shiite Muslim domain of Baltistan, or "Little Tibet," which the Anglocentric 1911 edition of the *Encyclopedia Britannica*—the reference book of empire—described as a thinly populated "mass of lofty mountains" capped by K2.[9]

With their climbing supplies and equipment prepackaged in two hundred sixty-two parcels of 50 pounds each, the Italians covered the 200 miles from Rawalpindi to Srinagar by all manner of carriage, oxcart, and horse wagon—some fast, some slow—using every vehicle that they could commission or commandeer, none of them motorized. On April 14, the two luxury landau carriages carrying the duke and his immediate party crossed from British India proper into the British-controlled protectorate, with a representative of the reigning maharaja, Pratap Singh, greeting them at the border. Francis Younghusband, then serving as the British Resident in Kashmir, paved the way, arranging an exemption from taxes and inspections for the expedition's supplies and equipment. He also engaged the local British agent A. C. Baines to obtain and oversee porters, ponies, and fresh food for the expedition in the protectorate.

Located at the heart of the lush, mile-high Vale of Kashmir, an oval plain encircled by lofty mountains, Srinagar was something of a Shangri-La for the British in hot, densely populated India during the early 1900s. Those with the means rushed there in late spring, typically living on houseboats, before moving higher into the mountains for midsummer. "To our party, who had left Italy barely twenty days before, the first impression was one of slight disappointment," De Filippi confessed. "But to travelers who come to Kashmir after months or years spent in the parched and burning plains of India, or after wearying journeys across the barren waste of Central Asia, it must seem a paradise indeed."[10]

The duke referred to Kashmir as "this Switzerland of India" and compared Srinagar, with its canals, to Venice. "The inhabitants are tall and well-proportioned with European features and bright eyes," he noted.[11] Arriving in Srinagar on the third day after leaving Rawalpindi, the Italians remained there until all the various vehicles carrying their supplies caught up with them over the next week.

Departing Srinagar by canal to the start of the overland route across the Himalayas from Kashmir to Central Asia, the Italians traveled on ornate shikara-style barges supplied by the maharaja, each rowed by more than a dozen red-festooned oarsmen. A small colony of houseboats and tents waited at the trailhead for the duke's arrival, along with ninety-three packhorses supplied for the next leg of the journey. This ancient route over the 11,500-foot-high Zoji Pass linked the humid Sind Valley in the south with the arid Dras Valley in the north. Twenty-five miles in, the expedition reached snow and transferred the load from packhorses to Kashmiri porters—two hundred seventy-one in all, each carrying one of the expedition's 50-pound parcels plus his own supplies for the fixed fee of one rupee per day. "Their feet are clad in sandals of plaited straw," De Filippi noted. "Their legs are either bare or covered with puttees." Snowdrifts exceeded 3 feet deep in places, storms struck frequently, and avalanches posed a constant threat. De Filippi described this stretch as "an interlude of high mountain life between the green garden of Kashmir and the parched and torrid valley of the Indus basin."[12] The expedition carried £450 in small coins simply to pay its hundreds of individual indigenous porters.

Just short of the pass's summit, thirty more porters sent by Baines from the far side met the expedition to help with the final steep ascent and beat a path through the snow. Then the entire three-hundred-person entourage descended the Dras River Valley to the Indus River, which it followed northwest to Skardu, the capital of Baltistan, a Shiite Muslim prefecture of the Protectorate of Jammu and Kashmir that includes the Karakoram. "There is probably no range of mountains on the face of the earth whose two slopes reveal features so absolutely opposed to one another," De Filippi observed about the traverse. "The traveller has crossed the great northern barrier of India, and has suddenly entered a country which is physically identical with Tibet."[13]

The vivid green of the Kashmir and Sind valleys gave way to the dull gray of the Dras and Indus valleys. The duke called them "stony, arid, and monotonous."[14] Once over the pass and out of the high-country snow, saddle ponies were waiting for the duke and his Italian party, while a mix of packhorses and fresh porters took up the load. Three days or 50 miles brought them to the Indus River, and then five more days northwest took them to Skardu, which an earlier British traveler had depicted as "a scattered collection of houses and hamlets" perched on a bleak plateau 150 vertical feet above the riverbank.[15]

"The striking peculiarities of the Dras valley had made a strong impression on us. But not until we reached the Indus valley did we realize to the full the nature of this land of desolation and sterility," De Filippi wrote. "Geological evolution is proceeding with such obvious plainness that the traveller feels as though he were beholding a country in a state of formation and witnessing the modelling of the earth's crust."[16] The stark mountains, sharp cliffs, and stone-filled valleys seemed of recent creation and ongoing formation. Reaching Skardu on May 8, the party had made the 225-mile passage across the Himalayas in eleven days.

FROM SKARDU, THE WAY went north and then east through the Shigar and Braldoh river valleys to Askoley, the last settlement before the eastern Karakoram. After crossing the Indus on barges, the duke's party began this five-day stretch with one hundred twenty-six porters and fifty-six packhorses but left the horses behind when crossing the Braldoh River on small rafts constructed from branches tied to inflated animal skins. At both Skardu and Shigar, local rajas welcomed the duke with bands, banquets, and polo matches. Although the route was lined with tall peaks, the valley walls were too high and the clouds too low to reveal the full panorama.

Askoley, which the Italians depicted as "a poor village indeed, and certainly one of the dirtiest in all Baltistan," stood over 10,000 feet high.[17] Behind it was a bleak, stony valley blocked by snows for eight months each year. Beyond that lay the world's largest subpolar glacial network. The Italians felt they had reached the end of the known world, with only terra nova ahead. Theirs was the first party to reach the village in 1909 and they received a warm welcome. Virtually every able-bodied man and boy in the region, and some that were not able-bodied, asked to serve as porters into the Karakoram. Local shepherds went ahead with sheep and goats to supply the expedition with fresh milk and meat. Displaced, the Kashmiri porters returned home. The British had warned the duke not to mix Kashmiri with Balti porters because the former were Sunni and the latter Shiite, and each accused the other of performing human sacrifice and other bloody rites. After working with them, the duke dismissed such charges and concluded that both could serve as proper mountain porters.

On May 15, the duke dispatched nearly a hundred fifty Balti porters with half of the expedition's supplies into the broad, rock-strewn valley running east from Askoley. The Italians followed a day later with over two hundred more Balti porters, making it the largest expedition ever to enter the Karakoram. "We now once more made our way across the shingle and pebbles of the valley bottom, but no longer the narrow gorge it was below Askoley, but over a mile wide and quite level," De Filippi wrote.[18] After passing the 300-foot-thick snout of the Biafo Glacier, which entered from a tributary valley on the north, they continued until the various parts of the expedition converged on May 17 at the base of the 2-mile-wide Baltoro Glacier, which all but blocked the valley floor. Its surface covered by rocky debris carried down by tributary glaciers and fallen from the steep mountains standing on either side, the glacier lay "like a huge black monster crouching with flattened back in the bottom of the valley," according to De Filippi.[19] Furrows of white showed through the gray mantle. A slow-moving river of ice nearly 40 miles long, the Baltoro Glacier descended at a steady 3.5-degree grade from 16,000 feet above sea level at its eastern summit to 11,000 feet at its western terminus. Once the expedition entered the glaciated regions of the Karakoram, it never encountered another person.

Marching east up the glacier, the expedition now labored alternately across its rough surface and a narrow marginal moraine winding along its south side. The Italians preferred the glacier; the porters favored the moraine. Either way, it was hard going on tortuous footing, especially for the livestock, which had nothing to eat for three days. After about 30 miles, the moraine rose above the glacial surface and broadened out at a large rockfall called Urdukas or, then, Rdokass. With boulders as large as houses, level terraces where scrubby grasses gave a matlike surface, and a mountain stream, Urdukas provided a made-to-order supply center for a large expedition with livestock. About two-thirds of the way between Askoley and the dramatic confluence of three glaciers at what Martin Conway called the Place de la Concorde, or "Concordia," after a similar juncture in the Alps, the duke made Urdukas a hub for his operations in the Karakoram. Due to its placement in the steep-sided Lower Baltoro, it offered only a limited view of the surrounding peaks and none whatsoever of K2, though the camp did boast a stunning vista of the valley walls.

His goal nearby if not yet within sight, the duke settled in for a two-month-long siege of K2 and the eastern Karakoram. No longer needing a large retinue, he sent two hundred Balti porters back to Askoley. Another one hundred fifty went on with him to establish a base camp at the southern foot of K2, with all but ten of these then returning to Askoley. The shepherds with their flocks and twenty-five porters remained with Baines at Urdukas to resupply the climbing party. No more lavish expedition had ever entered the Karakoram. Indeed, only from this point on did the duke give up his portable bed for a sleeping bag. Fresh meat, milk, and eggs continued, however.

With the vast resources of the Italian crown supporting his effort, the duke tried to anticipate every contingency, but like the fabled King Canute, he could not control the elements. Weather remained his main concern, though he did what he could to deal with it. "The night was very cold," the duke wrote about the first evening spent by the Italians at Urdukas. "In our triple-layered sleeping bags of goatskin, camelhair, and eiderdown, we could defy Arctic temperatures. Not so our porters, who were forced to take shelter from the cold by crouching under waxed canvas."[20] In a foretaste of what was to come, a furious late-spring blizzard held up the duke's party at Urdukas for two days.

On May 23, the Italians and their Balti porters started their 15-mile, two-day trek from Urdukas to Concordia, where the Godwin-Austen and Vigne glaciers flow into the Baltoro. "The meeting point of these three glaciers forms an immense basin offering a spectacle of incomparable Alpine beauty," the duke reported.[21] It provides readier access to and better views of more lofty summits than any place on earth—a 360-degree panorama that includes seven of the world's highest peaks, all over 25,000 feet, some 10,000 feet higher than Mont Blanc. Nevertheless, K2 steals the show.

"Suddenly," De Filippi wrote upon stepping into the Concordia basin, "the wide Godwin-Austen valley lay before us in its whole length. Down at the end, alone, detached from all the other mountains, soared up K2, the indisputable sovereign of the region, gigantic and solitary." Arriving late on May 24, the Italians were dumbstruck by their first view of it. "For a whole hour we stood absorbed."[22] In the gathering darkness, K2 stood in full profile, some 12,000 feet from base camp to summit. A steep, four-sided pyramid of gray granite and gleaming glaciers, it reminded the Italians of a massively oversized Matterhorn. The duke was in sight of his pole.

"It was a world of ice and cliffs, a grand view that, while it would please an artist, alarmed the alpinist," he wrote.[23]

———

THE NEXT MORNING GAVE the Italians their first panoramic view of the surrounding landscape. The clouds that had partially obscured it during the prior evening gave way to a diffuse mist that seemed to sharpen features rather than dull them. "Like a crystal breathed upon" was how De Filippi described the morning air, through which they now saw the towering mountain chains and broad glacial valleys radiating outward from the central basin. "So inconceivably vast are the structural lines of the landscape, that the idea comes into one's mind of being in the workshop of nature, and of standing before the primeval chaos and cosmos of a world as yet unvisited by the phenomenon of life," he wrote. "It is comparable to the polar regions in this respect, but in no other, for instead of the monotonous horizons of the far north, all the landscape around K2 has the richest variety of design."[24]

Vastness is the operative word linking the Karakoram to the polar regions. Just as Peary, Shackleton, and Mawson complained that they could not judge heights or distances in the far north or south, so too the Italians inevitably found landmarks in the Karakoram farther away and larger than they first appeared. "We had no standards of comparison, and the glaciers and valleys are so well adjusted in their proportions to the surrounding mountains that it was hard to realize the absolute size of any object," De Filippi wrote. "All of this was revealed to us gradually, by dint of daily contemplation and detailed observation, most of all by repeated failures in estimating heights and distances. Thus it happened that our amazement, instead of diminishing with familiarity, grew greater every day."[25] He remained at Concordia with Negrotto and Sella for the day to map and photograph the surroundings.

Drawn more to adventure than scenery, on May 25 the duke marched ahead for 6 miles over the Godwin-Austen Glacier with the alpine guides and most of the Balti porters to set up their base camp beneath K2's southern face. "The location could not be better," the duke wrote. "Sheltered from avalanches and winds, the view is dominated by the lower part of the Godwin-Austen Glacier and the great Concordia basin" spreading outward to the south and the 2-mile-high rock face of K2 rising abruptly in the north.[26]

The others followed a day later. "The immense [mountain] chains rose all about us," De Filippi wrote of his trek up the glacial valley. "The mountains have all the bold design to be seen anywhere in the Alps—the barren precipices, the snowy slopes and the upward thrust of slender peaks, the ample curving cornices, the multiform broken architecture of séracs, and the overweighted glaciers hanging on vertical rocks," but on a grand scale "that seems to beggar the human imagination."[27] Despite the summits on both sides, including the massive 26,400-foot Broad Peak to the east, it was K2, looming directly ahead, that mesmerized them.

By the time the other Italians reached the base camp, the duke had already reconnoitered the southwest flank of K2 with two guides and sent Alexis Brocherel with three others along its east side. While no one found an obvious route to the summit, the duke reported, "The news brought back by Brocherel, while not optimal, was more encouraging than ours."[28] He had found a rocky ridge running from the southeast to the mountain's eastern shoulder that appeared possible if not promising, though from below he could not discern a path from the shoulder to the top. For his part, the duke had discovered a long route around to a northwestern ridge that might shelter a climbable snowfield on its far side. Some 16,500 feet above sea level at the base camp, any route to the 28,250-foot summit would be treacherous.

After reviewing the options, the duke chose Brocherel's route on what became known as the Abruzzi Spur. His plan involved making a high camp at a reddish outcrop on the ridge about 3,500 vertical feet above the valley floor, and then climbing to the shoulder, which stood over 25,000 feet high. Simply reaching it would set a new altitude record. The duke made this attempt with seven Italian guides, leaving the others below.

As it turned out, the duke could not even reach the reddish outcrop. Setting out on May 30, he camped for the first night at 18,245 feet. From there, the guides tried to find a way up on three successive days, going farther each day—surely over 20,000 feet on one or two occasions—but returned despondent. The rock crumbled beneath their feet, the ridge narrowed to a precarious crest, the weather deteriorated, and the perspective baffled them. "Slabs of rock which at a few yards distant looked like gentle and easy inclines, turned out to be little less than perpendicular," they reported, and the reddish outcrop receded before their eyes.[29]

"The guides finally came to the reluctant conclusion that it was useless to proceed further, not because they had encountered insurmountable obstacles," De Filippi explained, "but because it was hopeless to think of bringing so long and formidable an ascent to a successful issue, when from the very first steps they had met with such difficulties."[30] From what the guides told him, the duke noted, "I understood that to carry our supplies even with reduced loads and to overcome the difficulties that would be encountered, it would have taken weeks, not days."[31] Despite the setback, he had chosen the best way. Forty-five years later, an Italian party used the Abruzzi Spur to make the first-ever successful ascent of K2. It remains the standard route.

Returning to the base camp on June 4, the duke now tried his western route. All of the Italians and most of the Balti porters moved around K2's southwestern flank to an advance camp at 18,176 feet near the midpoint of a tributary glacier that the duke named Savoia for his homeland. "At this height," De Filippi observed with some surprise, "we not only found ourselves in perfect condition, but could actually breathe more easily here than at the [16,500-foot] base camp."[32] A scientist as well as a physician, De Filippi was gaining deeper insight into acclimatation and altitude sickness. At this point, he attributed the easier breathing in part to relatively better air circulation at the higher camp.

Thickly covered with fresh snow, the 10-mile-long Savoia Glacier hugged the mountain's west face, which rose from base to summit at a staggering 60-degree pitch. "We could see its entire west wall, splotched with snow, but so steep that no glacier could cling to it," De Filippi observed.[33] Making this move into the Savoia Valley in marginal weather, the Italians soon saw conditions worsen so much that they could not even see the summit, much less try to reach it. The wind rose to gale force, avalanches thundered down the mountainsides, heavy snow fell, and the temperature plummeted to near zero.

Forced by the weather to remain in camp much of the time, they took advantage of every clear opportunity. On the one truly fine day during this period, June 7, while Sella took some of the most stunning photographs ever captured of K2, the duke with three guides set off for the saddle at the valley's northern terminus. There, he hoped to view the mountain's north face and perhaps find a route up it. After a long march through knee-deep snow, this effort ended with a near-vertical climb up an ice wall to the pass at nearly 22,000 feet. From here, they could go no farther. The far side dropped off steeply, towering pinnacles blocked the ridge, and a cornice barred access to or even a view of the north face.

On June 8, the Italians withdrew to their base camp on the Godwin-Austen Glacier, where they remained for four days preparing for their next move. Since reaching the Karakoram, they had not had more than two consecutive days of good weather. For his part, De Filippi lamented, he had never felt "so alone, so isolated, so completely ignored by nature," and he had been with the duke on both the Saint Elias and the Ruwenzori expeditions.[34] Now they would probe K2's east face.

Still hoping to summit, the duke established a new advance camp 4 miles farther north on the steeply rising, deeply crevassed Godwin-Austen Glacier. "K2, with its steep flanks swept clean by avalanches and its summit cone covered with ice, reveals itself here in all its splendor," the duke wrote.[35]

At over 18,600 feet above sea level, the camp stood beneath a dip in the valley's eastern wall opposite K2. The party climbed to this dip for an unobstructed view of the mountains and glaciers to the east, resulting in Sella's panoramic photograph of the Gasherbrum massif's three highest 26,000-foot peaks and the distant Teram Kangri. Such images, climbing historians Maurice Isserman and Stewart Weaver observed, "For the first time made it possible for armchair mountaineers to picture in the mind's eye the physical scale of the Himalaya." With them, they added, "Photography disclosed its full potential and began to displace lengthy narrative as the conventional way of marking individual and collective achievement in the mountains."[36]

Massive spring avalanches crashed down continuously from the nearby heights during the party's two-week stay in the upper Godwin-Austen, unnerving everyone. Storms raged. Looking at the mountain from the east, De Filippi commented on its changed appearance. "The whole cone is covered with ice, above which just show the low, little accented rocky ridges converging to the top. The wall, at a very steep angle of inclination, is live ice for 7,000 feet up, and crowned by séracs," he wrote. "It is absolutely inaccessible."[37] All hope of climbing K2 from this side evaporated. If anyone is to reach the summit, the duke observed, "It will not be a climber, but an aviator."[38]

Instead, the duke and Sella led alternating marches over the Godwin-Austen Glacier to its terminus at the 20,500-foot-high, aptly named Windy Gap, which opened onto the land beyond. Each carried cameras to capture images of what they could not reach. Trying again to gain a view of K2's elusive north face, the duke and three guides attempted to climb the narrowing ridge running northwest from Windy Gap to Staircase Peak, but were blocked by steep ice and deep crevasses after gaining little more than 1,000 feet. There, at 21,650 vertical feet, the duke snapped the expedition's classic photograph of K2. Although impatient in the role, he was a fine photographer too.

Infinitely patient in his work, Sella revolutionized the art of mountain photography. By seizing every chance in the midst of appalling weather and using fragile, large-format glass-plate negatives developed in the field, he captured a series of historic panoramas from Windy Gap toward the north and east. "In Sella's photographs there is no faked grandeur," Ansel Adams later commented. "The vastness of the subjects and purity of Sella's interpretations move the spectator to a definitely religious awe."[39] None of these photos were easily won. The duke made his by climbing to precarious positions, then snapping away. Sella, in contrast, photographed mountains much as portraitists photograph children—waiting with forbearance for the subjects to reveal themselves in telling moods.

During their fifteen days in the upper Godwin-Austen, howling wind, intense cold, and frequent snowstorms frustrated the Italians at every turn. Only a few days offered even brief moments of good visibility; many offered none. "For an entire week encamped under K2," the duke reported, "we never saw the summit."[40] De Filippi wrote of wind piercing the thickest woolens. Ever the perfectionist, Sella stood for hours in exposed positions, teeth chattering and feet stomping, hoping for the clouds to part enough to show a mountain as only an artist could see it. The Balti porters suffered miserably in their loose garments and visibly shook from the cold when they paused from marching.

By the end of June, having given up on K2, the duke looked instead for a nearby mountain where he could set a world altitude record. Returning to Concordia and turning east onto the Upper Baltoro Glacier, he settled on majestic Chogolisa, with its rectangular, pup-tent-like shape and twin 25,000-foot summits, the lower of which Martin Conway had named Bride Peak when he saw it in 1892. Proceeding ahead as far as Concordia, Sella took advantage of a rare break in the weather to climb ridges on either side of the basin and make a complete photographic panorama of surrounding mountains and valleys.

FOR THE DUKE'S ASSAULT on Chogolisa, the expedition moved its base camp to the south side of the Upper Baltoro below the mountain's east face. The 26,500-foot summit of the Gasherbrum massif, Conway's Hidden Peak, originally K5, stood across the valley—the eleventh-highest mountain in the world. The broadly pyramidal 24,000-foot Baltoro Kangri, Conway's Golden Throne, rose to the east. Were it not for clouds and storms, it would have been a stunning campsite. De Filippi and Negrotto remained there for thirteen days while the duke and six guides pushed up Chogolisa in ever worsening weather. Hoping to photograph it, Sella joined the first part of the climb, but returned with only one grand panorama after realizing that the worsening weather would bar him from taking further pictures. July had brought the summer monsoon, with heavy snows turning to heavier rains in the valley. Snows persisted on the mountain, where the duke's party repeatedly sought shelter in small climbing tents. "Avalanches fell continually from the wall, fed from the uninterrupted heavy snows, during the whole time of our stay here," De Filippi reported. "In the warm part of the day it seemed as though the whole mountain were actually falling apart, so huge were the masses of ice, rock and snow that hurled themselves down from it."[41] Those below could only imagine what the climbers above were experiencing.

Once again fooled by perspective, the duke misjudged the ascent. Originally, he planned to climb Chogolisa's broad northern face, which looked like a snowfield from a distance. On close inspection, the lower portion consisted of chaotic torrents of steep séracs— "foaming white cataracts like frozen Niagaras" was how De Filippi depicted them—clearly impossible for porters to climb.[42]

Instead, the duke opted for an eastern route up a steep glacial icefall and over a snow slope to the Chogolisa saddle, then across a dome-shaped shoulder toward the mountain's eastern summit, Conway's Bride Peak. "The route was long and not easy to the saddle, with the final part unknown," the duke observed, "but it was the only one that would allow taking supplies up to the shoulder."[43] This was central to his plan. The Balti porters would transport supplies to an advance camp on the mountain. The duke anticipated that this portion of the ascent would take two days at most. It took eight.

Terrain and weather combined to slow the initial ascent to a crawl. "The glacier was broken up into large blocks, between which were wide and treacherous openings disguised by the snow," De Filippi explained. The climbers "could never tell whether the latter would be firm beneath their tread, or whether a bottomless gulf would open where they set their feet." The snow atop the ice stood knee-deep at best, waist-deep at worst. Plowing through it, the Italians observed, was "infinite labour at every step."[44] Snowshoes scarcely helped. After three days, a furious snowstorm kept the climbers in camp for three more, so that by the sixth day, July 8, they had ascended only 1,300 vertical feet. Two days with improved weather over the snow slope took them to the saddle at nearly 21,700 feet, temporarily freeing the Balti porters to head down. "They had performed the work of real Alpine porters, coming up over the séracs with full loads of luggage, and had lived in camps on the snows without fires and contrary to all the habits of their normal lives," De Filippi reported.[45] The Italian guides were impressed: locals could learn their work and replace them in the Himalayas and Karakoram.

The duke with six guides stood less than 4,300 vertical feet from the summit. He estimated the ascent would take two more days, but again failed to reckon with terrain and weather. Their legs sinking (or "postholing") into the deep snow, they crossed the saddle on July 11 and were poised to summit on the 12th when the weather again turned against them. Ascending a narrow ridge above 23,000 feet, their steps favored the steep slope on the left to avoid the overhanging cornice on the right and occasionally dislodged snowslides with their footfalls. One misstep on either side meant death.

Then, at 23,458 feet, the fog became too thick to see ahead, send-

Ernest Shackleton as he portrayed
himself in the frontispiece of
his 1909 book, *In the Heart of the
Antarctic*.

King Edward VII, Queen
Alexandra, and the Prince of Wales
(the future King George V), on the
Nimrod with Ernest Shackleton,
1908.

The *Nimrod* in the Ross Sea ice pack, 1908.

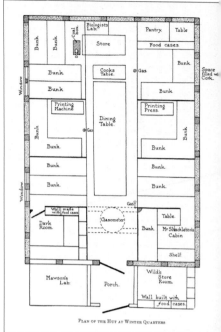

PLAN OF THE HUT AT WINTER QUARTERS

Above: An interior diagram of the *Nimrod* Expedition's winter quarters at Cape Royds, showing the elevated gas-lighting system and cramped living space.

Left: The *Nimrod* Expedition's shore party at their winter quarters with the Victrola, 1908.

Bernard Day driving the Arrol-Johnston automobile on the sea ice at Cape Royds, 1908.

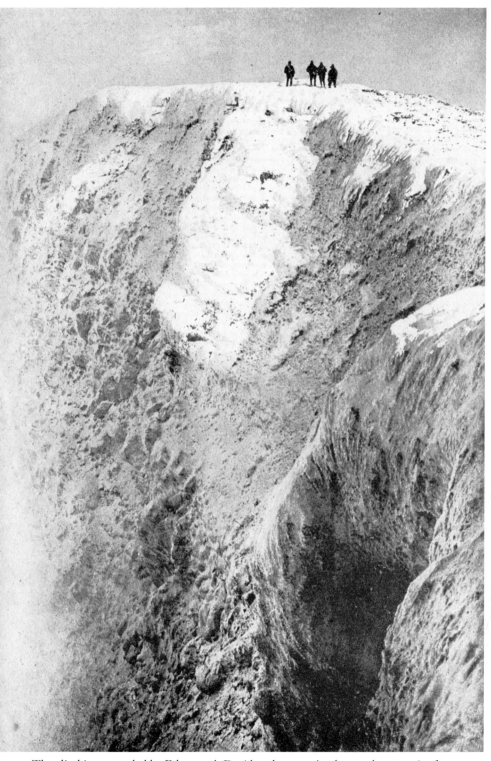

The climbing party led by Edgeworth David at the crater's edge on the summit of Mount Erebus, 1908.

Ernest Shackleton, Eric Marshall, Jamison Adams, and Frank Wild with their ponies Socks, Grisi, Quan, and Chinaman, marching south across the Ross Ice Shelf, 1908.

Looking south from Mount Hope toward the Beardmore Glacier with its "Golden Gateway" on the right, 1908.

Lower Glacier Depot near the base of Beardmore Glacier, 1909.

(*From left to right:*) Ernest Shackleton, Frank Wild, and Jamison Adams in a photograph taken by Eric Marshall at the flag marking their farthest south on the Polar Plateau, January 9, 1909.

Forbes Mackay, Edgeworth David, and Douglas Mawson, with their tent and sledge, on the Great Ice Plateau, 1909.

Photograph of Douglas Mawson, ca. 1915.

Portrait of Edgeworth David, 1922.

The route of the northern sledge party from Cape Royds to the south magnetic pole, 1908–09.

(*From left to right:*) Forbes Mackay, Edgeworth David, and Douglas Mawson in a photograph taken at the flag marking the south magnetic pole, January 16, 1909.

The southern sledge party upon its return to the *Nimrod*, 1909.

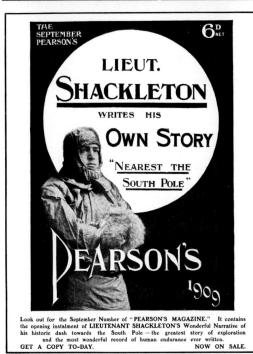

"The greatest story of exploration": An advertisement for Ernest Shackleton's magazine account of the *Nimrod* Expedition, 1909.

The author's photograph of the *Nimrod* Expedition's Cape Royds hut as it appeared in 2004, with stables and a car port on the left and Mount Erebus rising in the background.

ing them back to camp in the saddle. Storms kept them there for four days. On July 13, the duke sent three guides down for added supplies, and on July 17, he headed back up the ridge with three others, Joseph Petigax and Henri and Emil Brocherel. Again slowed by the heavy snow, they made it to 22,483 feet, where they spent the night in two small tents, setting a new record for the highest documented campsite.

July 18 opened clear enough to start but with a light mist that grew steadily heavier. Visibility dropped as the duke and his team made their way along the knife's edge between the cornice on the right and the sheer slope on the left. "The snow was very tiring, being over two feet deep, and the grade was steep. The foot went down so far at every step that one felt there was no solid ground beneath," De Filippi reported from the duke's account. "Nothing could be seen beyond a few yards, but they realized that bottomless gulfs opened on every side."[46]

After four hours in worsening conditions, they gained a rock outcropping they had measured at 24,278 feet from below. Climbing it with their hands and feet put them at 24,600 feet above sea level, a new world record, but still some 500 feet below the summit. "The fog became dense, the day hot, the snow bad," the duke observed.[47] A steeply rising, utterly unknown snow-covered ridge stretched into the mist ahead, with unseen drop-offs on either side. "It would have been madness to go on," De Filippi declared.[48]

They waited for two hours for the fog to clear, but it persisted. "Petigax wanted to continue," the duke wrote, "but I thought it would be too risky to proceed under these conditions."[49] Knowing that his party must return to camp by nightfall, he sensibly ordered a retreat. "When this happens in the Alps, we can try again," a commentator for Britain's Alpine Club later noted; "in the Himalaya, we can't."[50]

With the weather worsening and no relief in sight, 24,600 feet became the duke's "pole by default," and an admitted disappointment to him. Nevertheless, his altitude record held for thirteen years, until broken by British mountaineers George Mallory, Howard Somervell, and Edward Norton on Mount Everest in 1922. As in the response to Shackleton's falling just short of reaching the South Pole earlier in 1909, however, near misses can become virtual achievements in the public mind. At the time, Shackleton and the duke received nearly as much acclaim for what they did as they most likely would have received for doing more. Not summiting on Chogolisa, the *Alpine Journal* declared, "was sheer bad luck." First ascents are not the sole goal; it added, "Records do count for something."[51]

Beyond the record, the duke, Petigax, and the Brocherels showed what humans could do. Except for the fickleness of the weather, they would have summited on Chogolisa. Without supplementary oxygen or suffering any physical effects except loss of appetite, they spent a longer period at higher altitudes than any previous group.

At the time, the American climber and physician William Workman posited that humans could not sleep at over 20,000 feet, yet the duke and his guides stayed ten days above that height and one night each above 21,000 and 22,000 feet, after which they climbed another 2,000 vertical feet, all in adverse conditions. "None of them had difficulty in breathing; there were no headaches, and their pulses were normal," De Filippi reported. Even the Balti porters reached the highest camp at 22,483 feet, which De Filippi deemed "as especially worthy of remark."[52] Throughout this entire span, they had only one full day of fine weather. Further, the expedition remained for eight weeks at over 16,000 feet, with nearly three of these above 18,000 feet.

At half past three on the afternoon of July 18, 1909, in thick fog, the climbing party started down from its highest point to the Chogolisa saddle, where the others waited. On the morning of July 19, in a heavy snowstorm, the enlarged party began the descent to base camp on the Upper Baltoro. On the afternoon of July 20, in torrential rains, the full party commenced the three-day march from the Upper Baltoro camp to the expedition's supply center at Urdukas on the Lower Baltoro, from where all headed home.

After two months among the world's highest glaciers and mountains in abominable weather, the Balti porters were overjoyed at the prospect of going home, De Filippi noted. "The rest of us were silent and depressed."[53]

CHAPTER 11

Returnings

REACHING THE UTTERMOST EDGES of the earth is only halfway home. One by one over the course of 1909, after they had gone as far as possible toward their poles, Mawson and David, Shackleton, Peary, the Duke of the Abruzzi, and those with them turned back. Some carried ample supplies; others had much less. Although they were crossing familiar territory, conditions changed with the seasons, and no one knew what to expect.

HAVING ATTAINED THE SOUTH magnetic pole on January 16 after pushing far beyond their point of safe return with the supplies available, David, Mawson, and Mackay were the first to turn back and in the most hurry. In his narrative account, David called it an abrupt "right-about turn."[1] They did not even take time to confirm their location at the pole, and by this point were relying on Mawson's projections of the probable position of a receding target. Growing increasingly desperate on the outward trek, they had left behind everything required for the return journey at drops along the way, and now needed to find them on the polar ice sheet.

"It was a weary tramp back over the hard and high sastrugi," David wrote in his first entry about the return trip, "and we were very thankful when at last we saw a small dark cone, which we knew was our tent, rising from above the distant snow ridges."[2] Covering 24 miles out and back on this critical day, the men reported sleeping soundly and with a certain satisfaction. The worst was yet to come.

Two scientists and a physician, this party calculated and recalculated its odds and options. "At the Magnetic Pole," David wrote, "we were fully 260 statute miles distant, as the skua flies, from our depot on the Drygalski Glacier," where they hoped to meet the *Nimrod*.[3] Of course, this was just their hope. No one knew if the *Nimrod* could make it back to the Antarctic in 1909, and if it did, whether its captain could find a small party at an undetermined location on an icebound, 200-mile-long seacoast.

Heading now for the Drygalski depot, they were aiming to hit the coast roughly 150 miles north of the planned rendezvous at or near Marble Point, which lay directly across McMurdo Sound from the expedition's winter quarters at Cape Royds. Shackleton's year-old instructions to David simply said, "If by February 1 after the arrival of *Nimrod*, there is no evidence that your party has returned, the *Nimrod* will proceed north along the coast, keeping as close to the land as possible, on the look-out for a signal from you flashed by heliograph." Shackleton only added this alternative pickup as "a safeguard in event of any accident."[4] These plans assumed that David's party would be working in the Dry Valley near Marble Point by January. Yet David, with the off-and-on acquiescence of Mawson and Mackay but rarely with the support of both at once, fixed his party's course for the pole at the expense of all else.

By pushing the quest for the magnetic pole into January, contrary to Mackay's advice, the team faced a desperate circumstance. They were now in a race to the coast against the *Nimrod*. Reaching their depot at the landward end of the Drygalski Ice Tongue, or barrier, by February would require them to average 16 miles per day on the return trip, which was more than they had covered *any* day on the outbound trek, and this presumed traveling without detours. The *Nimrod* might be late, which would extend the window for rescue, but they could no more count on this than be sure the ship would arrive at all. Mackay put their odds of getting back home at not more than 50 percent and had long since lost faith in David's ability to lead.

"The strain of the whole thing, the exhaustion and actual muscular pain, the cold, the want of food and sleep, the monotony, the anxiety as to what will happen in the end," Mackay confessed in his diary, "make me think that this must be the most awful existence possible."[5]

The first thirteen days went as well as David and Mawson hoped and better than Mackay expected. Following their old track over the mostly level or lightly undulating ice sheet, the party maintained the necessary average of 16 miles per day, even though it often required sledging late into the evening. Some days the surface was soft and slow; some days crusted over; and some days so hard and icy that the men could not stand without wearing crampons. Most days, the temperature hovered around minus 20°F in the mornings and never broke zero, but at least the weather held and no blizzards struck.

Mawson's diary entries spoke of snow blindness, bruised legs, many falls, and frostbite. "In agony," Mawson wrote on January 22. "Surface abominable," he added on the 25th.[6] One leg troubled him greatly.

The scenery remained a 360-degree panorama of snow and sky until the coastal mountains came into view. Then the glacial surface began tilting away toward the coast, accented by occasional sharp drops. "Every now and then the sledge would take charge and rush down this marble staircase, bumping very heavily over the steps," David noted on the 26th.[7]

Three days later and still on schedule, the party reached its depot below Mount Larsen at the head of the steep glacier's descent to the sea. Shortly after reaching the depot, with their load augmented by additional equipment and geological specimens, the men made a near-fatal mistake. Having failed to find a way up the main glacier's snout on the outbound journey, they had gone around it by way of a side outlet that they called the Backstairs Passage. Mackay wanted to take this same route down, arguing that "the devil one knew was better than the devil one didn't know."[8] He was right, but the others over-ruled him.

With time running out, shorter and steeper should work going down, even if it failed going up, David and Mawson argued, and re-membering how soggy and disrupted the ice-encrusted shoreline was in December, they dreaded how much worse it might be after two months of summer thaw. The Backstairs Passage angled north-west, away from their Drygalski depot, while the glacier's main ice-fall pointed more directly toward it, or so David reasoned. By this stage of their long ordeal, trust had broken down completely between David and Mackay, with only the affable and imposing Mawson, who frequently talked with each man separately and criticized both of them privately in his diary, holding the party together. Nothing they had experienced to date prepared them for what followed.

The glacier sloped ever more steeply downward as the party moved past the outlet passage. Staying to their right, near a granite cliff, the men avoided the worst of the crevasses and pressure ridges but faced the sharper slope. Twisting tarred rope around the runners to keep the sledge from running ahead, they slowly worked their way down to the coastal icefield. "Mawson's leg was now so bad that it was only with considerable pain and difficulty that he could proceed," David noted, "and both Mackay's and my eyes were affected a good deal by snow-blindness and were painful."[9]

Upon reaching the base of the glacier, David reported, "We now found ourselves on an ice-surface quite unlike anything which we had hitherto experienced." The ice had frozen in upturned tiles of varying sizes and thicknesses. "As we stepped forwards, our feet usually crashed through the ice tiles, and our legs were imbedded in the formation up to our knees," he wrote. "Another moment one would find the tiles thick enough and strong enough to support one, but their surfaces being at an angle of 45° to the horizontal, our feet would slip down them sideways."[10] The upturned edges tore at the sledge's runners. Having started the day at 9 A.M. but desperate to advance, they kept on through the midnight sun to 2 A.M., when they camped on a frozen lake.

The men awoke on January 31 to find 4 inches of fresh snow, making the tile ice tougher to navigate. Soon pressure ridges, crevasses, and meltwater canyons began intersecting the route toward the Drygalski depot, forcing them to climb across, hack through, or detour around obstacles. At the outset they relayed their load, tripling the distance, and at one point they carried it item by item over a steep pressure ridge. The depot stood less than 20 miles away, but progress toward it slowed to a crawl.

Crossing a newly frozen lake, Mawson crashed through the ice, soaking himself to the waist. Everyone suffered physically and mentally, but David, who turned fifty-one on the 28th, struggled the most. Judged by his actions, Mawson observed, "He is apparently half demented."[11] Mackay called him a bloody fool for falling into a plainly visible crevasse and issued an ultimatum. Either David must voluntarily relinquish command of the expedition to Mawson, Mackay demanded, or he, as the party's doctor, would declare David mentally unfit for command. Mawson was again left to mediate, but only managed to bide some time.

"It was an awful day of despair, disappointment, hard travelling, agonizing walking—forever falling down crevasses," Mawson noted in his diary.[12] Frantic to reach the depot, the men sledged around the clock until collapsing in camp at 7 A.M. the following morning with roughly 16 miles still to go.

The next two days were even worse. First, the men knew that

it was now February and the ship could pass at any moment without their being in position to flag it down. (Although they could not know this, the *Nimrod* had successfully returned from New Zealand and was just then sailing slowly up the Victoria Land coast looking for them.) Second, the men awoke on February 1 to a blizzard that kept them in camp until afternoon and then limited their progress to a mile and a half before they gave up at 8 P.M. Looking back at their track a day later, David likened it to a corkscrew. Third, serving as cook for the week, Mackay reported that they had only "two day's [*sic*] rations on *very* short allowance" left.[13] Finally, with clear weather returning on February 2, after about 10 miles with all three men in harness and Mackay kicking David from behind to keep him moving, they ran into the deepest meltwater canyon yet, with sea ice at its base. Mawson called it an "arm of [the] sea."[14] Predictably, Mackay blamed their latest predicament on "our having approached the depôt on a wrong bearing" because of how they descended the glacier.[15] In his eyes, David could do nothing right.

By this point, the party was only a few miles west of the coast, with the *Nimrod* slowly approaching from the south but blocked from sight by the Drygalski Ice Tongue. The men needed to go southwest to their depot on the northern side of the ice tongue's base, however, which meant crossing or circumventing the canyon. Initially they tried to cross it, which involved lowering the sledge down a vertical 40-foot bank. Due to an overhanging cornice, they could not scale the far side and retreated the way they came, where they camped after twenty-three hours of continuous effort and no progress. David's feet were so frozen during much of their march that Mawson depicted him as "walking on his ankles" for most of the day.[16] Bowing to Mackay's ongoing demand, David now formally transferred command to Mawson, leading Mackay to crow, "I have deposed the Professor."[17] Mawson privately reassured David as much as possible, but by then the senior scientist was most likely beyond caring.

The issue facing the men was not so much about whether they

would reach the depot but what to do if the *Nimrod* did not come or had already passed. Mackay wanted to race south around the rough coastline to winter quarters at Cape Royds over 200 miles away but knew that David could not survive the trip. Mawson must make that decision, Mackay felt. Mawson and David simply wanted to get to the depot and hoped that the ship could rescue them from there. In either event, they had no option other than to round the canyon, which meant turning east away from the coast until they found a crossing.

The crossing came in about 2 miles, where an icefall had created a tenuous bridge across the canyon. Then the party turned west along the canyon toward the coast, which it reached after roughly 4 miles at 10:30 P.M. on February 3, shortly after the *Nimrod* had sailed past during a sudden snow squall without sighting either them or their well-marked depot. "We were now all thoroughly exhausted and decided to camp," David wrote. "The spot we had selected seemed specially suitable, as from the adjacent ice mound we could get a good view of the ocean beyond the Drygalski Barrier."[18] Scarcely a mile from their depot, they had a clear view of any approaching ship and took turns keeping watch.

Since descending into the seawater canyon and now on the coast, concern over the lack of food gave way to visions of plenty. "We have penguins and seals galore within sight," Mackay rejoiced on February 3.[19] That day, Mawson's diary spoke of "fried up penguins with seal blubber" and David's extolled one Emperor penguin stew as "the most satisfying meal we had had for many a long day."[20] At least hunger was no longer a problem.

After each man stood one watch while the others slept, they were eating together inside the tent about 4 P.M. on February 4. "Mac was just having a final fill up of blubber and we were discussing immediately shifting camp to higher depot when a shot rang out," Mawson wrote.[21]

"A gun from the ship!" he exclaimed as they all broke for the tent door, tripping over each other on the way.[22]

After sailing north for another day searching the coast, the *Nimrod* had turned back south when First Officer John King Davis suggested reexamining the region around the Drygalski Ice Tongue obscured by the snow squall. Worried about the ship's dwindling coal reserves, the captain only reluctantly agreed. There, a lookout on board now spotted the party's depot but not yet its tent.

"It would have been hard, indeed, for any one, not situated as we had been, to realize the sudden revulsion of our feelings," David commented. "In a moment, as dramatic as it was heavenly, we seemed to have passed from death to life."[23]

Leading the way across the ice to flag down the ship without thinking to don a harness, Mawson abruptly dropped from sight into a deep crevasse. The others were so weak that they needed to wait for the ship's crew to raise him.

"Mawson has fallen down a crevasse," Mackay now shouted to those on board, "and we got to the Magnetic Pole."[24] Fortunately, Mawson had landed on his back unhurt upon a ledge only about 18 feet down.

"What a joyous grasping of hands and hearty all-round welcoming followed," David added. "After our one hundred and twenty-two days of hard toil over the sea ice of the coast and the great snow desert of the hinterland, the little ship seemed to us as luxurious as an ocean liner."[25] He hobbled aboard with the aid of two walking sticks. "They were a curious looking little group," the captain said of the three. "Abnormally lean because they had been reduced to very short commons for some six weeks, they were the color of mahogany with hands that resembled the talons of a bird of prey."[26]

After hearing their story, the captain marveled at all they had done. "There is nothing in polar travel to compare with the exploits of the party led by Professor David because so ambitious a project has never been undertaken with such slender resources," he declared.[27] Another officer wrote that David looked dazed and that all three of "their faces were skinned and frostbitten."[28] To their colleague from the Mount Erebus climb, Philip Brocklehurst, they now appeared in "a very bad state and dreadfully weak."[29] Upon reaching the ship, David promptly asked about Shackleton. No one on board knew the fate of his party. It was still out.

EVEN AS THE NORTHERN party was being rescued, Shackleton and his men were barely halfway back from their farthest south. The return trek had devolved into a fight for survival. "Ours is an invalid camp," Frank Wild wrote in his diary from the Ross Ice Shelf on February 4. "We are all too ill to march, all four down with acute diarrhea. Adams had to turn out seven times last night and there has not been an interval of a few minutes between the times that someone has been outside in agony."[30] Marshall and Shackleton called it dysentery and blamed it on meat from Grisi, the second pony shot, which they had picked up two days earlier from a depot left behind over two months earlier. The meat was rancid, but they had little else to eat.

"So we shall all be hungry all the way to the Bluff [depot], probably three weeks, and if this illness does not prove short, we shall *never* get there," Wild added.[31] "I believe we all thought the end had come."[32]

Sicker than Wild, Shackleton simply jotted, "Terrible day. No march possible; serious outlook." He could not write more.[33] Marshall likened the campsite to "a battlefield."[34] That night, Shackleton asked Wild to sing the well-known dirge "Lead, Kindly Light," but Wild could only make it through one verse.[35]

The return trip had started out bleakly nearly a month earlier and soon became desperate. By the time his party turned back on January 9, Shackleton had already pushed himself and his men to their limits. They thought they had turned in time, however, which was to Shackleton's credit, given the explorer's strong impulse to reach the goal at all costs.

"If we'd gone on one more hour," Jameson Adams later commented, "we shouldn't have got back."[36]

Yet a day after their turning, Wild wrote in his diary, "Given average luck and weather, we ought to get to Hut Point about 27 February, which would be in time for the *Nimrod*."[37] Before setting out, Shackleton had left orders authorizing the ship to steam north for New Zealand on March 1, and in no event later than March 10. If the southern party remained out, they were to leave a relief party with ample provisions behind at Cape Royds for a second winter in case the lost party turned up later or needed rescue. For Shackleton and his men, this schedule made their return a timed race against harsh conditions and the limits of human endurance.

The first ten days of the march back across the Polar Plateau, while difficult, buoyed their hopes. The unrelenting winds that had hindered their advance going south propelled their retreat going north. With the temperature hovering between 10° and 25° below zero and a makeshift sail attached to their battered sledge, the party averaged 20 miles per day over the undulating ice. Gravity helped as well, as the plateau sloped evermore downward as the party approached the Western Mountains, where the Beardmore Glacier began its steep descent to the Ross Ice Shelf.

"There has been tremendous wind here, and the sastrugi are enormous," Shackleton wrote near the outset of this stretch. "This strong blizzard wind has been an immense help this way, though not outward for us," he added near its end.[38]

The men could also follow their outward sledge tracks, which stood up in the windswept snowscape and obviated the need for navigation. "What a blessing we have the tracks to follow or we should be in Queer Street," Marshall wrote in his trademark religious tone. "A great treat to have wind at one's back instead of heading into it."[39]

The critical problem was hunger, for the men were on part rations with no prospect of more until they reached their upper glacier depot. "What a thing hunger is," Wild wrote on January 12; "all day long we cannot help thinking about food, and at night we dream about it."[40]

On the last two days before reaching the depot, the plateau began turning down in a series of intermittent crevasses, pressure ridges, and icefalls. As far as distance covered, the steeper descent more than compensated for the obstructions. The party registered its two record days for the entire journey on January 18 and 19, covering over 26 miles on the former and an amazing 29 miles on the latter, despite repeated falls by everyone, a broken sledge runner, and Shackleton suffering from frostbitten feet. "I don't know how Shackleton stands it," Wild wrote on the 19th; "both his heels are split in four or five places, his legs are bruised and chafed, and today he has had a violent headache though falls, and yet he gets along as well as anyone."[41]

Adams also marveled about the man they were calling "The Boss": "The worse he felt, the harder he pulled."[42]

And there was no denying their progress. "We have been running with the sledge at times overtaking us," Wild wrote on February 19. "We have crossed hundreds of crevasses wide and narrow, all at the run, and have had no accidents. We are camped tonight about eight miles from our upper glacier depot."[43]

The men reached the depot shortly after noon on January 20, just as the terrain shifted from an increasingly sloped and disrupted ice sheet to a steep glacier descent with heavily crevassed névé and patches of slick blue ice. At times, they lowered the sledge by rope down particularly deep icefalls. "A gale was blowing, and often fierce gusts came along, sweeping the sledge sideways, and knocking us off our feet," Shackleton reported. "On several occasions one or more of us lost our footing, and were swept by the wind down the ice-slope, with great difficulty getting back to our sledge and companions."[44] Perhaps because of his bad feet, Shackleton suffered the most frequent and serious falls. Their rapid progress continued through to the head of Beardmore Glacier, however.

"Good bye to the plateau," Marshall commented at this point, "thank god we are off it."[45]

Here began the hell that persisted through the "invalid camp" on February 4. With lower altitude, the temperature rose daily until it exceeded the freezing point, making for a slow snow surface mixed with patches of slippery blue ice. We were "often up to our knees in soft snow," Marshall reported. "The pace slowed as we approached the lower reaches of the Glacier, which had become masked, in our absence, by heavy fall of soft snow," he added. "Only when completely exhausted did we camp."[46]

Repeatedly one man or another would drop into a crevasse to the length of his sledging harness, leaving the others to haul him back to the surface. "Whilst hanging in the harness I prayed the rope would break so that I could have a nice long rest," Wild later recalled.[47]

Supplies again began running low just four days after passing the upper glacier depot, with 40 miles of deeply crevassed glacial ice still remaining before the lower glacier depot. "No biscuit, only cocoa, tea, salt and pepper left, very little of those also," Shackleton reported on January 25. "Must reach depot to-morrow."[48]

The next morning, the men consumed their only remaining solid food—a porridge made from leftover maize for the long-gone ponies—and then marched for twenty hours through knee-deep snow with a broken sledge. "Except for the swish of the deep snow as we shuffled through it, complete silence reigned broken at times by the tinkle of falling ice into the crevasses over which we were passing," Marshall recalled. He depicted the pace as "funereal."[49]

As the party's physician, Marshall kept the men going with repeated doses of a cocaine-laced drug called Forced March, which he had saved for just such an emergency. "While it lasted, the effect was dramatic," Marshall reported about his first use of these energy pills.[50] They ran out at 2 A.M. on the 27th, however, and the men collapsed. Following a five-hour rest, they man-hauled for five more hours on no solid food before collapsing again.

This time, they were close enough to the depot for Marshall to flounder ahead and bring back 4 pounds of food and their first tobacco for weeks. "Reached depot in 25 min[utes] after falling into 3 crevasses covered by recent heavy fall of snow," he related.[51] Three lumps of sugar gave him the energy to get back. "After nearly 60 hours without food the response in energy was strikingly effective," Marshall observed.[52]

Shackleton depicted these two days as "the hardest and most trying we have ever spent in our lives."[53]

Wild called them "one long awful nightmare."[54]

Having nearly reached the level ice shelf with the promise of two more pony-meat caches ahead, the half-starved men thought the worst was over except for the worry of not reaching Cape Royds before the *Nimrod* sailed north. "From now onwards it was a race against time and the onset of the Antarctic winter," Marshall wrote.[55] If so, it was an obstacle course. First, Shackleton dropped into one last crevasse with such a hard jerk on his harness under his fragile heart that it badly shook him. Then a blizzard struck with hurricane-force gusts that kept them in camp for a day and froze their wet gear into a solid mass of ice. After the sky cleared, they reached the depot housing Grisi's remains on February 2, and shortly afterward all fell ill.

They felt the full impact on February 3 after feasting the evening before on slabs of Grisi's horseflesh. With food in short supply, it was now rushing through their bowels at a rate of up to once each hour. "I have taken sufficient drugs to kill three men, and it has had scarcely any effect," Wild complained.[56] "My diary noted that more than one member turned out eight to nine times that night," Marshall reported about the first evening spent at their so-called invalid camp.[57] "Adams passing much blood due to horsemeat," Shackleton added on May 4. "Outlook serious."[58] The only benefit from this depot came in retrieving the sledge left there when they put down Grisi. It replaced their broken one for the long stretch remaining.

———

THE SOUTHERN PARTY RESUMED its trek north on February 5, still suffering the effects of acute hunger and food poisoning. "Shackleton and I are now the best in health and Adams is the worst," Wild wrote. He called it "a poor day's march," but Marshall noted that at least they were able "to get along a little, in spite of frequent halts."[59]

By this point it was march or die, with meager rations for a week or more to the next depot, where the first pony, Chinaman, had been butchered. "Dead tired. Short [of] food; very weak," Shackleton wrote on February 7. "All thinking and talking of food," he added on both the 9th and 10th. Each entry was short and mostly about food or weather.[60]

"Our hunger is awful too awful to describe," Wild lamented. "My greatest desire now seems to be to sit on the hearth rug at Mother's feet and be petted."[61]

Aided by a strong southerly wind, which at one point Wild described as "howling like hell" and Marshall depicted as sent by God to assist them, the men averaged 12 miles per day despite their weakened state.[62] They reached the next depot on February 13 with no food to spare. By this point, close calls of this sort had become the norm for the southern party and would remain a trademark of Shackleton's expeditions. "All the way back it was just touch & go whether we should reach the next depot in time or not," Wild wrote.[63]

The Chinaman depot, as Shackleton called it, contained horsemeat, a pool of frozen blood congealed in snow, and some tobacco, but little else. "For dinner we had the whole of Chinaman's liver," Wild wrote, with Marshall adding that "more smokes are a great treat."[64] The blood-and-snow mixture "was like beef tea when boiled up," Shackleton noted. He called it "splendid."[65]

Without gaining much for their larder and still on short rations, the men pushed on toward the open sea, where they hoped to catch the *Nimrod* before it sailed. They estimated that they had roughly two weeks to go, with their own depot A in one week and another depot supposedly laid at Minna Bluff by a supply party from winter quarters a few days farther along. Again, they carried barely enough food to reach the next depot, with no measure for error. Surviving on about a cup of horsemeat and a few biscuits per day, they were "more hungry than ever," Wild wrote.[66] He suffered nightmares about sitting down at a royal banquet but protocol preventing him from eating.

"The harness around our weakened stomachs gives us a good deal of pain when we are brought up suddenly," Shackleton complained, yet they made the 100 miles to depot A in seven days, despite plunging temperatures and a blinding blizzard.[67] They reached it with no food remaining except a few scraps of meat from Grisi that they dared not eat unless worse came to worst.

"It is neck or nothing with us now," Shackleton wrote on February 21 as his party raced north from depot A in a blizzard with scarcely enough food to reach the bluff depot, if indeed it existed. "Our food lies ahead, and death stalks us from behind. This is just the time of year when the most bad weather may be expected."[68] The sun now set each night bringing palpable darkness. The temperature dropped to minus 35°F. They resorted to eating the scraps from Grisi that night, which renewed Wild's diarrhea.

Bluff depot had become the focus of the men's hopes and pivot to their survival. They reached it on February 23 without any measure for error. "It was the most cheerful sight our eyes have ever seen, for we had only a few biscuits left," Shackleton noted. Just weeks earlier, teams from winter quarters had stocked it with all the foods they could imagine. "There were Carlsbad plums, eggs, cakes, plum puddings, gingerbread and crystallized fruit," Shackleton reported with childlike glee. "I am writing in my bag with biscuits beside me, and chocolates and jam."[69]

With food no longer a worry, concern now focused on reaching open water before the ship sailed. No one on the *Nimrod* or at winter quarters could know if the southern party would return, however, and by this point most of them feared that it would not. Rather than risk having the ship iced in for the winter, Shackleton had authorized it to steam north for New Zealand as early as March 1 and leave a small rescue party behind for the winter at Cape Royds. Yet until the sea ice became firm, Shackleton could not get beyond Hut Point on foot. His party had to get that far and hope the *Nimrod* would rescue it there.

Resting only for one night and with time of an essence, the men set off again on the morning of February 24. A day later, however, a fierce blizzard kept the party in camp for a day, and Marshall's dysentery returned with full force. Despite Marshall's condition, the men arose as soon as the blizzard ended and were marching by 4 A.M. on February 26. They continued with only three brief stops until 11 P.M. and were back at it again by six the next morning. "Marshall suffered greatly, but stuck to the march. He never complains," Shackleton wrote on the 27th.[70]

After these two days netted some 30 miles, Shackleton decided to leave Marshall in camp with Adams and dash ahead with Wild over the 33 more miles to Hut Point, desperately seeking rescue for all before the ship departed. Leaving without sleep soon after the party set up camp at 4 P.M. on the 27th, Shackleton and Wild carried food for one meal, which they finished early the next day. Finding the sea ice out south of Hut Point, they left their sledge and scrambled 7 miles over a hilly, snow-covered shore route to arrive at the old hut late on February 28.

"Weary footsore & famished, those hills seemed miles high instead of the actual 1,000 feet," Wild later recalled.[71]

They found the hut empty, with a note stating that all the others were safe on the ship, which would shelter at the ice tongue between Hut Point and Cape Royds until February 26. The note said nothing about how long the ship would remain beyond that date. "If the ship was gone," Shackleton wrote, "our plight, and that of the two men left out on the Barrier, was a very serious one."[72] By now, all on board the *Nimrod* thought that the southern party was lost, with the captain openly speaking of its members as dead.

Shackleton and Wild became desperate to save themselves and the two remaining on the ice shelf. With the sea ice out, they could not reach the ice tongue except by a long overland route. Instead, they tried to set an outbuilding ablaze to signal their presence at Hut Point to anyone at the ice tongue or Cape Royds. Exhausted from marching 50-odd miles in thirty-eight hours without sleep, they could not get the asbestos-laden shed to burn, so rested until the next morning, March 1, when they tried again with some success.

Departing from the ice tongue that same morning to land a small relief party at Cape Royds before heading north with the others, a ship's officer aboard the *Nimrod* spied activity at Hut Point and began shouting. It could only be the southern party. "We all tumbled out, and rushed forward to the foc's'l head," Forbes Mackay recalled. "We all danced about and cheered and waved our arms, and then fell to punching each other."[73] The ship turned south at full speed. Seeing its masts appear overwhelmed Shackleton and Wild. "No happier sight ever met the eyes of man," Wild wrote, "and about an hour later we were being greeted by our comrades, the most optimistic of whom had given us up as dead."[74]

Less than three hours later, after what he called "a good feed of bacon and fried bread" but no further sleep, Shackleton led three men back onto the ice shelf to rescue Marshall and Adams.[75] Tested by their own sledging ordeal, Mawson and Mackay joined the rescue effort. Shackleton ordered Wild to remain behind in case of an accident. The party returned on March 4 with Marshall and Adams.

"By the narrowest margin," Marshall wrote, "we accomplished a journey of 1,613 miles (more than half of which was pioneer work) in 126 days."[76]

With sea ice forming across the Ross Sea, the *Nimrod* departed that very day for New Zealand, leaving behind everything not already packed and on board.

SCARCELY A MONTH AFTER Shackleton reached the *Nimrod*, Peary made his U-turn and headed back to the *Roosevelt*. With enough food to eat, plenty of dogs to pull, a well-cut trail with existing shelters, and sufficient time, because the ship could not depart until the ice broke out in July, Peary had many advantages over Shackleton. The American's worst fears were open leads and prolonged bad weather of the type that had stymied his 1906 effort. Those were chance occurrences. He had planned for everything one could anticipate in polar exploration. The result was a dash that met his own high expectations.

Peary claimed to cover the 150-odd miles from the pole to the camp where his last support party turned back in just three days. "No explorer, before or since, has claimed to cover these sorts of distances across polar pack ice over the same number of consecutive days," Wally Herbert later wrote.[77] They justifiably contributed to the doubts about Peary's claims, especially since later explorers had better equipment. Yet Peary would need to travel at record speeds on the return trip if he had gone all the way to the pole and back to the ship in the given time since he left Bartlett's farthest-north camp on April 2.

Fueling his critics, the first two of these three days are blank in his diary, which resumed on April 9, shortly before the polar party reached the old camp. "From here to the Pole and back has been a glorious sprint, with a savage finish," he wrote at this point. Yet in his diary, he only described that savage finish of minus 20°F temperatures, gale-force winds, dogs on the gallop, and "ice rafting all under and all around us under pressure of the gale."[78] Even his harshest critics accept the story from here on back.

In his various narrative accounts of his expedition, which built on his sledging diary but added much detail, Peary fleshed out the initial segment of his return trip in part with an explanation of his plan to double-march all the way back. "That is," he wrote, "to cover one of our outward marches, make tea and eat our luncheon in the igloos at that camp; then cover another march, eat, and sleep a few hours in the igloos of the next outward camp, and go on again." Over a track smoothed out by multiple outbound and inbound sledge trips, this plan struck Peary as feasible. "We could double our speed," he projected. "We need waste no time in building igloos."[79] The polar party mostly kept to this schedule except for a few days when exhaustion led Peary to order only a single march.

In the end, he found that his party could cover an average of five outward marches in three returning days. The dogs, he noted, received double rations when they made double marches. "I was able to do this on account of the reserve supply of food which we had in the dogs themselves," Peary wrote in a terse description of the culling process.[80] Of course, any dog culled from the pack received no rations at all.

Matthew Henson, who never doubted that the party had attained the pole, filled out the start of the homeward account somewhat differently. "It was with quivering voice that Commander Peary gave the order to break camp. Already the strain of the hard upward-journey was beginning to tell, and after the first two marches back, he was dead weight," Henson would write of the expedition. Although Henson here suggested and at other times stated that Peary rode all the way back, this account at least affirmed that Peary continued to direct the party.[81] A later account coauthored by Henson has Henson, not Peary, beginning "the task of leading the enfeebled party back," covering "the distance of three of their outward marches" in his first southward dash, and "feverishly" guiding the march toward land.[82] "After Peary finished making his observations [at the pole], he just about collapsed. He couldn't walk. We had to put him on the sledge," Henson told journalist Lowell Thomas thirty years after the event. "All his strength had been concentrated on getting to the Pole. Once he got there his strength gave out."[83] Over time and countless retellings, Henson likely embellished his own role in the return journey, especially after Peary publicly disparaged Henson's ability to lead a return trek. The part about Peary riding back, which Henson consistently maintained and others suggested, seems probable.

Peary and Henson agreed on one key point. Both depict the party speeding back at a breakneck pace from Bartlett's farthest north with remarkably few delays. "For the most part we found the trail renewed by our support parties easily recognizable and in most cases in good condition," Peary reported. The wind typically either came from a northerly direction, which propelled them and the sea ice southward, or calmed to a whisper. Every lead they encountered was narrow or newly iced over, closed quickly, or was readily circumvented or ferried across on ice cakes. "Perhaps we took chances," Peary wrote, "perhaps not. One thing in our favor: our sledges were much lighter than on the upward journey, and we could now 'rush' them across thin ice that would not have held them a moment then."[84] At times, new ice quivered under the weight of the sledges, but only once did a dog team break through and require rescue. "Only calm weather or northerly wind keeps it practicable," Peary said of the young ice.[85]

Henson's accounts were more dramatic but had the same ending. "We crossed lead after lead, sometimes like a bareback rider in the circus, balancing on cake after cake of ice, but good fortune was with us all of the way," Henson noted. "It was not until land of recognizable character had been lifted [into view on the horizon] that we lost the trail, and with land in sight as an incentive, it was no trouble for us to gain the talus of the shore ice and find the trail again."[86]

Peary's account has the polar party losing the main trail within sight of land but still following the thin path cut by Bob Bartlett's final support party, which also lost the main trail. Late on April 22, the polar party reached the fringe of freshwater glacial ice near Cape Columbia, their original point of departure. "When the last sledge came to the almost vertical edge of the glacier's fringe, I thought my Eskimos had gone crazy," Peary wrote. "They yelled and called and danced until they fell from utter exhaustion." Ootah, who was with Peary on his purported second traverse at the North Pole, now declared, "The Devil is asleep or having trouble with his wife, or we should never have come back so easily."[87] It was a heavenly moment.

The party rested for two days in the igloos at Cape Columbia before taking the well-worn trail back to the *Roosevelt*, where they arrived on April 27. "It has been a very comfortable return and we have had full rations," Peary noted in his diary, "but a little difference in the weather and all would have been changed." The same entry contained the more stylized assertion "I have now the last great geographical prize, the North Pole, for the credit of the U.S., the Service to which I belong, myself, and my family." No mention here of Henson or the Inuits. "It has been accomplished with a clean cut, dash, spirit, and I believe thoroughness, characteristically American," Peary concluded. "I am content."[88]

The support parties had more trouble with leads than the polar party, so much so that Bartlett's final party reached the *Roosevelt* only three days before Peary, even though it started back from its final camp with a ten-day head start. Goodsell's division turned back first, with MacMillan's right behind. They traveled together with some injured members. Despite crossing one thin-ice lead with the Inuits walking on all fours to distribute their weight and Goodsell flipping headlong over a pressure ridge, they made some 200 miles back to the ship in twelve days. Borup's division went next and had the most problems with open leads. Held up by one and going around others, Borup wrote of crossing one on thin ice "swaying in waves beneath the sledges and ourselves" and the rear of a sledge breaking through another, "drenching everything."[89]

Marvin had turned next, on March 25, with two Inuit sledge drivers, Kudlooktoo and Inukitsoq, but only the Inuits returned. They told the story that Marvin went ahead on foot one morning and broke through thin ice, from which Peary concocted a richer account of it happening at the Big Lead with Marvin scouting the way forward while the drivers broke camp and harnessed the dogs. Two decades later, after converting to Christianity, Kudlooktoo confessed to shooting Marvin, allegedly for mistreating Inukitsoq and threatening to leave him behind. After so many years, no attempt was made to prosecute, and not everyone believed the story. For his part, at one point on his return journey, Bartlett fell through young ice with the air temperature at minus 32°F and was saved by his Inuit drivers, who rolled him in a musk-ox robe and carried him to the nearest igloo for warmth.

After reaching the *Roosevelt* in late April, Peary remained on board until the ship broke free of the ice in July and sailed south through Nares Strait. Stopping at Cape Saumarez to drop off Inuits from the expedition, Peary first heard that Frederick Cook had survived. Although surprising, this news alone did not trouble Peary—but that soon changed.

Mooring at Etah on August 17, Peary learned more from Harry Whitney, the wealthy American hunter who had wintered in Cook's old hut, and the two members of the *Roosevelt*'s crew left there to guard supplies. Cook had returned to his hut four months earlier with two Inuits, Ahwelah and Etukishuk, claiming the pole. "Human beings could not be more unkempt," Whitney recalled. "They were half starved and very thin."[90] Cook had crossed Ellesmere Island with a large band of drivers, dogs, and sledges in February 1908, this much Peary knew, and sent most back from Axel Heiberg Island's Cape Hubbard. Now Cook claimed to have sledged with the two Inuits and their dogs over the sea ice from Cape Hubbard to the pole during April 1908. On their return trip, after the sea ice carried them too far west, the three men rounded Ellesmere Island on the south, wintered in an underground den at Devon Island, and lived off the land until they could march back to Etah, by this time with one sledge and no dogs. Entrusting Whitney with his records, Cook carried on south toward the Danish outpost of Upernavik, where on August 9, 1909, he boarded a passenger ship bound for Copenhagen.

Certain that Cook could not have made such a journey, Peary took immediate countermeasures. "To us, up there at Etah, such a story was so ridiculous and absurd that we simply laughed at it," Henson wrote. He knew Cook from two prior expeditions and, like Peary, considered "him not even good for a day's work."[91] Bartlett called it "utterly impossible." He knew the perils of polar travel from two prior expeditions and, like Peary, believed Cook could not "have crossed a thousand miles of Polar Sea ice without supporting parties."[92] Peary ordered a team led by Bartlett to obtain testimony from Ahwelah and Etukishuk, who readily recanted. They never ventured onto the Arctic ice pack with Cook, they now said, and their one seaward march from Cape Hubbard ended on the glacial fringe in clear sight of land. Peary also barred Whitney from taking Cook's records back with him on the *Roosevelt*.

In what became something of a race to the media if not to the pole, Cook first reached a telegraph station on September 1, five days before Peary. He broadcast his claim around the globe via the *New York Herald* before Peary could report to his mouthpiece, the *New York Times*. Defending his priority at the pole, Peary faced an uncertain homecoming.

AS THESE SURPRISING EVENTS were unfolding in the Arctic, the Duke of the Abruzzi started his expedition's trek home from the eastern Karakoram on July 20. Traveling faster than either American, and with abundant resources for a summertime trek back to Kashmir and beyond, the duke reached Italy before Peary or Cook arrived in the United States. He was at home by September to hear the first public announcement of Peary's achievement.

"May I congratulate you on the result of your expedition," the duke wired Peary. "Am very glad you have succeeded." Peary may have bested the Italians' farthest north, but now the duke held the altitude record, and a front-page article in the *New York Times* print-ing his telegram noted both points.[93]

The Italians' march home began by retracing their route over the Baltoro Glacier to their supply base at Urdukas and from there to Askoley. Rain continued most of the way, with rivers of water erod-ing the ice and even more stones covering the surface than before, making the path tortuous and tiring. One hundred Balti porters came from Askoley to Urdukas to assist in withdrawing the expedi-tion's equipment and provide a royal welcome for the mountaineers. "All manner of luxuries were waiting for us" in Urdukas, Filippo De Filippi wrote in the expedition's official report, "chief among them, to our minds, being a bath of deliciously hot water."[94] Urdukas itself was abloom with flowers, the only bright spot on the initial part of the return journey. The broad valley beyond, when they reached it, was still barren despite the rushing torrent of the river that now ran through it. Monsoon rains and glacial meltwater had transformed the valley almost beyond recognition. Having ascended its dry, sandy floor in late May, on the descent in midsummer the caravan of Italian climbers and Balti porters hugged the valley's edges and crossed trib-utary gorges on rope bridges. Local officials turned out to welcome the duke to Askoley, with the last half hour into town "lined with bowing and saluting," De Filippi reported.[95]

The season permitted the returning party to cut the long trek from Askoley to the Kashmiri capital of Srinagar in half by using mountain passes open only in late summer. These high passes pro-vided the final challenges for the duke's expedition because from Srinagar in summer the route into British India was a virtual highway for vacationers escaping the heat.

The first pass, Sorko La, crossed over a glacier to an altitude of 16,700 feet with a long slope up and a steep drop down. This took the party to Shigar, where the local raja greeted the Italian climb-ers with riding ponies for the next leg of the trip. Then the party went on to Skardu, with the duke and five core members of his party rafting down the swollen river on three traditional zhaks composed of a latticework of branches tied to inflated pig- and goatskins while the others walked around. Sella filmed the rafting adventure on a motion-picture camera that he attached to his zhak. "We were seized by the current and given over to the mercy of the waves, veering now toward one bank, now to the other, tossed about like corks, whirled in the eddies," De Filippi wrote. "The river banks seemed to fly past us, our course was so rapid."[96] They made the 12-mile passage in one exhilarating ninety-minute ride.

At Skardu, the expedition shifted back from Balti to Kashmiri porters for the trek over the 15,500-foot-high Berji Pass and across the arid Desoli Plain to central Kashmir. The snow-covered pass gave the duke and his party one last opportunity to view K2 from a distance, with Sella remaining behind for a day trying without success to capture a final panoramic photograph of the entire range. Mist and renewed bad weather prevented it.

From this point, the party traveled over several low passes, gradually descending for four days into the ever more densely settled regions of Kashmir and reaching its central valley on August 11. Government houseboats waited to carry the Italians through the valley's scenic lakes and canals to Srinagar following their twenty-day trek from the base of Chogolisa. "We were once more in the heart of Kashmir—noisy, garrulous, bombastic, servile, yet withal charming Kashmir," De Filippi concluded his account. "Our exertions were over."[97] From Srinagar to Mumbai and then back to Europe by ship took another month, with the duke arriving to a tumultuous welcome in Marseilles on September 12.

By coincidence, the first detailed report of Peary's North Pole expedition appeared on that same day in the *New York Times*, sent to the newspaper by Peary as an exclusive account from a telegraph station in Labrador. On September 21, multitudes turned out to greet Peary's ship in Sydney, Nova Scotia. "The throngs began to cheer as the *Roosevelt* drew near the densely packed wharf," the *Times* reported, "while the esplanade and the slopes of the hills at the water front were reverberant with lusty cheers."[98]

The next morning, Peary boarded a train bound for Maine. Crowds assembled at every stop as the train passed through the state, with five thousand in Waterville and still more at Peary's boyhood hometown of Portland, where he spent the night of September 23 before returning to his Eagle Island retreat. Again by coincidence, on that same evening, a black-tie banquet at the Waldorf-Astoria Hotel, hosted by the Arctic Club and attended by 1,185 persons, welcomed Cook back to his native New York.

On March 22, the *Nimrod* reached New Zealand, where Shackleton telegraphed his news to the world. David arrived in Sydney, Australia, by steamship from New Zealand on March 30 to a hero's reception. Mawson followed two weeks later to similar applause. The British crown prince, the future George V, personally welcomed Shackleton to London in June, while the ailing King Edward VII hailed the explorer's southern sledge journey as "the greatest geographical event of his reign."[99] By summer's end, the grand expeditions of 1909 had returned from the earth's edges to worldwide acclamation.

The Last Biscuit

"THE FASCINATING THING ABOUT Mr. Shackleton's report," the *New York Evening Globe* commented one day after its publication on March 24, 1909, "is the story of the struggle rather than the results of the struggle. All of us feel loftier in our inner stature as we read how men like ourselves pushed on until the last biscuit was gone."[1] At the dawn of the twentieth century, after the rise of industrialized technologies that promised to make all results possible and before the Great War that made even the most self-sacrificing human struggle seem meaningless while, at the same time, tarnishing technology's gleam, the *Globe*'s comment captured the essence of heroism as extraordinary efforts by ordinary people.

Shackleton, like Robert Peary (but not Mawson, Henson, or the others who were not expedition organizers), had an advance contract with a leading newspaper for an exclusive first report on his expedition. For both men, income from these contracts helped to finance their efforts. For newspapers—then at the height of the publishing wars that marked the era in journalism—disasters, battles, and harrowing expeditions sold best. Publishers paid top dollar for exclusive accounts. On March 22, the *Nimrod* stopped for a day at Steward Island, just south of New Zealand, where a special telegraph operator waited to dispatch Shackleton's report to London's *Daily Mail*, much as Peary would lay over in Labrador six months later to telegraph his first account to the *New York Times*. Of royal lineage, and needing no funds beyond those of his family and his nation, the Duke of the Abruzzi had no such contracts, made no such stops, and gave no reports on his expedition beyond official ones to the Italian Alpine Club and the Italian Geographical Society. As he had done for the Mount Saint Elias and Ruwenzori expeditions, the duke turned the task of writing the official account for the Karakoram expedition to Filippo De Filippi. His handsomely illustrated volume joined Shackleton's and Peary's books in parlors and libraries around the globe.[2]

A MASTER STORYTELLER AND a family man with a gift for attracting women and befriending men, Shackleton knew what the public wanted and, in his report for the *Daily Mail*, dished it out in due measure. Newly discovered mountains and the world's largest glacier; waist-deep snow with crevasses that swallowed ponies and left men hanging by their harnesses; man-hauling 500-pound sledges over blue ice; and struggle, always struggle, filled this first narrative. "For sixty hours," he wrote at one point, "the blizzard raged, with 72 degrees of frost and the wind blowing at seventy miles per hour. It was impossible to move. The members of the party were frequently frostbitten in their sleeping-bags." The race to survive ran through the account, underscored by the repeated refrain "food had again run out."[3] These were Shackleton's own words. The ghostwriter who helped transform his sledging diary and this first narrative into a bestselling book, *In the Heart of the Antarctic*, would not join him until New Zealand.

To capitalize on its investment, the *Daily Mail* solicited dozens of celebrity endorsements for Shackleton's feat, which it published along with the queen's "very hearty congratulations,"[4] though her telegram mistakenly credited Shackleton rather than Mawson with hoisting her flag at the magnetic pole. Mountaineer Martin Conway hailed the ascent of Mount Erebus as "a great achievement," while Albert Markham of former farthest-north fame called the polar trek "a wonderful performance."[5] Fridtjof Nansen, Roald Amundsen, and Robert Scott added their tributes, though for personal reasons each was pleased that Shackleton had fallen short of the pole. By the time his first report had circled the globe, Shackleton had stepped out of Scott's shadow and into the limelight of worldwide fame.

After the humiliation of the Boer War and with the rising German challenge to its military superiority, the British Empire needed heroes, and Shackleton seamlessly fit the bill. First in New Zealand, then in Australia, and finally in England, he was cheered by the masses and feted by the elites in the upstairs-downstairs Edwardian swirl. "I am representing 400 million British subjects," Shackleton said before his departure, and upon his return, they all seemed to adopt him.[6]

It was the struggle more than the results that won plaudits. "An amount of pluck and determination has been displayed by Lieut. Shackleton and his companions which has never been surpassed in the history of Polar enterprise," the Royal Geographical Society proclaimed.[7] The *Standard* spoke of his "intrepid heroism," the *Morning Post* of his "extraordinary endurance."[8] "The benefit," the *Spectator* said of Shackleton's expedition, "is to be seen in the proof it gives that we are not worse than our forefathers; that the blood of the Franklins, the Parrys, and the Rosses still flows in a later generation; and that men of the various ranks and various callings are still found ready to encounter great risks and endure prolonged privation and suffering for no gain to themselves beyond the joy of mastering difficulties."[9] A knighthood followed. It scarcely mattered that Shackleton had failed to reach the pole. "His adventures," the *Nation* observed, "appear to have been brilliant, if not extremely valuable."[10]

Shackleton wanted to go back as soon as possible to finish the job. He discussed it with Frank Wild during the grueling return march and received Wild's commitment to return. The fame, money, lectures, and elite social invitations only made him want to go more. "The world was pleased with our work, and it seemed as if nothing but happiness could enter life again," Shackleton wrote with some candor, but he recognized the fleeting nature of celebrity and knew that it needed feeding by new fame.[11]

Scott was already planning an expedition to the South Pole, however, and Amundsen one to the North Pole that he secretly flipped south upon hearing the claims of Peary and Frederick Cook. Little glory lay in coming in second to a place whose reputed value lay in getting there first. As a British entrant in this race, Shackleton queued behind Scott. When Amundsen succeeded on December 14, 1911, and then Scott reached the pole five weeks later but perished with his party on the bitter march back, Shackleton was doubly eclipsed. Scott had followed Shackleton's route up Beardmore Glacier and across the Polar Plateau. He also adopted Shackleton's means by favoring ponies over dogs for pulling sledges but, like Shackleton, ultimately fell back on man-hauling. Amundsen, in contrast, followed Shackleton's instincts (rather than his route) by starting his trek at the Bay of Whales—Shackleton's intended winter quarters—and then taking the shorter, quicker path to the pole along the Ross Ice Shelf's eastern edge. With the stories of Amundsen and Scott overshadowing his *Nimrod* accounts, Shackleton all but faded from sight. Repeated efforts to augment his book and lecture earnings by investment schemes and business ventures failed.

Seeking new feats in the Antarctic before interest waned, Shackleton planned the Imperial Trans-Antarctic Expedition for 1914–16. The ambitious plan involved sending a support party to the old British huts on Ross Island to lay resupply depots as far as the Beardmore Glacier while he took the main party to the Weddell Sea, from which he would march across the continent to the Ross Sea. The Ross Island party was stranded at Scott's old huts when its ship drifted out to sea in a gale, however, and Shackleton's ship, the *Endurance*, was icebound and crushed before reaching the Weddell Sea coast.

These setbacks provided the path to lasting glory for Shackleton, whose leadership skills always rose in crisis situations. With an air of confidence that masked his own fears, Shackleton led his men on a storied five-month journey across drifting sea ice and by lifeboats to Elephant Island. From there, Shackleton and five others sailed 800 miles across the notoriously turbulent Southern Ocean by open boat to a whaling station on South Georgia Island. The leadership displayed by Shackleton during this epic trek and open-boat voyage was much like that shown by him on the *Nimrod* Expedition's southern journey, writ large for everyone to see. Yet there was more. On the fourth attempt, in the teeth of midwinter storms, he rescued all his men on Elephant Island and turned his attention to the Ross Sea sector, where three had already died. But after joining the imperial effort to rescue the survivors, Shackleton returned to an England consumed with the bloodiest war of its history. Amid the Great War, no one much cared about polar heroics. Lasting fame for the *Endurance* Expedition came too late for Shackleton to enjoy. Following World War I, he tried one last time for Antarctic glory with an expedition in 1921–22, but died at the age of forty-seven from a heart attack on South Georgia Island. Rather than bring his body back to England for a hero's funeral, Shackleton's wife, Emily, asked that it be buried on South Georgia near his beloved Antarctic. The tombstone bears Shackleton's favorite words, drawn from the poet Robert Browning, that a man should strive "to the uttermost for his life's set prize." Years later, Frank Wild's ashes were interred on the right-hand side of The Boss's grave.

FOLLOWING THE *NIMROD*'S RETURN, Australians reserved their heartiest adulation for Edgeworth David and Douglas Mawson, who became the young commonwealth's first national heroes. For them, it was about both struggle and results, because they had made it to the magnetic pole, whatever that was worth.

David reached Sydney first, arriving by steamer from New Zealand on March 30. A crowd gathered at the harbor before dawn to meet his ship; six hundred more filled the university's Great Hall at noon for a reception. "Almost everyone who was anybody in the University was present," one reporter noted.[12] "Professor David, on rising, was obliged to stand mute for five minutes while cheering, shouting, stamping, and hand-clapping was maintained by the energetic undergrads."[13] Two days later, it was the city's turn, at a town-hall reception where, due to overcrowding, as many were turned away as gained entrance. Newspapers reported that David's wife was refused admission on the grounds that six ladies had tried the same ruse already. "To-day his name with Lieutenant Shackleton's was acclaimed throughout the civilized world," the Lord Mayor said of David.[14] For his part, David characteristically demurred: "In all sincerity and without the pride that apes humility, I say that Mawson was the real leader and the soul of our expedition to the magnetic pole. We really have in him an Australian Nansen, of infinite resource, splendid physique, [and] astonishing indifference to frost."[15]

Then it was Mawson's turn, arriving in Sydney on April 16 and reaching Adelaide five days later. Both his childhood and adopted hometowns turned out to welcome him. Meeting him at the train station and drawing him on a handcart through the streets, hundreds of University of Adelaide students chanted:

> *Raw feet, raw feet, down a hole,*
> *Rough seat, rough seat, on the pole;*
> *Seal fat, seal fat, come and see,*
> *Douglas Mawson, D.Sc.*[16]

Like Shackleton, Mawson now felt the explorer's pull back toward the ice.

Declining an invitation to go with Scott, Mawson organized his own expedition for 1911–13 to explore unknown portions of coastal Antarctica due south of Australia. The trek became the stuff of Australian folklore after one of Mawson's two sledging companions disappeared into a crevasse with his dogs, sledge, and most of the supplies, leaving the other two to march some 300 miles to the main base. Eating their remaining dogs as virtually their only food and sleeping under a tent cover, only Mawson made it back, and he suffered abominably from extreme hunger and exhaustion; severe skin, hair, and nail loss (including the entire layer of skin on the soles of both feet); snow blindness; and depression. His second colleague became delirious before dying, likely due to hypervitaminosis A from eating so much dog's liver. At one point after dropping into a sheer-walled, seemingly bottomless crevasse, the now-alone Mawson gained the strength to pull himself up on his harness rope by thinking, "There was all eternity for the last and, at its longest, the present would be but short."[17] Given up for lost by this time, Mawson arrived at his base only hours after the supply ship had sailed, leaving him with a small rescue party in the Antarctic for a second brutal winter. His account of the ordeal, *The Home of the Blizzard*, became a polar classic.[18] After distinguished service as a munitions officer during World War I, Mawson settled down to a celebrated career as a research geologist in South Australia. He led joint British, Australian, and New Zealand expeditions to the Antarctic from 1929 to 1931, resulting in the formation of the Australian Antarctic Territory in 1936. Mawson remained an active member of the Australian Antarctic Executive Planning Committee until his death in 1958. The first issue of Australia's $100 note featured a picture of him in polar garb on the front.

David also served in the Great War, volunteering at age fifty-seven to organize and lead a corps of Australians engaged in mining and tunneling for trench warfare on the Western Front. He received the Distinguished Service Order and was promoted to the rank of lieutenant colonel following his role in the mining of German positions during the Battle of Messines in 1917. David never went back to Antarctica but, like Mawson, remained a champion of Australian discovery and exploration there.

DUE TO COOK'S PREVIOUSLY published claims, Peary returned from the Arctic in 1909 to an unexpectedly cool reception. It was not that Americans did not care that one of their countrymen had reached the North Pole. If anything, from Peary's perspective, they cared too much, and jumped to a rash conclusion based on a superficial reading of the character of the claimants. The "polar controversy," as it became known, unfolded in one tumultuous week in September 1909, with Peary on the defensive, after which he was either powerless to recover fully or too broken to try. The heroic eluded him.

On August 9, while Peary was in Smith Sound and first learning of his rival's claim from local sources, Cook secured passage on a Danish ship from Greenland to Copenhagen. After the captain heard Cook's astonishing news, he stopped in the Shetland Islands on September 1 at the first port with a telegraph station so that Cook could tell the world. Cook sold his story to the *New York Herald*. Forty years earlier the *Herald* had sent Henry Stanley to find David Livingstone in Africa; thirty years earlier it had dispatched the ill-fated *Jeannette* Expedition to the Arctic. No publication had a better reputation for expedition coverage, and Cook now offered it his exclusive newspaper account for a mere $3,000. To Cook, credibility mattered more than cash. The *Herald*'s legendary publisher, James Gordon Bennett, could scarcely believe his good fortune and threw the full weight of his global publishing empire behind Cook's account. The story broke on September 2 with front-page coverage that continued for weeks. As it appeared in the *Herald*, Cook's tale had all the hallmarks of a polar narrative except much detail on key parts of the trek.

Cook's claim to have reached the pole a year earlier with two Inuit sledge drivers circled the globe in hours and became the top story everywhere. The polar community split. Adolphus Greely and *Fram* captain Otto Sverdrup, both of whom had felt Peary's wrath, accepted it at face value, even as the *Jeannette* Expedition's George Melville and Arctic veteran George Nares dismissed it out of hand. Amundsen gave some credence to his former Antarctic colleague's story, while Shackleton and the leader of the Duke of the Abruzzi's northern party, Umberto Cagni, deemed it plausible. Nansen and Scott wanted more evidence. For many, the distances covered, speed traveled, and sparse records raised doubts. Peary would challenge Cook on all three counts, leading Cook's defenders to take Peary to task on them as well. On September 4, however, Copenhagen welcomed Cook with open arms, and three days later the Royal Danish Geographical Society awarded him its highest medal. Offers of up to half a million dollars for book rights and lectures lay before him.

While still in Copenhagen, Cook first learned from the press that Peary had returned from the Arctic claiming the pole. Cook hailed his rival's achievement. "The pole is big enough for two," he declared. Cook could afford to be gracious because, without challenging his priority, Peary's success made his own appear more plausible. If one could make it across the Arctic sea ice by dog sledge in a season, more could as well. "Probably other parties will reach it in the next ten years," Cook added.[19] By this time, the American public had largely decided for Cook, and the new president, William Howard Taft, who knew far less about exploration than his predecessor, sent him a congratulatory telegram. "Thus, in the course of a single week, were the claims of two rival American explorers dramatically proclaimed to the world," the *London Daily News* reported.[20]

On September 21, 1909, Cook returned by ship to a hero's reception in his hometown of thirty years, Brooklyn. "It is estimated that several hundred thousand people assembled along the route of the parade," the *New York Herald* reported. "Buildings were decorated, schoolchildren sang and waved flags and the people shouted, 'We believe in Cook!'"[21]

Peary responded with a rage that cost him dearly. He reached Indian Harbor, Labrador, on September 5 and telegraphed his first reports a day later. "Stars and Stripes nailed to the Pole," he wired to the Associated Press news service. "I have the pole," he added to the *New York Times*.[22] Showing as much concern for debunking Cook's claim as for telling his own story, Peary wired the Associated Press a day later regarding Cook, "The two Eskimos who accompanied him say he went no distance north and not out of sight of land."[23] Peary added about Cook in a telegram to the *Times*, "He has not been at the pole on April 21st, 1908, or any other time. He has simply handed the public a gold brick."[24] Differentiating himself in racial terms that others turned against him, Peary proclaimed himself as "the only white man to have ever reached the pole."[25] He promised a detailed exposé of Cook's claim upon his return and dared his rival to publish his proof. Peary even sent a telegram critical of Cook to the *Herald*, which its editors published alongside tributes to Cook and their own damning commentary on what they depicted as Peary's "savage charges against Dr. Cook."[26] Controversy sold newspapers, Bennett knew, and he cast his man as the hapless victim of the powerful interests backing Peary.

Those interests rallied to Peary's side. The *Times* led the drumbeat against Cook, complete with the front-page comment "His claim to have reached the north pole belongs to the realm of fairy tales" and new testimony that Cook had lied about his first ascent of Denali.[27] Peary's longtime backers in the National Geographic Society, Peary Arctic Club, American Museum of Natural History, and Explorer's Club took up his defense, with the society impaneling a committee to certify his account. The polar community generally accepted Peary at his word but often without dismissing Cook's claim. "Peary undoubtedly got to the pole" was how Shackleton now put it; "between him and Dr. Cook the pole certainly has been reached."[28] Nares and Melville came down foursquare for Peary, however, with Nares declaring that Peary's "well-known arctic veracity" should settle the matter and Melville exclaiming, "Isn't it bully!"[29] Geographic societies in Europe lined up behind Peary as well, especially after December, when Cook failed to supply sufficient evidence to an agreed-upon panel of Danish experts charged with investigating his claim. The Explorer's Club used that ruling to expel Cook. It even led Amundsen to wonder aloud about his old Antarctic colleague, "Is he a swindler, or merely ignorant?"[30]

The testimony of explorers, experts, and institutions mattered little to the American people, Peary found. He lost the public's favor with his initial reaction, and Cook won it with his affable response. "It is perfectly apparent that Commander Peary has repelled and Dr. Cook has gained public sympathy," a Buffalo newspaper commented near the outset of the controversy.[31] As the back-and-forth wore on, informal surveys bore out this initial assessment. In late September, the *Detroit Free Press* found that 93 percent of its readers supported Cook over Peary, while the *Pittsburgh Press* reported that, of the 75,000-odd readers responding to its survey, over 73,000 believed that Cook reached the North Pole first and nearly 60,000 did not think Peary ever got there. "If this ratio holds good all over the country, Dr. Cook may well afford to remain indifferent to any decision finally arrived at by scientists," the newspaper noted.[32]

Such findings did not come solely from pro-Cook sources or simply reflect antiestablishment bias. Late in 1909, the publisher of the serial version of Peary's narrative, Benjamin Hampton, asked eighty professors, lawyers, doctors, and other midwestern opinion leaders, twenty of them women, about their views on the controversy and found that all but two were decidedly "anti-Peary."[33] America's leading mass-circulation weekly, *The Saturday Evening Post*, satirized the controversy in a fictional play synopsis tellingly subtitled "A Typical American Drama of the Present Day," which revealed how middle-class Americans most likely viewed the episode. The play's befuddled Cook character claims to cover 244 miles to the pole in a matter of hours, while its tyrannical Peary character sends back supporting parties so that he alone can get there. Then he commands "his faithful Negro servitor" and four Eskimo helpers, "Forward, march, to the nearest telegraph station."[34] From England, essayist G. K. Chesterton offered the pointed double couplet:

> *Earth's icy dome, the skull that wears*
> *Terrible crystals for a crown,*
> *Is billed at last with Cook's renown.*
> *And Peary's personal affairs.*[35]

Surveying the scene, the *San Francisco Chronicle* observed, "The verdict of the country is that Dr. Cook is a gentleman and Commander Peary is a cad and that without reference to whether either of them reached the Pole."[36]

America's foremost progressive theologian and dean of the University of Chicago divinity school, Shailer Mathews, drew moral lessons from the episode. "The time was when the search for the North Pole stood for the very acme of uncommercialized heroism," Mathews noted in a popular essay published at the height of the controversy. "And now! The call of the North Pole to heroism has become a quarrel by wireless telegraph." He complained of both claimants, "We find one man with an all but incredible story of endurance which runs counter to the entire run of experience in arctic traveling, and the other man refusing to share the honor of standing on the North Pole with another white man." This was too much for Mathews. "A hero should be as great as his exploits," he wrote. "Even a cad can risk his life for the sake of going on the lecture platform."[37]

Peary retreated before the onslaught. Without conceding anything to Cook, he declined to accept public honors or speaking invitations until competent authorities resolved the controversy in his favor. While Cook took to the lecture circuit, Peary retired to his private island in Maine. He began venturing onto the public stage only after the National Geographic Society ruled for him and the

Danish commission against Cook, but even then only for limited engagements in friendly venues.

In 1911, over vocal opposition, Congress recognized Peary's claim by retroactively raising his rank to rear admiral and retiring him from the navy with pay, effective on the day he claimed the pole. By then, Cook had faded from public view, only briefly to reenter it when charged, tried, convicted, and jailed for fraud in a securities scam during the 1920s. Amundsen visited him in federal prison. Peary died in 1920 still bitter about his treatment after claiming the North Pole. He did little of public note in the intervening years except to advocate for the use of aircraft during World War I. Instead, the once very public man lived quietly with his family in Maine and Washington. Cook died in 1940 still professing that he got to the pole first. Each man left his defenders and detractors. Over time, even the *New York Times* and National Geographic Society qualified their support for Peary's claim. If neither claimant reached the North Pole, then Amundsen most likely got there first by sailing over it by airship in 1926, making him the first person at both poles.

THE DUKE OF THE Abruzzi returned to Europe just as the public controversy over the North Pole broke. His arrival managed to snag lead headlines in the *New York Herald* for one day of that critical first week, but gave place to the Cook-Peary controversy on every other day. Even then, the second paragraph of the *Herald* article turned to press inquiries about the duke's views on the polar controversy and an aide's terse reply, "He never gave interviews to the press and would consequently say nothing." The following paragraph reported on the duke's private comments about the topic to local officials. He did not know enough about Cook to have an opinion, the *Herald* noted, but "in regard to Commander Peary he said that everybody would trust him."[38] Even in the duke's presence, interest focused more on Peary and Cook than on his own record climb. After five full paragraphs debating Peary and Cook, the article turned to rumors about the duke's romance with Katherine Elkins. Gossip had him returning to meet her in Paris in defiance of the king's wishes.

Royalty has its privileges, which the duke enjoyed, but it also came with its burdens, which the duke accepted. He returned to active duty as an admiral in the Italian navy and led a task force during his nation's ensuing war with the Ottomans over control of Libya. World War I followed. Italy fought on the side of Britain and France, with the duke serving as commander in chief of allied naval forces in the Adriatic. Victory in both wars cost Italy dearly, and soon the royal House of Savoy became little more than a front for Mussolini. His days of serious climbing over, the duke shifted his focus to exploring the headwaters of the Shebelle River in the Ethiopian highlands and building a sustainable agricultural community in Italy's African colony of Somaliland, where he died in 1933. He never married Katherine Elkins, although he always loved her, and upon her death, three years after his, she was buried wearing his bracelet.

By leaving Italy during Mussolini's rule, the duke retained more dignity than other members of the House of Savoy. Character matters in the judgement of history, and the duke maintained his good name by living up to the highest standards of his rank in his public service as well as in his mountaineering. David and Mawson, too, were men of character who pushed themselves to the limits of human endurance. As shown by the promises he made and broke to Scott, Shackleton was more of a hustler and opportunist than these others, yet his extraordinary resolve and resourcefulness became clear in crisis. "For a joint scientific and geographical piece of organization, give me Scott," polar explorer Apsley Cherry-Garrard later observed, but "if I am in the devil of a hole and want to get out of it, give me Shackleton every time."[39] Of the top explorers of 1909, only Peary left a mixed legacy. Few doubted his courage and determination. Even in his lifetime, however, many questioned his treatment of the Inuit and the truth of his claims. These doubts have only grown with time, so much so that the historical marker at his Eagle Island home, while hailing Peary as "America's foremost Arctic explorer," never mentions whether he reached the North Pole. Character indeed matters.

THE MEANING OF HEROISM changes with time and conditions. If Peary had reached the North Pole as he claimed, his efforts to defend his priority against Cook's claim would not have offended a later generation. He would have remained the gentleman, while Cook became the cad. An earlier generation might not so readily have forgiven Shackleton's decision to turn back a few days short of his goal, and instead expected from him the same resolve that David showed in reaching his. David's heroism peered back toward the nineteenth century; Shackleton's looked forward to the twentieth century. Shackleton clearly had the Victorian response in mind when he asked his wife whether she preferred a live donkey to a dead lion, yet he became the lion of the Edwardian era, as struggle replaced success for an empire in decline. Even in his day, the Duke of the Abruzzi's heroism in setting farthest-north and altitude records seemed of an earlier age, when royals led their troops in battle and suffered at the front, but Theodore Roosevelt's Rough Rider charges and expedition heroics demonstrated its ongoing appeal.

The geography and place of heroism also changes. At least since the days of Samuel Taylor Coleridge and Mary Shelley, ice has held a special spot in the British and American imagination, with both the poles and highest peaks exerting an intense attraction. "The ice was here, the ice was there, / The ice was all around," Coleridge wrote in his epic *The Rime of the Ancient Mariner*. "The ice did split with a thunder-fit; / The helmsman steered us through!"[40] Volume upon volume, in both fiction and first-person narratives, lined nineteenth-century European and American bookshelves with tales of heroics and hubris in the high Arctic and alpine regions. They became spaces where nature tested the mettle of men and found it as often cowardly as courageous. Their ships entrapped by the Arctic ice, explorers could face the defining choice of eating either their boots or each other. Peary could learn from the native people, while Nares did not. Shackleton and Mawson could display heroic leadership skills that became legendary, while Adrien de Gerlache and Carsten Borchgrevink all but disappear from history. After going there himself as a young ship's surgeon, British writer A. Conan Doyle could knowingly speak of the Arctic as "a training school for all that was high and godlike in man" yet pen a story where an icebound ship's captain goes stark raving mad and dashes after visions to his death "on the great field of ice."[41]

Having reached new heights in latitude or altitude in 1909, Shackleton, Peary, and the Duke of the Abruzzi shrank and shifted the space for heroism. Once Peary or Cook made it there first, the North Pole was no longer an ultimate destination for explorers. David and Mawson wiped the south magnetic pole off the list as well. Having shown the way to the south geographic pole, Shackleton left room for Amundsen and Scott to cover the remaining miles, but their efforts—one triumphant, one tragic, both epic—caused a further retreat in the space for heroism. The duke's altitude record and long duration at extreme heights helped to shift the focus of the climbing elite toward the Himalayas and Karakoram for mountaineering glory, with the region becoming known as "The Third Pole." Summiting Everest, once it became open to Westerners by 1920, emerged as the ultimate goal. There, after dozens of efforts modeled in part on the duke's K2 expedition, Edmund Hillary and Tenzing Norgay gained lasting fame for their heroic first ascent in 1953.

The edges of the earth no longer held unreached places for humans to explore. Interstices and outer spaces replaced them in the geography of exploration and adventure. Aviation, of course, offered a place for heroics before 1909, but it literally took off with improvements in aircraft during and after World War I. Amundsen quickly adopted it as a means for Arctic exploration, ending in his death during a rescue flight in 1928. The American Richard Byrd became a national hero for his pioneering flights toward the North and South Poles during the late 1920s, while Charles Lindbergh attained the status of a living legend for completing the first solo flight across the Atlantic Ocean on May 21, 1927. With the refinement of jet and rocket engines following World War II, test pilots like Chuck Yeager set altitude and speed records beginning in the late 1940s, while Soviet cosmonaut Yuri Gagarin and American astronaut John Glenn gained worldwide acclaim for orbiting the earth during the early 1960s. Of course, modern heroes emerge from fields such as science, technology, business, warfare, and public service that have nothing to do with exploration. Following his celebrated Arctic explorations, for example, Nansen gained added glory for his relief work with refugees after World War I, leading to his receipt of the Nobel Peace Prize in 1922.

The earth's edges—north, south, and altitude—continue to attract, of course, but the ice encasing those alluring extremes has retreated as well. By their words or deeds, Peary, Shackleton, and the duke (despite their willing use of mechanical means and steam travel to get them to their starting points) eschewed modern technology in their quest to show what humans could achieve. "Man and the Eskimo dog are the only two mechanisms capable of meeting all the varying contingencies of Arctic work," Peary declared.[42] Shackleton relied on ponies and man-hauling. The duke tested the ability of humans to live unaided at high altitude. By feeding climate change, however, human technology has transformed even the earth's edges that these men explored. The duke's Karakoram is warming rapidly, even though a heavy covering of rubble has so far kept the valley glaciers intact. Greenland's ice sheet, where Nansen and Peary first made their marks, has melted at the astonishing rate of nearly 270 gigatons of ice per year during the twenty-first century. The Arctic ice pack can no longer serve as a foundation for sledging from the northernmost points of land to the pole itself as it did in the days of Nansen, the Duke of the Abruzzi, and Peary. The multi-year-old ice floes that they relied on have virtually disappeared.

Whereas in 1903–06 Amundsen became the first explorer to sail through the Northwest Passage, in 2015 I lectured on the first cruise ship to take the route. The landscape remains forbidding and starkly beautiful, but warming has diminished the ice dramatically, turning adventures into commonplace trips. Both the Northwest and Northeast Passages will soon be open for commercial navigation, at least during the summer months, and I met families, some with small children, who transit them in private sailboats. Humans still do great things every day, but our times call for different types of heroics.

Even the places these explorers left behind only a century ago have changed beyond recognition. County Kildare, where the staunchly unionist Anglo-Irish Shackleton was born, is now part of an independent Irish state. The colonial Sydney of David and Mawson's day, British to the core, has become a global city with more of its residents born in Asia than in Europe and a rapidly growing percentage of its citizens of non-British ancestry. Civil war has reduced the Duke of the Abruzzi's once-thriving agricultural community in Somalia to rubble, while the thousand-year reign of his House of Savoy abruptly ended with a popular referendum in 1946.

Of all the places shaped by these men, only Peary's Eagle Island home remains much as he left it. Built over several stages under Peary's watchful eye, in retirement it became his refuge from controversy and a monument to his Arctic dreams. His desk still stands in his office facing the sea with the clock from the *Roosevelt* keeping time on the wall. The island's location at "Long. 70°03'10" W"—Peary's Columbia Meridian to the pole—appears above the main doorway with a compass image painted on the floor below. Scattered about for visitors to see, as if Peary just put them down, are faded publications with titles such as *Peary and the North Pole: Not a Shadow of a Doubt* and *How Doctor Cook tried to pervert American History*. Sitting on the front steps looking over the sea while writing these words, I can all but see the *Roosevelt* steaming past with its prow pointing north. "Bully," they would shout, "give it to 'um, Teddy, give it to 'um!"[43]

Notes

Preface: The Wonderful Year 1909

1. "After the Unknown in Many Parts of the World," *The New York Times Sunday Magazine*, February 2, 1908.
2. [Charlotte Brontë], *Jane Eyre: An Autography* (London: Smith, Elder, 1847), 1:3–4.
3. Ibid., 1:206.
4. Daily Mail, *The Wonderful Year 1909: An Illustrated Record of Notable Achievements and Events* (London: Headley Brothers, 1910), 82.
5. Robert E. Peary to Theodore Roosevelt, August 17, 1908, Theodore Roosevelt Papers, reel 84, Manuscripts Division, Library of Congress.

Chapter 1: The Aristocracy of Adventure, Circa 1909

1. "Imperial and Foreign Intelligence," *Times* (London), March 23, 1908.
2. "Imperial and Foreign Intelligence," *Times* (London), April 13, 1908.
3. Mirella Tenderini and Michael Shandrick, *The Duke of the Abruzzi: An Explorer's Life* (Seattle: Mountaineers Books, 1997), 100.
4. Ibid.
5. "Court Circular," *Times* (London), October 14, 1908.
6. "Abruzzi-Elkins Wedding Expected," *New York Times*, October 12, 1908.
7. The American polar explorer and mountaineer Frederick Cook, upon claiming the North Pole in 1908, wrote in his expedition diary, "Now that the NP has been reached, it is natural to seek about for other poles to conquer." He listed three: the South Pole, the south magnetic pole, and the "Pole of highest alt[itude]. nearest heaven." [Robert M. Bryce, *The Lost Polar Notebook of Dr. Frederick A. Cook* (Monrovia, MD: Openlead Books, 2013), 190.] Cook had

already claimed the first ascent of Denali, North America's highest peak. His claim to reach the North Pole led others to reevaluate and most to reject his claims for both summiting Denali and reaching the North Pole. Until debunked, however, these claims made him a world-famous celebrity. Because of Cook's keen sense of what generated publicity, sold books, and attracted lecture audiences, his equation of the high Himalayas with a pole is telling. In their book on the Duke of the Abruzzi, mountaineers Mirella Tenderini and Michael Shandrick quoted a member of the Scottish Royal Geographical Society as asking the duke, following his North Pole expedition, when he would take on the "Third Pole," which they defined as "an altitude record in the Himalaya." [Tenderini and Shandrick, *Duke of the Abruzzi*, 87.] In his book *To the Third Pole*, German mountaineering historian G. O. Dyhrenfurth dated the published use of the term *the Third Pole*, which he defined "to include all of the highest mountains of the world—the 'Eight Thousanders' of the Himalaya and the Karakoram," to 1933. [G. O. Dyhrenfurth, *To the Third Pole: The History of the High Himalaya* (London: Werner, 1955).] Whatever its origin, the term is now widely used to refer to the Himalayas and the Karakoram regions of south-central Asia.

8. "Abruzzi, In France, Keeps Plans Secret," *New York Times*, September 13, 1909.

9. Sherard Osborn, "On the Exploration of the North Polar Region," *Proceedings of the Royal Geographical Society* (1865): 9:62.

10. Ibid., 57–58 (quoting Sabine letter).

11. C. R. Markham, "On the Best Route for North Polar Exploration," *Proceedings of the Royal Geographical Society* (1865) 9:143.

12. "The Arctic Expedition," *Times* (London), May 13, 1875.

13. A. H. Markham, "On Sledge Travel," *Proceedings of the Royal Geographical Society* (1876) 21:114.

14. Ibid., 114–15, 119.

15. "The Arctic Expedition," *Times* (London), October 18, 1876.

16. Fridtjof Nansen, *Farthest North: The Exploration of the Fram, 1893–1896* (1898; repr. Edinburgh: Birlinn, 2002), 25 (quoting Greely).

17. Frederick Jackson, *A Thousand Days in the Arctic* (London and New York: Harper and Brothers, 1899), 2:62.

18. Fergus Fleming, *Off the Map: Tales of Endurance and Exploration* (New York: Grove Press, 2004), 391 (quoting Whymper's review of Nansen's book about the expedition).

19. Luigi Amedeo of Savoy, *On the "Polar Star" in the Arctic Sea* (London: Hutchinson, 1903), 1:viii.

20. "The Abruzzi Polar Expedition," *Times* (London), October 18, 1900 ("the Duke was simply worshiped by his men").

21. Robert E. Peary, *Northward Over the "Great Ice"* (New York: F. A. Stokes, 1898), 1:346.

22. For the duke's discussion of this plan, including the use of Peary's rate of speed and methods of formulating it, see Amedeo, *"On the "Polar Star,"* 1:13–18.

23. Ibid., 1:15.

24. Ibid., 1:vii.

25. Ibid., 1:167.

26. Ibid., 1:21.

27. Ibid., 2:441.

28. Ibid., 2:452.

29. Ibid., 2:444.

30. Ibid., 2:468.

31. Ibid., 2:470.

32. Ibid., 2:479.

33. Ibid., 2:479–80.

34. Ibid., 2:488.

35. Ibid., 2:484.

36. Ibid., 2:483.

37. Ibid., 2:486.

38. Ibid., 2:490.

39. Ibid., 2:529.

40. Ibid., 2:525.

41. Ibid., 2:577.

42. Ibid., 2:597. See also page 586, where Cagni writes, "We kill Ladro, and put the heart, kidney, and a leg into the pot, and find them excellent. The well-scraped leg-bone, the head, the intestines, and the skin form the meal of the twelve surviving dogs. The remainder of the victim is put in a kayak, to serve for our food to-morrow and the day after."

43. Ibid., 2:540.

44. Ibid., 2:573.

45. Ibid., 2:571.

46. Ibid., 1:269.

47. Ibid., 1:346.

48. "Duke of Abruzzi Honored," *New York Times*, September 12, 1900. See also, for example, "Nearest to North Pole," *New York Times*, September 7, 1900. This article carried the erroneous subtitle "The Duke of Abruzzi Penetrated Farther North Than Nansen" and mentioned Cagni only in its listing of all members of the expedition, without noting his role in the sledge journey.

49. In the titles of its articles reporting on the expedition's successes, the *Times* of London, then the English-language paper of record for the world, headlined the duke's role. For example, "The Duke of the Abruzzi," *Times* (London), September 12, 1900; "The Abruzzi Expedition," *Times* (London), October 18, 1900; "The Abruzzi Expedition," *Times* (London), November 6, 1900.

50. For example, a beautifully edited and illustrated 2005 volume of first-hand accounts by adventurers and explorers includes a selection written by Cagni about his farthest north, but the selection is both titled and cited to "Duke of Abruzzi" or "Abruzzi, L.," so that most readers would presume that the account was by and about the duke. [Fergus Fleming and Annabel Merullo, eds., *The*

Explorer's Eye: First-Hand Accounts of Adventure and Exploration (Woodstock, NY: Overlook Press, 2005), 126–29.]

Chapter 2: The Audacity of Adventure, Circa 1909

1. "Cook Not Near Pole, Says Peary; Proofs Still Held Back by Cook," *New York Times*, September 9, 1909.

2. For example, "Peary Denounces Cook," *New York Times*, September 11, 1909.

3. For example, "The Goal of Centuries Achieved by Peary," *New York Times*, September 11, 1909.

4. Peary later wrote about this point in his life, "My interest in the Arctic work dates back to 1885, when as a young man my imagination was stirred by reading accounts of explorations by Nordenskjold in the interior of Greenland. These studies took full possession of my mind and led to my undertaking, entirely alone, a summer trip to Greenland in the following year." [Robert Peary, *The North Pole* (New York: Frederick A. Stokes, 1910), 25.]

5. Robert E. Peary to Mary P. Peary, August 16, 1880, quoted in Robert M. Bryce, *Cook and Peary: The Polar Controversy, Resolved* (Mechanicsburg, PA: Stackpole Books, 1997), 19. Though a well-documented, highly reliable book, this letter is acknowledged by its author and my own research as not being in the Peary Papers at the National Archives.

6. Fridtjof Nansen, *The First Crossing of Greenland* (London: Longmans, Green, 1890), 1:505–6 ("The distance of a hundred miles from the margin of the ice cannot, therefore, be established as beyond all doubt"). Nansen also questioned Peary's estimate of altitude because it was based on an aneroid barometer rather than a boiling-point barometer.

7. Robert Peary, *Northward Over the "Great Ice"* (New York: Frederick A. Stokes, 1898), 1:39.

8. Robert E. Peary to Mary P. Peary, February 27, 1887, Mary W. Peary Papers, Correspondence, A1/I-BB/box 2, Robert E. Peary Papers, National Archives (hereafter cited as Peary Papers).

9. Robert E. Peary to Mary P. Peary, February 1, 1891, Mary W. Peary Papers, Peary Papers.

10. For historical analysis suggesting that Peary might have knowingly exaggerated this claim, see Bryce, *Cook and Peary*, 85–86 and Wally Herbert, *The Noose of Laurels: Robert E. Peary and the Race to the North Pole* (New York: Atheneum, 1989), 89–90 ("With the nagging doubt about his discoveries in North-East Greenland . . .").

11. A. H. Markham, "Arctic Exploration," *Report of the Sixth International Geographical Congress* (London: John Murray, 1896), 193.

12. Robert E. Peary to Mary P. Peary, December 22, 1892, Mary W. Peary Papers, Peary Papers.

13. Robert E. Peary, "The Great White Journey," in Josephine Diebitsch Peary, *My Arctic Journal: A Year Among Ice-Fields and Eskimos* (London: Longmans, Green, 1894), 239.

14. J. B. Pond, *The Eccentricities of Genius: Memories of Famous Men and Women of the Platform and Stage* (London: Chatto & Windus, 1901), 295–97.

15. Robert E. Peary's notes, reprinted in Herbert, *Noose of Laurels*, 206. Herbert uses the name Aleqasina but quotes Peary's spelling as Alakahsingwah and estimates her age as "about ten years old." [Ibid., 205–7.] Many authors spell the name Allakasingwah or use the nickname "Ally." A discussion of the relationship, including the conclusion that it began during the year after Josephine Peary left in 1894, is in Bruce Henderson, *True North: Peary, Cook, and the Race to the Pole* (New York: W. W. Norton, 2005), 134–35.

16. Peary, *Northward Over the "Great Ice,"* 1:500. As part of his ethnological research, Peary sought to photograph as many of the local Inuit as possible, often posing them nude or in native clothing. When he first sought to photograph Allakasingwah, Peary noted that she "evinced extreme reluctance to having her picture taken, and only a direct order from her father accomplished the desired result." [Robert E. Peary's notes, reprinted in Herbert, *Noose of Laurels*, 206.]

17. Pond, *Eccentricities of Genius*, 297.

18. Robert E. Peary, "Moving on the North Pole," *McClure's Magazine*, March 1898, 424.

19. "Peary's Arctic Expedition, 1897," Papers Relating to Arctic Expeditions, A1/1-V/box 11, Peary Papers, National Archives.

20. Peary, *Northward Over the "Great Ice,"* 1: 508–9.

21. Peary, "Moving on the Pole," 425.

22. R. E. Peary, *Nearest the Pole: A Narrative of the Polar Expedition of the Peary Arctic Club in the S. S. Roosevelt, 1905–1906* (New York: Doubleday, 1907), 285.

23. Peary, "Moving on the Pole," 425.

24. "Transactions of the Society, January–March, 1897," *Journal of the American Geographical Society of New York* 29 (1897), 118–19 (Peary's acceptance speech).

25. Ibid., 120–21.

26. Peary, "Moving on the Pole," 422.

27. Robert E. Peary, *Secrets of Polar Travel* (New York: Century, 1917), 197.

28. Peary, *Northward Over the "Great Ice,"* 1:lxii.

29. Peary, "Moving on the Pole," 422–24.

30. Bradley Robinson, *Dark Companion*, rev. ed. (New York: Fawcett, 1967), 125 (an account purportedly related by Henson).

31. Peary, *Nearest the Pole*, 308.

32. Herbert, *Noose of Laurels*, 114.

33. R. E. Peary, "Report of Expedition of 1898–1902," in Peary, *Nearest the Pole*, 306.

34. Ibid., 307.

35. Ibid., 307–8.

36. Robinson, *Dark Companion*, 128.

37. John Edward Weems, *Peary: The Explorer and the Man* (Boston: Houghton Mifflin, 1967), 337 n. 5.

38. Robinson, *Dark Companion*, 131.

39. Ibid.

40. Otto Sverdrup, *New Land: Four Years in the Arctic Regions* (London: Longmans, Green, 1904), 1:116.

41. Ibid., 117.

42. Peary, "Report of Expedition," 311.

43. Robert E. Peary to Josephine D. Peary, August 28, 1899, Josephine D. Peary Papers, Family Correspondence, P/4/box 4, National Archives (hereafter cited as J. D. Peary Papers).

44. Peary, "Report of Expedition," 325–26.

45. Ibid., 227.

46. Ibid.

47. Supporting the view that this extended trek east after his polar quest ended served to complement his earlier work in North Greenland, at this point in his written account Peary wrote, "In this journey I had determined, conclusively, the northern limit of the Greenland archipelago or land group, and had practically connected the coast southward to Independence Bay." [Ibid., 332.] Peary had still not given up referring to (and perhaps seeing) the northern end of Greenland as an archipelago.

48. See, for example, Herbert, *Noose of Laurels*, 123: high praise from an otherwise critical judge.

49. Robert E. Peary to Josephine D. Peary, April 4, 1901, J. D. Peary Papers.

50. Ibid.

51. Ibid., March 1901.

52. Ibid., January 23, 1901.

53. Frederick A. Cook, "Hell Is a Cold Place," chap. 5, p. 9, unpublished manuscript, Writings, reel 7, Frederick Cook Collection, Library of Congress.

54. Peary, "Report of Expedition," 341.

55. Ibid., 341–42.

56. Ibid., 345 ("Grand Canal").

57. Ibid., 343.

58. Ibid., 344.

59. Robert E. Peary, Diary, May 24, 1902, Papers Relating to Arctic Expeditions, A1/I-V/box 14, Peary Papers.

60. "Says Pole Will Be Found," *New York Times*, November 20, 1902.

61. Ibid.

62. "Peary Supply Ship Sails," *New York Times*, July 29, 1900.

Chapter 3: The Allure of Adventure, Circa 1909

1. "Lecture by Lieutenant Shackleton," *Sydney Morning Herald*, December 7, 1907.

2. "The Antarctic Expedition," *Evening News* (Sydney), December 7, 1907.

3. "Antarctic Exploration," *Age* (Melbourne), December 4, 1907.

4. Ibid.

5. "The South Pole Expedition," *Sydney Morning Herald*, December 16, 1907.

6. "Lieutenant Shackleton," *Sydney Stock and Station Journal*, December 10, 1907.

7. See, for example, "Farthest South," *Sydney Morning Herald*, December 9, 1907.

8. "The South Pole," *Evening Journal* (Adelaide), December 2, 1907.

9. "The Antarctic Expedition," *Argus* (Melbourne), December 4, 1907.

10. "Lecture by Lieutenant Shackleton," *Sydney Morning Herald*, December 7, 1907.

11. "South Pole Expedition," *Sydney Morning Herald*, December 2, 1907.

12. These terms are drawn from a widely quoted ad that Shackleton supposedly posted to solicit men for his expedition. Although the ad is an urban legend, the terms it used aptly describe the conditions that his men faced.

13. "Through Antarctic Ice," *Express and Telegraph* (Adelaide), December 2, 1907.

14. "To the South Pole," *Sunday News* (Sydney), December 8, 1907.

15. "The Dash for the Pole," *Sydney Morning Herald*, December 6, 1907.

16. "To the South Pole," *Sunday News* (Sydney), December 8, 1907.

17. "The Dash for the Pole," *Sydney Morning Herald*, December 6, 1907.

18. "Farthest South," *Sydney Morning Herald*, December 9, 1907; "An Appeal to Australia," *Sydney Morning Herald*, December 14, 1907.

19. M. E. David, *Professor David: The Life of Sir Edgeworth David* (London: Edward Arnold, 1937), 118. The unnamed opposition leader quoted was most likely Charles Frazer of Western Australia. News reports of the day do not contain this quote, which is taken from a biography by Edgeworth David's wife.

20. "Is Antarctic Exploration Possible?" *The Spectator* (London), September 28, 1895.

21. Ibid.

22. "Discussion on Antarctic Exploration," *Report of the Sixth International Geographical Congress* (London: John Murray, 1896), 163.

23. C. E. Borchgrevink, "The Voyage of the 'Antarctic' to Victoria Land," in ibid., 171–74.

24. Karl vo den Steinen, [Discussion], in ibid., 176.

25. C. E. Borchgrevink, *First on the Antarctic Continent, Being an Account of the British Antarctic Expedition, 1898–1900* (London: George Newnes, 1901), 242–45.

26. William G. FitzGerald, "Mr. C. E. Borchgrevink," *Strand Magazine*, September 1900, 238.

27. Borchgrevink, *First on the Antarctic*, 280.

28. G. Allen Mawer, *South by Northwest: The Magnetic Crusade and the Contest for Antarctica* (Edinburgh: Birlinn, 2006), 166.

29. Borchgrevink, *First on the Antarctic*, 245.

30. J. Austin Hussey to H. R. Mill, July 27, 1922, Scott Polar Research Institute, MS 100/49/3 D, University of Cambridge, Cambridge, UK (hereafter cited as SPRI).

31. J. Austin Hussey to H. R. Mill, May 15, 1922, MS 100/49/1 D, SPRI.

32. Edward Wilson, *Diary of the "Discovery" Expedition to the Antarctic Regions 1901–1904* (New York: Humanities Press, 1967), 150–51.

33. Robert F. Scott, *Voyage of "Discovery"* (London: Smith, Elder, 1905) 2:20.

34. Ibid., 2:23.
35. Wilson, *Diary of the "Discovery,"* 226.
36. Ibid., 228.
37. Scott, *Voyage of "Discovery,"* 2:52.
38. Ibid., 2:79–80.
39. Ibid., 2:125.
40. "Antarctic Exploration," *Times* (London), September 10, 1904.
41. Robert Scott to Hannah Scott, February 24, 1903, MS 1542/8/1 D, SPRI (depicting Shackleton as "a very good fellow and only fails from his constitution point of view").
42. Scott, *Voyage of "Discovery,"* 2:121. See also, Robert to Hannah Scott, February 24, 1903, SPRI: "Our own journey to the South was, of course, the severest, the distance travelled was the longest, the time longest, and our food allowance the least. For Wilson and myself, saddled as we were with an invalid for three weeks at the end, it was especially trying."
43. G. W. Gregory, "The Work of the National Antarctic Expedition," *Nature* 63 (1901): 610–11.
44. Robert to Hannah Scott, February 24, 1903, SPRI.
45. David Branagan, *T. W. Edgeworth David: A Life* (Canberra: National Library of Australia, 2005), 19.
46. "Man and the Great Ice Age," *Sydney Morning Herald*, August 29, 1893.
47. Diary of Cara David, June 23, 1897, David Family Papers, MS 8890, National Library of Australia, Canberra.
48. Douglas Mawson to Margery Fisher, [1956?], Mawson Papers, 5.1.54 (48 DM), South Australian Museum, Adelaide.
49. Ernest Shackleton to Emily Shackleton, January 22, 1908, MS 1581/1/3 D, SPRI.
50. Douglas Mawson to Edgeworth David, September 28, 1907, Correspondence of Douglas Mawson, MS 3022/1, Mitchell State Library of New South Wales, Sydney.
51. For example, one earlier article wrote about David, "Professor David is a young man, pale and studious in appearance. He is possessed of a lively sense of the duties and responsibilities of his position." ["T. W. E. David," *Illustrated Sydney News*, December 16, 1893.] In these respects, except for growing older, David never changed.
52. Paquita Mawson, *Mawson of the Antarctic: The Life of Sir Douglas Mawson* (London: Longmans, 1964), 23 (quoting J. W. Turner).
53. Philip Ayres, *Mawson: A Life* (Melbourne: Melbourne University Press, 1999), 209 (quoting Mawson).
54. Ibid.
55. D. Mawson, "The Geology of the New Hebrides," *Proceedings of the Linnean Society of New South Wales*, pt. 3 (October 25, 1905): 402.
56. D. Mawson, "Preliminary Note on the Geology of the New Hebrides," *Reports of the Australian Association for the Advancement of Science* 10 (1904): 214.

57. Mawson, *Mawson of the Antarctic*, 27.

58. "Yesterday's Celebrations," *Sunday Times* (Sydney), May 7, 1905.

59. Mawson, *Mawson of the Antarctic*, 27 (quoting H. G. Foxall).

60. Douglas Mawson to Margery Fisher, [1956?], Mawson Papers.

Chapter 4: The Great Game

1. "Proceedings of the Royal Scottish Geographical Society," *Scottish Geographical Magazine* 24 (1908): 95.

2. Mirella Tenderini and Michael Shandrick, *The Duke of the Abruzzi: An Explorer's Life* (Seattle: Mountaineers Books, 1997), 87. See also "Duke of the Abruzzi's Visit," *Glasgow Herald*, December 21, 1907, which quoted the lord provost's toast to the duke on behalf of the townspeople of Glasgow: "That second highest peak of the Himalayas was still unclimbed, and either in connection with that, or some other expedition that would be of advantage to science and geography, they gave him their heartiest wishes."

3. "Proceedings of the Royal Scottish," 95.

4. William Wordsworth, "The Prelude, Book Sixth: Cambridge and the Alps," lines 524–25, 529–30, 542–45.

5. Samuel Taylor Coleridge, "Hymn before Sun-rise, in the Vale of Chamouni," lines 3, 13–16, 26.

6. Mary Shelley, ed. *The Works of Percy Bysshe Shelley*, Essays and Letters Volume (London: Edward Moxon, 1874), 100.

7. Mary Shelley, *Frankenstein; or, The Modern Prometheus* (London: Lackington at al., 1818), 256–57.

8. Percy Bysshe Shelley, "Mont Blanc: Lines Written in the Vale of Chamouni," lines 35-36, 80–84.

9. Lord Byron, *Manfred: A Dramatic Poem* (London: Murray, 1817), 10.

10. Albert Richard Smith, *The Natural History of the Gent* (London: David Bogue, 1847), 22–23.

11. C. G. Floyd, "The Ascent of Mount Blanc," *Times* (London), August 26, 1851.

12. Ibid.

13. Albert Smith, "Ascent of Mont Blanc," *Times* (London), August 20, 1851.

14. "The Ascent of Mount Blanc," *Times* (London), November 30, 1852.

15. Ibid.

16. A Tourist, "To the Editor of the Times," *Times* (London), September 5, 1854.

17. Peter H. Hansen, "Albert Smith, the Alpine Club, and the Invention of Mountaineering in Mid-Victorian Britain," *Journal of British Studies* 34 (1995): 310 (quoting a club officer who then, to illustrate his meaning, purportedly pointed at a workman outside the association's Saville Row clubhouse and sneered, "I mean that we would never elect that fellow even if he were the finest climber in the world.")

18. "London, Monday, October 6, 1856," *Times* (London), October 6, 1856.

19. Roger W. Patillo, *The Canadian Rockies: Pioneers, Legends and True Tales* (Aldergrove, B.C.: Amberlea, 2005), 176.

20. Edward Whymper, *Scrambles Among the Alps in the Years 1860–'69* (Philadelphia: J. B. Lippincott, 1872), 148.

21. Ibid., 151.

22. Ibid., 152.

23. Ibid., 153.

24. Edward Whymper, "The Matterhorn Accident," *Times* (London), August 9, 1865.

25. "London, Thursday, July 27, 1865," *Times* (London), July 27, 1865.

26. Charles Dickens, "Foreign Climbs," *All the Year Round* 14, 1865, 137.

27. E. T. Cook and Alexander Wedderburn, eds., *The Works of John Ruskin* (London: George Allen, 1905), 18:21.

28. Ibid., 18:90.

29. Anthony Trollope, *Traveling Sketches* (London: Chapman & Hall, 1866), 90–91.

30. H. B. George, *The Oberland and its Glaciers: Explored and Illustrated with Ice-Axe and Camera* (London: A. W. Bennett, 1866), 197.

31. "London: July 29, 1865," *Illustrated London News*, July 29, 1865.

32. Theodore Roosevelt to Anna Roosevelt, August 5, 1881, Theodore Roosevelt Collection, MS Am 1834 (187), Harvard College Libraries.

33. Friedrich Nietzsche, *Thus Spake Zarathustra, a Book for All and None*, trans. Alexander Tille (London: Allen & Unwin, 1908), 86. Later English translations restructured this famous sentence, but this version was the standard English one in 1909, having been published in New York in 1896 and London in 1908, and thus likely the one that Roosevelt and Churchill read.

34. Leslie Stephen, "Alpine Climbing," in *British Sports and Pastimes, 1868*, ed. Anthony Trollope (London: Virtue, 1968), 274–75.

35. Roderick Impey Murchison, "Address to the Royal Geographical Society of London," *Journal of the Royal Geographical Society of London* 22 (1852): cxxiii–cxxiv.

36. "Livingstone," *New York Herald*, July 2, 1872.

37. H. M. Stanley, "The Uganda Protectorate, Ruwenzori, and the Semliki Forest: Discussion," *Geographical Journal* 19 (1902): 40.

38. Duke of the Abruzzi, "The Snows of the Nile," *Geographical Journal* 29 (1907): 133–34.

39. Ibid., 135.

40. Ibid., 138–39.

41. "The Ascent of Ruwenzori," *Times* (London), January 9, 1907.

42. "London, Wednesday, January 9, 1907," *Times* (London), January 9, 1907 (quoting the Roman newspaper *Tribuna*).

43. "Duke of the Abruzzi Conquers the Mountains of the Moon," *New York Times*, October 7, 1906.

44. "The Snows of the Nile: Discussion," *Geographical Journal* 29 (1907): 147.

45. See, for example, Martin Conway, "The Duke of the Abruzzi's Climb," *The Speaker*, January 19, 1907, 466 ("As an amateur [the duke] ranks among the best and is so recognized in the confraternity of mountaineers") and Tenderini and

Shadrick, *Duke of the Abruzzi*, 86, which quotes Edward Whymper's comment that, although the Ruwenzori could have been climbed by a less skilled mountaineer, the duke contributed "the perfect management, the adoption of the right means to attain the ends, and the completeness of the manner in which the results were attained."

46. "Italian Warship Brings Royal Duke," *New York Times*, May 26, 1907.

47. "Warship Visited by Eager Crowds," *New York Times*, May 31, 1907.

48. "Duke D'Abruzzi Alpine Club Guest," *New York Times*, May 29, 1907.

Chapter 5: The Peary Way

1. "Holiday Throngs Visit Peary's Ship," *New York Times*, July 5, 1908.

2. "Bids Peary Goodby: President and His Family Inspect *Roosevelt* before She Sails," *New York Tribune*, July 8, 1908.

3. Theodore Roosevelt to Daniel Coit Gilman, December 18, 1903, in *The Letters of Theodore Roosevelt*, ed. Elting E. Morison (Cambridge: Harvard University Press, 1951), 3:671.

4. Theodore Roosevelt to R. E. Peary, September 9, 1903, Theodore Roosevelt Papers, reel 332, Manuscripts Division, Library of Congress.

5. Wally Herbert, *The Noose of Laurels: Robert E. Peary and the Race to the North Pole* (New York: Atheneum, 1989), 156.

6. R. E. Peary, [Cullun Geographical Medal Acceptance Speech], *Bulletin of the American Geographical Society* 29 (1897): 121.

7. Theodore Roosevelt to Walter Wellman, March 17, 1898, in *Letters of Theodore Roosevelt*, 1:796.

8. Theodore Roosevelt to Cecil Arthur Spring Rice, April 11, 1908, in *Letters of Theodore Roosevelt*, 6:796.

9. "Presentation to Commander Peary," *Report of the Eighth International Geographic Congress* (Washington: Government Printing Office, 1905), 111.

10. "Resolutions Adopted by the Eighth International Geographic Congress," *Eighth International Geographic Congress*, 107.

11. Robert E. Peary, "Address of the President of the Congress," *Eighth International Geographic Congress*, 77, 79.

12. Ibid., 78, 80.

13. R. A. Harris, "Evidences of Land Near the North Pole," *Eighth International Geographic Congress*, 397.

14. Frederick A. Cook, "A Comparative View of the Arctic and Antarctic," *Eighth International Geographic Congress*, 708.

15. Frederick A. Cook, "Results of a Journey Around Mount McKinley," *Eighth International Geographic Congress*, 762.

16. Cook titled his book about climbing on Denali "To the Top of the Continent." Frederick A. Cook, *To the Top of the Continent: Discovery, Exploration and Adventure in Sub-arctic Alaska* (New York: Doubleday, 1908).

17. Frederick A. Cook, "The Voyage of the *Belgica*," *Eighth International Geographic Congress*, 710.

18. R. E. Peary, *Nearest the Pole: A Narrative of the Polar Expedition of the Peary Arctic Club in the S. S. Roosevelt, 1905–1906* (New York: Doubleday, 1907), 35. Peary also called the Inuits "my people" or "my faithful people" [ibid., 25, 26].

19. Ibid., 30. Peary reported slightly higher figures three pages later [ibid., 33].

20. Ibid., 33, 40.

21. Ibid., 44–45, 49.

22. Ibid., 50.

23. With respect to his 1908–09 expedition, Peary used the phrase "Peary system." [Robert E. Peary, "The Discovery of the North Pole," *Hampton's Magazine*, June 1910, 780.]

24. See, for example, Robert A. Bartlett, *The Log of Bob Bartlett: The True Story of Forty Years of Seafaring and Exploration* (New York: G. P. Putnam's Sons, 1928), 149.

25. Ibid., 117; Herbert, *Noose of Laurels*, 173.

26. Peary, *Nearest the Pole*, 105.

27. Ibid., 114.

28. Ibid., 115, 116, 118.

29. Ibid., 118, 119.

30. The numbers here are computed from Peary, *Nearest the Pole*, 119, 130, and "30,000 Seek to Greet Peary at his Lecture," *New York Times*, December 9, 1906.

31. Peary, *Nearest the Pole*, 126.

32. Ibid., 127.

33. Ibid., 124.

34. Ibid., 125–30; R. E. Peary, Diary (transcription), April 5, 1906, Robert E. Peary Papers, Papers Relating to Arctic Expeditions, Ai/I-V/box 18A, National Archives (hereafter cited as Peary Papers).

35. Herbert, *Noose of Laurels*, 175–85.

36. Peary, *Nearest the Pole*, 130–32.

37. Ibid., 134; Peary, Diary (transcription), April 30, 1906, Peary Papers.

38. Peary, *Nearest the Pole*, 144–47.

39. Henson placed the original number of dogs on the northern journey at one hundred thirty, but Peary put the number at one hundred twenty. Compare Matthew A. Henson, *A Negro Explorer at the North Pole* (New York: Frederick A. Stokes, 1912), 13, with "Bolder Dash for Pole Next Time, Says Peary," *New York Times*, November 29, 1906. Peary stated that only two of the dogs with his party survived the trip but more came back with the other parties. [Peary, *Nearest the Pole*, 166.]

40. Peary, *Nearest the Pole*, 228.

41. Ibid., 234.

42. Ibid., 190.

43. Ibid., 280.

44. Compare Peary, *Nearest the Pole*, 235–36, with Robert A. Bartlett, *The Log of Bob Bartlett* (New York: G. P. Putnam's Sons, 1928), 164–65.

45. Bartlett, *Log of Bob Bartlett*, 168.

46. Ibid., 166.

47. Henson, *A Negro Explorer*, 13.

48. "30,000 Seek to Greet Peary at his Lecture," *New York Times*, December 9, 1906.

49. Ibid; see also "Peary Takes Audience on Trip to the Pole," *New York Times*, December 13, 1906 (Peary Arctic Club dinner); "Jesup Disappointed," *New York Times*, November 3, 1906 (expressing initial disappointment).

50. "President Praises Peary's Hardy Virtue," *New York Times*, December 16, 1906.

51. Peary, *Nearest the Pole*, ix–xi. (Roosevelt's presentation speech and Peary's acceptance speech are reprinted in this book.)

52. "Peary Gets D.K.E. Flag to Plant at the Pole," *New York Times*, January 17, 1907.

53. Herbert, *Noose of Laurels*, 204.

54. "Bolder Dash for Pole Next Time, Says Peary," *New York Times*, November 29, 1906; "Peary Ready for another Pole Dash," *New York Times*, April 10, 1907.

55. "Peary Ready to Start but Still Lacks $4,000 of the Money He Wants," *New York Tribune*, July 6, 1908.

56. "Commander Peary Again to Seek the Pole," *The New York Times Magazine*, March 8, 1908.

57. "To Try New Route to Pole," *New York Times*, October 5, 1907.

58. "Dr. Cook's Feat Doubted," *New York Times*, November 10, 1907.

59. In his letter to Theodore Roosevelt, for example, Peary informed the president that "John R. Bradley, Cook's backer in this enterprise, . . . is a well-known gambler, known in certain circles as 'Gambler Jim'" and went on to suggest that Bradley was "a card sharp" and allowed both men and women to gamble at his Palm Beach casino. [Robert E. Peary to Theodore Roosevelt, July 15, 1908, Letters and Telegrams Sent 1908, P/1/box 11, Peary Papers.]

60. "Dr. Cook's Experiment," *New York Times*, October 4, 1907.

61. Robert E. Peary to Robert A. Bartlett, July 4, 1908, Letters and Telegrams Sent 1908 (telegram), Peary Papers.

62. Bartlett, *Log of Bob Bartlett*, 183.

63. Compiled from "Roosevelt Bids Peary Godspeed," *New York Times*, July 8, 1908; "Bids Peary Goodby: President and His Family Inspect *Roosevelt* before She Sails," *New York Tribune*, July 8, 1908; Robert E. Peary, *The North Pole: Its Discovery Under the Auspices of the Peary Arctic Club* (New York: Frederick A. Stokes, 1910), 27. Bartlett noted Roosevelt's "glistening teeth" [Bartlett, *Log of Bob Bartlett*, 183].

Chapter 6: Beyond the Screaming Sixties

1. "The King and the *Nimrod*," *Citizen* (Gloucester), August 5, 1907. As implied by the text, the king's question is quoted in the article; Shackleton's reply is suggested in it. See also "The King and the Home Fleet," *Times* (London), August 5, 1907.

2. "The King and the South Pole," *Daily Mail* (London), August 5, 1907.

3. "Dash for the Pole," *Waggo Waggo Express* (New South Wales), November 28, 1907.

4. "To the South Pole," *Clarence River Advocate*, November 23, 1907.

5. Ernest Shackleton to Emily Shackleton, February 12, 1907, Scott Polar Research Institute, MS 1537/2/12/15 D, University of Cambridge, Cambridge, UK (hereafter cited as SPRI).

6. Emily Shackleton to Hugh Robert Mills, March 27, 1922, MS 100/104/4 D, SPRI ("I adopted Browning's 'principle' that a man contends to the uttermost for his life's set prize be it what it may").

7. Ernest Shackleton to Hugh Robert Mills, December 26, 1906, MS 100/106/9 D, SPRI.

8. "New British Expedition to the South Pole," *Times* (London), February 12, 1907.

9. Ibid. For the circular, see Ernest H. Shackleton, "Plans for an Antarctic Expedition," MS 1456/13 D, SPRI. The circular describes the expedition as "mainly for the purpose of reaching the Geographical South Pole, and the South Magnetic Pole, and incidentally to do scientific work in the fields of Magnetism, Meteorology, Biology, and Geology." This circular reflected Shackleton's view and the common assumption that the south geographic pole lay roughly at sea level on the Ross Ice Shelf and the south magnetic pole was on the lofty Polar Plateau. It also spoke of using "dogs, ponies, and a specially designed motor car" to reach the two poles. Although the circular is not dated, polar historian Beau Riffenburgh estimated that Shackleton wrote it around January 1906. [Beau Riffenburgh, *Shackleton's Forgotten Expedition: The Voyage of the* Nimrod (London: Bloomsbury, 2004), 103.]

10. Raymond Priestley, "Diaries of the British Antarctic Expedition," January 1–8, 1908, MS 298/1/1, SPRI.

11. Ernest Shackleton, *The Heart of the Antarctic: The Story of the British Antarctic Expedition, 1907–1909* (Philadelphia: Lippincott, 1909), 1:40.

12. Fred Jacka and Eleanore Jacka, eds., *Mawson's Antarctic Diaries*, January 10, 1908 (Sydney: Allen & Unwin, 1988), 5. Mawson gave the room's dimensions as "24 ft x 6 ft"; David gave them as "about 15 ft by 8 ft by 8 ft"; but of the two, only Mawson was assigned to live in it. Compare with Edgeworth David, "With Shackleton," *Sydney Morning Herald*, March 21, 1908.

13. Shackleton, *Heart of the Antarctic*, 1:39.

14. Edgeworth David, "With Shackleton," *Sydney Morning Herald*, March 23, 1908.

15. Jacka and Jacka, *Mawson's Antarctic Diaries*, January 1, 1908.

16. Shackleton, *Heart of the Antarctic*, 1:41–42.

17. "With the *Nimrod*," *Sydney Morning Herald*, February 5, 1908 (excerpts from Shackleton's diary for the voyage).

18. Edgeworth David, "With Shackleton," *Sydney Morning Herald*, March 23, 1908.

19. Eric Marshall, Diary of the British Antarctic Expedition, January 9, 1908, MS 1456/8 D, SPRI.

20. Jacka and Jacka, *Mawson's Antarctic Diaries*, January 2–9 and 10, 1908, 4–5.

21. Marshall, Diary, January 9, 1908.

22. Arthur E. Harbord, Diary of the British Antarctic Expedition, January 8, 1908, quoted in Riffenburgh, *Shackleton's Forgotten Expedition*, 145.

23. "The *Nimrod*'s Return," *Maitland Weekly Mercury* (New South Wales), March 14, 1908 (printing a report from Shackleton).

24. Edgeworth David, "With Shackleton," *Sydney Morning Herald*, March 24, 1908. David also wrote that Buckley "loves adventure".

25. "Letter from Professor David," *Scone Advocate* (New South Wales), February 4, 1908.

26. "With the *Nimrod*," *Sydney Morning Herald*, February 5, 1908. The reporter went on to ask Cara David if she would have liked to accompany her husband on the expedition as she had for his expedition to Funafuti. "Yes," she replied, "but I could not leave the children."

27. Edgeworth David, "With Shackleton," *Sydney Morning Herald*, March 23, 1908 and April 2, 1908.

28. "Professor David," *Sydney Mail and New South Wales Advertiser*, February 5, 1908.

29. "With the *Nimrod*," *Sydney Morning Herald*, February 5, 1908.

30. Shackleton, *Heart of the Antarctic*, 1:63; Edgeworth David, "With Shackleton," *Sydney Morning Herald*, March 25, 1908. In these passages, Shackleton estimated the width of the iceberg belt at 80 miles while David put it at 100 miles. Mawson placed it at 100 miles [Jacka and Jacka, *Mawson's Antarctic Diaries*, January 16, 1908, 5].

31. Edgeworth David, "With Shackleton," *Sydney Morning Herald*, March 25, 1908.

32. Shackleton, *Heart of the Antarctic*, 1:69.

33. Ibid., 1:69; Edgeworth David, "With Shackleton," *Sydney Morning Herald*, March 26, 1908.

34. Edgeworth David, "With Shackleton," *Sydney Morning Herald*, March 27, 1908; Ernest Shackleton to Emily Shackleton, January 26, 1908, MS 1537/2/16/3 D, SPRI. One historian noted that this letter went on to say, "I felt each mile that I went to the West was a horror to me," but the bottom portion of the page where this sentence would logically appear is torn from the manuscript in the archives. In his private diary at the time and later in public, Eric Marshall chastised Shackleton for not doing more to keep his word to Scott about establishing his base at or near King Edward VII Land—writing in his diary, for example, that Shackleton "hasn't got the guts of a louse, in spite of what he may say to the world on his return." [Marshall, Diary, January 24, 1908, SPRI]. No other member of the expedition expressed this view, however, and various historians who have reviewed the episode side with Shackleton.

35. Shackleton, *Heart of the Antarctic*, 1:170.

36. Ibid., 1:174.

37. Ibid., 1:174.

38. T. W. Edgeworth David, "The Ascent of Mount Erebus," in *Aurora Australis*, ed. E. H. Shackleton (Cape Royds: The Penguins, 1908), [11].

39. Ibid., [12–13].

40. Ibid., [15].

41. Ibid., [24–28].

42. Ibid., [31].

43. Marshall, Diary, March 10–11, 1908, SPRI.

44. [Ernest Shackleton], "Erebus," in *Aurora Australis*, [95].

45. Æneas Mackintosh, Diary of the British Antarctic Expedition, February 1, 1908, quoted in Riffenburgh, *Shackleton's Forgotten Expedition*, 159.

46. Shackleton, *Heart of the Antarctic*, 1:159.

47. See, for example, Douglas Mawson to Margery Fisher, [1956?], Mawson Papers, 5.1.54 (48 DM), South Australian Museum.

48. [Raymond E. Priestley], "Trials of a Messman," in *Aurora Australis*, [51].

49. Philip Brocklehurst, Interview, December 16, 1955, MS 1456/64 D, SPRI.

50. Marshall, Diary, March 16, 1908, SPRI.

51. Depicting the spirit at winter quarters as "very good," Brocklehurst gave full credit to Shackleton, whom he described as "very tactful and very genial." Brocklehurst also praised Shackleton for picking suitable people and treating them equally. The only signs of trouble during the winter, Brocklehurst noted, were the incidents with Mackay, who he said "was very strong physically, but he was also very unreliable mentally." Brocklehurst, Interview, December 16, 1955, SPRI.

52. Shackleton, *Heart of the Antarctic*, 1:232–33.

53. Ibid., 1:221–22.

54. Ibid., 1:231–32.

55. Ibid., 1:239–40.

56. Jameson Adams, Interview, October 5, 1955, MS 1436/63 D, SPRI.

57. Shackleton, *Heart of the Antarctic*, 1:238–39.

58. Ibid., 1:140.

Chapter 7: The Savage North

1. "Peary Off to Join His Ship at Sydney," *New York Times*, July 9, 1908.

2. With respect to his 1908–09 expedition, for example, Peary used this term in Robert E. Peary, "The Discovery of the North Pole," *Hampton's Magazine*, June 1910, 780.

3. Robert E. Peary, *The North Pole: Its Discovery in 1909 Under the Auspices of the Peary Arctic Club* (New York: Greenwood Press, 1910), 20.

4. Ibid., xi.

5. Compare Robert E. Peary to George Borup, June 14, 1908, Robert E. Peary Papers, Letters and Telegrams Sent 1908, P/1/box 11, National Archives (hereafter cited as Peary Papers), with Robert E. Peary to George Borup, June 16,

1908, Peary Papers: "I have $40,000 of the needed $50,000 now assured. I must ask you to draw your own inference from this as to whether the expedition is likely to start or not."

6. Peary, *North Pole*, 108. Along this line, Peary wrote, "The gradual breaking in of the new men is one of the purposes of the short [sledge] trips in the fall. They have to become inured to such minor discomforts as frosted toes, and ears, and noses, as well as losing their dogs." [Peary, "Discovery," March 1910, 507.]

7. Matthew A. Henson, *A Negro Explorer at the North Pole* (New York: Frederick A. Stokes, 1912), 17, 64.

8. Robert E. Peary, "Moving on the North Pole," *McClure's Magazine*, March 1899, 418.

9. Robert E. Peary, "Address of the President of the Congress," *Report of the Eighth International Geographical Congress* (Washington: Government Printing Office, 1905), 79.

10. Robert E. Peary, "Peary's Plans for 1905–06," *National Geographic Magazine* 15 (1904): 425.

11. Peary, "Discovery," January 1910, 16. This series of articles, the first full-length account appearing under Peary's name after his return from the pole, was ghostwritten by a female writer, Elsa Barker, who had previously penned a highly gendered poem comparing Peary's quest for the North Pole with King Arthur's quest for the Holy Grail, in which the pole was depicted as a virgin that needed to be conquered by violence. [Elsa Barker, "Frozen Grail," *New York Times*, July 7, 1908.]

12. See, for example, Peary, *North Pole*, 48, 62.

13. Ibid., 60.

14. Ibid., 35, 100.

15. Peary, "Discovery," January 1910, 21.

16. Peary, *North Pole*, 41.

17. Ibid., 29–31, for example.

18. Robert Peary, quoted in Wally Herbert, *The Noose of Laurels: Robert E. Peary and the Race to the North Pole* (New York: Atheneum, 1989), 15; Pierre Berton, *The Arctic Grail: The Quest for the North West Passage and the North Pole, 1818– 1909* (Toronto: McClelland and Stewart, 1988), 527.

19. Peary, "Discovery," February 1910, 161, 173.

20. Peary, *North Pole*, 32.

21. Ibid., 44.

22. Henson, *A Negro Explorer*, 30.

23. Peary, "Discovery," January 1910, 24; Peary, "Discovery," February 1910, 169.

24. Rudolph Franke, *Erkebbusse eines Deutschen im hoben Norden* (Hamburg: Janssen, 1914), 71, as translated into English in Robert M. Bryce, *Cook & Peary: The Polar Controversy, Resolved* (Mechanicsburg, PA: Stackpole Books, 1997), 328. Bryce's book is the most complete and definitive account of Cook's polar expedition.

25. Ibid., 127 (also reprinted with correction of transcription errors in Bryce, *Cook & Peary*, 329).

26. Henson, *A Negro Explorer*, 26.

27. Peary explained his purposes in a letter to his wife: "I have landed supplies here, & leave two men ostensibly on behalf of Cook. As a matter of fact, I have established here the sub-base which last time I established at Victoria Head." [Robert E. Peary to Josephine D. Peary, August 17, 1908, Josephine D. Peary Papers, Family Correspondence, P/4/box 4, National Archives.]

28. "Fear Explorer Cook Is Lost in Arctic," *New York Times*, October 5, 1908.

29. In his final account of his expedition, Peary added, "A single party, comprising either a small or a large number of men and dogs, could not possibly drag (in gradually lessening quantities) all the way to the Pole and back (some nine hundred odd miles) as much food and liquid fuel as the men and the dogs of that party would consume during the journey." [Peary, *North Pole*, 206.] This passage does not appear in the earlier magazine version of his account.

30. For example, even the pro-Peary *New York Times* ran a feature article on Cook. "Here the imagination wanders in doubt," the sympathetic piece said of Cook's fate. "If Dr. Cook reached the Pole did he succeed in returning to the north Greenland coast?" "A Lost Artic Explorer and His Chance of Rescue," *The New York Times Sunday Magazine*, November 8, 1908.

31. Ross Marvin to L. C. Bement, August 15, 1908, in Bruce Henderson, *True North: Peary, Cook, and the Race to the Pole* (New York: W. W. Norton, 2005), 210.

32. "Letters to Peary Contradict Osbon," *New York Times*, November 16, 1908. Peary also urged the club to bill Bradley for the wages of the two seamen Peary left behind at Etah, calling them "a proper charge against Mr. Bradley" since they were ostensibly left to protect Cook's relinquished supplies and aid Cook should he return. [Robert E. Peary to Herbert L. Bridgman, August 17, 1908, Letters and Telegrams Sent 1908, P/1/box 11, Peary Papers.] "Out of consideration of her difficult position," as he put it, Peary did not want the costs to fall on Cook's wife, however. [Robert E. Peary to Herbert L. Bridgman, May 12, 1908, Letters and Telegrams Sent 1908, Peary Papers.]

33. "The Denmark Greenland Expedition," *Times* (London), August 17, 1908 ("The coast line took a much more easterly direction than was expected"); "The Erichsen Greenland Expedition," *Times* (London), August 7, 1908 ("Their provisions being exhausted, the explorers became so weak that they were unable to return to the station").

34. "Give Me My Father's Bones!" *World Magazine*, January 6, 1907, 3.

35. "Why Arctic Explorer Peary's Neglected Eskimo Boy Wants to Shoot Him," *San Francisco Examiner*, May 9, 1909.

36. Josephine D. Peary to Robert E. Peary, July 16, 1909, Family Correspondence, P/8/box 1, Peary Papers.

37. Prior to leaving Etah, Peary wrote to his wife, "The Cook circumstances have given me a good deal of extra work and trouble; but have worked out satisfactorily." He closed the letter with an affectionate reference that captured

their marital alliance: "We have been great chums dear." [Robert to Josephine Peary, August 17, 1908, Peary Papers.]

38. Peary, *North Pole*, 92.

39. Peary, "Discovery," February 1910, 340.

40. Ibid., 346.

41. Peary, *North Pole*, 125. Peary put the number of persons on the ship at sixty-nine. [Ibid., 88.] With twenty non-Inuits on board (after two were left at Etah to guard supplies), this would put the number of Inuits at forty-nine. Henson put the number at thirty-nine. [Henson, *A Negro Explorer*, 49.]

42. My discussion with Robert M. Bryce, author of *Cook & Peary* and an expert on Peary archival material, confirmed that Peary did not talk about God or religion except in nominal terms anywhere in his archived letters, though Bryce did note Peary's belief in signs and omens. I found nominal references to God in Peary's letters to key supporters who believed in God, such as Theodore Roosevelt and Morris K. Jesup. For example, Robert E. Peary to Theodore Roosevelt, 1908 telegram, Letters and Telegrams Sent 1908, Peary Papers ("Thank you and God bless you, Peary").

43. Peary, "Discovery," March 1910, 504.

44. Ibid., 514.

45. Peary, *North Pole*, 146–48.

46. Ibid., 157, 165.

47. Henson, *A Negro Explorer*, 50.

48. Ibid., 75.

49. Peary, "Discovery," April 1910, 662.

50. Henson, *A Negro Explorer*, 44.

51. Peary, *North Pole*, 170–71.

52. Henson, *A Negro Explorer*, 30.

53. Peary, "Discovery," May 1910, 773.

54. Henson, *A Negro Explorer*, 53.

55. Peary, *North Pole*, 214. Peary wrote that one of his "essentials of success" was "to have an intelligent and willing body of civilized assistants to lead the various divisions of Eskimos—men whose authority the Eskimos will accept when delegated by the leader." [Ibid., 202.]

56. Henson, *A Negro Explorer*, 67, 73–74.

Chapter 8: Poles Apart

1. Ernest Shackleton, Diary of the Southern Journey, October 29, 1908, MS 1456/10 D, Scott Polar Research Institute, University of Cambridge, Cambridge, UK (hereafter cited as SPRI). Written when the southern party departed, this diary entry expressly refers only to the geographic pole but logically applied to both. The version of this diary entry that Shackleton published deleted these words.

2. E. H. Shackleton, *The Heart of the Antarctic: Being the Story of the British Antarctic Expedition, 1907–1909* (Philadelphia: J. B. Lippincott, 1909), 2:73.

3. Ibid., 2:74.

4. In his authoritative book about the *Nimrod* Expedition, polar historian Beau Riffenburgh characterizes David's behavior as passive-aggressive. [Beau Riffenburgh, *Shackleton's Forgotten Expedition: The Voyage of the* Nimrod (London: Bloomsbury, 2004), 237.]

5. T. W. Edgeworth David, "Professor David's Narrative," in Shackleton, *Heart of the Antarctic*, 2:80.

6. Ibid., 2:83, 85.

7. Fred Jacka and Eleanore Jacka, eds., *Mawson's Antarctic Diaries*, October 5–6, 1908 (Sydney: Allen & Unwin, 1988), 9.

8. Ibid., October 8, 20, 29 and November 23, 1908, 9, 12, 15, 24, 25.

9. David, "Professor David's Narrative," 2:127.

10. Jacka and Jacka, *Mawson's Antarctic Diaries*, October 29 and November 24, 1908, 16, 25.

11. Ibid., October 29, 1908, 16.

12. Ibid., November 22 and 30, 1908, 24, 27.

13. Ibid., November 3, 1908 and January 6, 1909, 17, 36.

14. Joy Pitman, ed., *The Diary of A. Forbes Mackay, 1908–09*, January 12, 1909 (Jaffrey, NH: Erebus & Terror Press, 2015), 8.

15. Jacka and Jacka, *Mawson's Antarctic Diaries*, January 6, 1909, 37.

16. Pitman, *Diary of Mackay*, December 4, 1908, 3.

17. David, "Professor David's Narrative," 2:135, 142.

18. "The Gentle Professor," *Evening News* (Sydney), April 17, 1909.

19. Pitman, *Diary of Mackay*, December 10–11, 1908, 4.

20. Ibid., December 14, 1908, 4.

21. Ernest Shackleton to Emily Shackleton, October 29, 1908, MS 1537/2/18/7 D, SPRI.

22. Shackleton, Diary, October 29, 1908, MS 1456/10 D, SPRI.

23. Shackleton, *Heart of the Antarctic*, 1:289, 294.

24. Ibid., 1:278, 281.

25. Ibid., 1:289–90.

26. Ibid., 1:270.

27. Frank Wild, "Memoirs," typescript, Frank Wild Papers, MLMSS 2198, State Library of New South Wales, Sydney, 78.

28. Shackleton, *Heart of the Antarctic*, 1:285.

29. Ibid., 1:286.

30. Frank Wild, Diary of the Southern Journey, November 21, 1908, MS 944/1 D, SPRI, reprinted in Leif Mills, *Frank Wild* (Whitby, UK: Caedmon of Whitby, 1999), 78.

31. Ibid.

32. Eric Marshall, Diary of the British Antarctic Expedition, November 7, 1908, MS 1456/8 D, SPRI.

33. Shackleton, *Heart of the Antarctic*, 1:282.

34. Ernest Shackleton, "Full Narrative," *Daily Mail* (London), March 24, 1909.

35. Wild, Diary, November 3, 1908, 73.

36. Shackleton, *Heart of the Antarctic*, 1:291–92.

37. Marshall, Diary, December 14, 1908. Some readings of this passage decipher the last word as "panicking." Compare Riffenburgh, *Shackleton's Forgotten Expedition*, 223 ("pausing") with Roland Huntford, *Shackleton* (New York: Atheneum, 1986), 263 ("panicking"). The typed transcript at the SPRI archives clearly states "pausing."

38. Ibid., December 2, 1908.

39. Shackleton, *Heart of the Antarctic*, 1:303.

40. Wild, Diary, December 3, 1908, 82.

41. Marshall, Diary, December 3, 1908.

42. E. S. Marshall, "An Antarctic Episode," *Medical Press and Circular*, December 8, 1943, 359.

43. Shackleton, *Heart of the Antarctic*, 1:299.

44. Ibid., 1:310.

45. E. H. Shackleton, "Some Results of the British Antarctic Expedition, 1907–9," *Geographical Journal* 34 (1909): 489.

46. Shackleton, *Heart of the Antarctic*, 2:13–14.

47. Shackleton, "Full Narrative," *Daily Mail* (London), March 24, 1909.

48. Shackleton, *Heart of the Antarctic*, 2:4.

49. Wild, "Memoirs," 83.

50. Wild, Diary, December 6–7, 1908, 84–85.

51. Wild, "Memoirs," 83–84.

52. Wild, Diary, December 12, 1908, 88.

53. Wild, "Memoirs," 84.

54. Shackleton, *Heart of the Antarctic*, 1:312.

55. Ibid., 1:320, 323, 325, 328.

56. Ibid., 1:329.

57. Wild, Diary, December 25, 1908, 93.

58. Marshall, Diary, December 25, 1908.

59. Shackleton, *Heart of the Antarctic*, 1:331.

60. Marshall, Diary, December 25, 1908.

61. Pitman, *Diary of Mackay*, December 25, 1908, 5.

62. Jacka and Jacka, *Mawson's Antarctic Diaries*, December 20, 1908, 31.

63. T. W. Edgeworth David, Diary, December 19, 1908, P11, series 5, University of Sydney Archives.

64. Jacka and Jacka, *Mawson's Antarctic Diaries*, December 16, 1908, 30.

65. Ibid., December 25, 1908, 33.

66. Pitman, *Diary of Mackay*, January 13 and 15, 1909, 9.

67. Jacka and Jacka, *Mawson's Antarctic Diaries*, January 1, 3, and 6, 1909, 33, 35, 36.

68. Pitman, *Diary of Mackay*, December 29 and 30, 1908, 6.

69. Ibid., January 13, 1908, 8–9.

70. David, "Professor David's Narrative," 2:179.

71. Ibid., 2:180–81.

72. Shackleton, *Heart of the Antarctic*, 1:335.

73. Ibid., 1:332.

74. Ibid., 2:18.

75. Wild, Diary, December 29, 1908, 95.

76. Marshall, "Antarctic Episode," 360. "Degrees of frost" are degrees F below freezing, or 32°F.

77. Shackleton, *Heart of the Antarctic*, 1:338–39. At this point, Marshall wrote in his diary, "Shack's suffering from altitude, and getting very thin and weaker." [Marshall, "Antarctic Episode," 360.]

78. Wild, "Memoirs," 87–88.

79. Shackleton, "Some Results," 490.

80. Shackleton, *Heart of the Antarctic*, 1:337.

81. Marshall, Diary, January 6, 1909.

82. Shackleton, *Heart of the Antarctic*, 1:341.

83. Marshall, "Antarctic Episode," 360.

84. Shackleton, *Heart of the Antarctic*, 1:347.

85. Wild, Diary, January 7, 1909, 98.

86. Marshall, "Antarctic Episode," 360 (here Marshall stated that the party left camp at 3 A.M.).

87. Shackleton, *Heart of the Antarctic*, 1:343.

88. Ibid. (Here Shackleton stated that the party left camp at 4 A.M.).

89. Marshall, Diary, January 9, 1909.

90. Ibid. It was Roland Huntford, in his biography of Shackleton, who aptly characterized 100 miles from the pole as the party's "goal of consolation." [Huntford, *Shackleton*, 272.]

91. Jameson Adams, Interview, November 17, 1955, MS 1436/63 D, SPRI.

92. Shackleton, Diary, January 9, 1909. The version of this diary entry that Shackleton published ended with "we have done our best."

93. Emily Shackleton to H. R. Mill, August 16, 1922, MS 100/104/39 D, SPRI. She added, "We left it at that."

94. Marshall, "Antarctic Episode," 360.

95. Jameson Adams, Interview, October 5, 1955, SPRI, MS 1436/63 D.

Chapter 9: On Top of the World

1. George Borup, *A Tenderfoot with Peary* (New York: Frederick A. Stokes, 1911), 160.

2. Robert A. Bartlett, *The Log of Bob Bartlett* (New York: G. P. Putnam's Sons, 1928), 191.

3. Robert E. Peary, *The North Pole* (New York: Frederick A. Stokes, 1910), 205.

4. Robert E. Peary, "The Discovery of the North Pole," *Hampton's Magazine*, June 1910, 786.

5. Borup, *Tenderfoot with Peary*, 144; John W. Goodsell, *On Polar Trails: The Peary Expedition to the North Pole, 1908–09*, rev. and ed. by Donald W. Whisenhunt (Austin, TX: Eakin Press, 1983), 117.

6. Matthew A. Henson, "The Negro at the North Pole," *World's Work*, April 1910, 12, 835.

7. Peary, *North Pole*, 222.

8. Goodsell, *On Polar Trails*, 120.

9. Robert E. Peary, Diary, March 4, 1909, North Pole Diaries 1909, A1/1-V/box 1, Robert E. Peary Papers, National Archives (hereafter cited as Peary Papers).

10. Peary, "Discovery," May 1910, 787.

11. Peary, *North Pole*, 228 (first quote); Peary, "Discovery," July 1910, 4 (second quote).

12. Matthew A. Henson, *A Negro Explorer at the North Pole* (New York: Frederick A. Stokes, 1912), 89 (quoting Bartlett).

13. Peary, Diary, March 7, 1909.

14. Henson, "Negro at the North Pole," 12, 827.

15. Goodsell, *On Polar Trails*, 122.

16. Bartlett, *Log of Bob Bartlett*, 193.

17. Henson, "Negro at the North Pole," 12, 836.

18. Goodsell, *On Polar Trails*, 125.

19. Henson, "Negro at the North Pole," 12, 836.

20. Borup, *Tenderfoot with Peary*, 178.

21. Peary, "Discovery," June 1910, 784.

22. Goodsell, *On Polar Trails*, 121.

23. Peary, Diary, March 8, 1909.

24. Borup, *Tenderfoot with Peary*, 164.

25. Peary, "Discovery," July 1910, 4.

26. Peary, Diary, March 11, 1909.

27. Peary, *North Pole*, 233.

28. Peary, "Discovery," July 1910, 9.

29. Borup, *Tenderfoot with Peary*, 170–71.

30. Goodsell, *On Polar Trails*, 121.

31. Borup, *Tenderfoot with Peary*, 173–75.

32. Peary, *North Pole*, 236.

33. Henson, *A Negro Explorer*, 97.

34. Borup, *Tenderfoot with Peary*, 169.

35. Henson, *A Negro Explorer*, 98.

36. Borup, *Tenderfoot with Peary*, 166.

37. Peary, Diary, March 18, 1909.

38. Peary, "Discovery," July 1910, 12.

39. Ibid.

40. Ibid.

41. Bartlett, *Log of Bob Bartlett*, 195.

42. Borup, *Tenderfoot with Peary*, 179.

43. Peary, *North Pole*, 245.

44. Ibid.

45. Peary, Diary, March 23, 1909.

46. Peary, "Discovery," July 1910, 16.

47. Ibid., 17.

48. Peary, Diary, April 6, 1909. He wrote this about a later day but described it as "like the march after Marvin turned back."

49. Peary, "Discovery," July 1910, 18.

50. Henson, *A Negro Explorer*, 121.

51. Peary, "Discovery," July 1910, 18.

52. Peary, "Discovery," August 1910, 165–66.

53. Henson, *A Negro Explorer*, 117–18; Peary, *North Pole*, 257.

54. Peary, "Discovery," August 1910, 166. Peary's diary entry for this date is almost identical.

55. Peary, "Discovery," August 1910, 166.

56. Bartlett, *Log of Bob Bartlett*, 195.

57. Peary, Diary, April 1, 1909.

58. "Matt Henson Tells the Real Story of Peary's Trip to Pole," *Boston American*, July 17, 1910 (reprinted online from fragile Boston Public Library copy). The *Boston American* was part of the Hearst chain of newspapers, which at this point in the Peary-Cook controversy often contained articles highly critical of Peary. Although the article carried Henson's byline and presumably reflected his opinions, like Peary's published accounts it appears to have been heavily edited or revised by others. For similar recollections by Henson, see Lowell Thomas, "First at the Pole: Lowell Thomas Interviews Matthew Henson," *Lowell Thomas Interviews* ([New York: NBC Radio Network], 1939), 3. Thomas quotes Henson in 1939 as saying about Peary on the return trip, "He couldn't walk. We had to put him on a sledge." See also Robert H. Fowler, "The Negro Who Went to the Pole with Peary," *American History Illustrated*, April 1966, 47–49, who quotes Henson in 1953 as saying about Peary on the outbound trip, "I know the last 133 miles he didn't walk."

59. "Matt Henson Tells the Real Story," *Boston American*, July 17, 1910.

60. Peary, "Discovery," August 1910, 170.

61. Ibid.

62. Ibid. Here Peary disparaged Henson, adding, "He would not have been so competent as the least experienced of my white companions in getting himself and his party back to the land." See also Peary, *North Pole*, 273.

63. For example, compare Goodsell, *On Polar Trails*, 126, with Peary, *North Pole*, 276. Goodsell estimated that, due to its winding way, the trail was about 25 percent longer than a straight-line course.

64. Thomas, "First at the Pole," 2.

65. Ibid.

66. Peary, "Discovery," August 1910, 171–72.

67. Peary, *North Pole*, 271. Both this source and the one cited in the prior note agree that Peary left camp "a little after midnight" on April 2, but his diary puts the time at 5 A.M. [Peary, Diary, April 2, 2017.] The comment about the responsiveness of his men also appeared in Robert E. Peary, "How Peary Reached the North Pole," *New York Times*, September 12, 1909. Peary's later published accounts were revised by editors under his supervision from the text of this

New York Times article, which was compiled from drafts wired by Peary on his return journey from his first port of call with a telegraph. Among Peary's published accounts, the *New York Times* article is the closest to being the product of his own hand.

68. Peary, *North Pole*, 274.

69. Peary, "Discovery," August 1910, 173.

70. Peary, "How Peary Reached the North Pole," *New York Times*, September 12, 1909.

71. Peary, *North Pole*, 277, 281–82.

72. Peary, "Discovery," August 1910, 174; Peary, *North Pole*, 284.

73. Peary, *North Pole*, 285.

74. Peary, Diary, on back of pages beginning with April 4, 1909 entry.

75. Peary, "Discovery," August 1910, 175.

76. Ibid., 174.

77. Peary, Diary, April 6, 1909.

78. Henson, "Negro at the North Pole," 12, 837.

79. Ibid.

80. Ibid.

81. Peary, *North Pole*, 287.

82. Ibid., 287. The sense is the same in Peary, "Discovery," August 1910, 175.

83. Peary, "Discovery," August 1910, 176.

84. Ibid.

85. Henson, "Matt Henson Tells the Real Story," *Boston American*, July 17, 1910.

86. Peary, "Discovery," August 1910, 176.

87. Robert E. Peary, "Certificate of Peary as to the Movements of the Expedition from April 1st 1909 to April 7th 1909," Papers Relating to Arctic Expeditions, Ai/I-V/box 25C, Peary Papers.

88. Wally Herbert, *The Noose of Laurels: Robert E. Peary and the Race to the North Pole* (New York: Atheneum, 1989), 270. Herbert estimated the distance as "at least fifty miles, and probably more than sixty." In reaching this conclusion, Herbert noted that "Peary did not prove by his altitudes of the sun that he had, beyond doubt, reached the North Pole, for the simple reason that Pole observations can very easily be faked." [Ibid., 250.] To a reporter, Henson later said that, at the North Pole camp, he told Peary that from his own tracking of the distance, "I have a feeling that we have just about covered the 132 miles since Captain Bartlett turned back. If we have not traveled in the right direction, then that is your own fault." [Henson, "Matt Henson Tells the Real Story," *Boston American*, July 17, 1910.] Herbert suspected that Peary did not take Henson along on his various trips from his North Pole camp because Henson might have detected the fraud, and noted that the critical evidence is either missing from Peary's diary or inserted rather than integral to it. [Ibid., 246–50.]

89. For an analysis of this study, see Robert M. Bruce, *Cook & Peary: The Polar Controversy, Resolved* (Mechanicsburg, PA: Stackpole Books, 1997), 758–61.

90. Henson reported that he proposed the three cheers, which Peary then led. [Henson, *A Negro Explorer*, 133; Henson, "Negro at the North Pole," 12, 837.] Peary stated that he proposed the three cheers, which Henson then led. [Peary, *North Pole*, 296.]

91. Peary's initial telegraph to the Associated Press news service after arriving at the first harbor with telegraph service read, "Stars and Stripes nailed to the Pole." ["Peary Discovers North Pole after Eight Trials in 23 Years," *New York Times*, September 7, 1909.]

Chapter 10: The Third Pole

1. A. Ferrari, "La Spedizione del Duca Degli Abruzzi al Karakorum-Himalaya," *Rivista del Club Alpino Italiano* 28 (1909): 113, 115.

2. H. W. Tilman, *The Seven Mountain-Travel Books* (London: Bâton Wicks, 2003), 431 (repr., *Mount Everest, 1938*, Cambridge U.K.: Cambridge University Press, 1948).

3. Filippo De Filippi, *Karakoram and Western Himalaya, 1909* (New York: Dutton, 1912), 1, 3. The second quote referred generally to the remote western Himalayas but was clearly meant to include the Karakoram.

4. Ibid., 9.

5. Maurice Isserman and Stewart Weaver, *Fallen Giants: A History of Himalayan Mountaineering from the Age of Empire to the Age of Extremes* (New Haven: Yale University Press, 2008), 43 (quoting Matthias Zurbriggen). A highly recommended book.

6. See Ferrari, "La Spedizione del Duca," 115 (noting that the expedition traveled with the broad support and protection of the British government and its officers and local authorities).

7. Luigi Amedeo di Savoia, Duca degli Abruzzi, "Esplorazione nei Monti del Karakoram," *Bollettino della Societa Geografica Italiana* 4:11 (1910): 436.

8. De Filippi, *Karakoram and Western Himalaya*, 18.

9. Thomas Hungerford Holdich, "Ladakh and Baltistan," *Encyclopedia Britannica* 16 (New York: Encyclopedia Britannica, 1911), 58.

10. De Filippi, *Karakoram and Western Himalaya*, 29–30.

11. Luigi Amedeo di Savoia, "Explorazione nei Monti," 438.

12. De Filippi, *Karakoram and Western Himalaya*, 52, 55–56. De Filippi referred to the expedition's Kashmiri and Balti porters as "coolies," but the journal of the Italian Alpine Club called them by the more accurate term "porters," which is used here. [Ferrari, "La Spedizione del Duca," 114.]

13. Ibid., 72.

14. Luigi Amedeo di Savoia, "Explorazione nei Monti," 440.

15. Fredric Drew, *The Jummoo and Kashmir Territories: A Geographical Account* (London: E. Stanford, 1875), 362.

16. De Filippi, *Karakoram and Western Himalaya*, 92–93.

17. Ibid., 157.

18. Ibid., 162.

19. Ibid., 171.

20. Luigi Amedeo di Savoia, "Explorazione nei Monti," 446.

21. Ibid., 447.

22. De Filippi, *Karakoram and Western Himalaya*, 218.

23. Luigi Amedeo di Savoia, "Explorazione nei Monti," 447.

24. De Filippi, *Karakoram and Western Himalaya*, 219, 225.

25. Ibid., 225.

26. Luigi Amedeo di Savoia, "Explorazione nei Monti," 448.

27. De Filippi, *Karakoram and Western Himalaya*, 226–27.

28. Luigi Amedeo di Savoia, "Explorazione nei Monti," 450.

29. De Filippi, *Karakoram and Western Himalaya*, 238.

30. Ibid.

31. Luigi Amedeo di Savoia, "Explorazione nei Monti," 451.

32. De Filippi, *Karakoram and Western Himalaya*, 246.

33. Ibid., 247.

34. Ibid., 252.

35. Luigi Amedeo di Savoia, "Explorazione nei Monti," 453.

36. Isserman and Weaver, *Fallen Giants*, 70.

37. De Filippi, *Karakoram and Western Himalaya*, 258.

38. Luigi Amedeo di Savoia, "Explorazione nei Monti," 454.

39. Ansel Adams, "Vittorio Sella: His Photographs," *Sierra Club Bulletin* 31 (December 1946): 16–17.

40. Luigi Amedeo di Savoia, "Explorazione nei Monti," 455.

41. De Filippi, *Karakoram and Western Himalaya*, 296.

42. Ibid., 297.

43. Luigi Amedeo di Savoia, "Explorazione nei Monti," 459.

44. De Filippi, *Karakoram and Western Himalaya*, 305.

45. Ibid., 310–11.

46. Ibid., 318.

47. Luigi Amedeo di Savoia, "Explorazione nei Monti," 461.

48. De Filippi, *Karakoram and Western Himalaya*, 319.

49. Luigi Amedeo di Savoia, "Explorazione nei Monti," 461.

50. "Reviews and Notices," *Alpine Journal* 27 (1913): 114.

51. Ibid.

52. De Filippi, *Karakoram and Western Himalaya*, 316, 322.

53. Ibid., 324.

Chapter 11: Returnings

1. T. W. Edgeworth David, "Professor David's Narrative," in E. H. Shackleton, *The Heart of the Antarctic: Being the Story of the British Antarctic Expedition, 1907–1909* (Philadelphia: J. B. Lippincott, 1909), 2:182.

2. Ibid.

3. Ibid., 2:183.

4. Shackleton, *Heart of the Antarctic*, 2:75.

5. Joy Pitman, ed., *The Diary of A. Forbes Mackay, 1908–09,* January 22, 1909 (Jaffrey, NH: Erebus & Terror Press, 2015), 11.

6. Fred Jacka and Eleanore Jacka, eds., *Mawson's Antarctic Diaries,* January 23–25, 1909 (Sydney: Allen & Unwin, 1988), 42.

7. "Professor David's Narrative," 2:189.

8. Ibid., 2:193.

9. Ibid., 2:193–94.

10. Ibid., 2:194–95.

11. Jacka and Jacka, *Mawson's Antarctic Diaries,* January 31, 1909, 45.

12. Ibid.

13. Pitman, *Diary of Mackay,* February 1, 1909, 12.

14. Jacka and Jacka, *Mawson's Antarctic Diaries,* February 2, 1909, 45.

15. Pitman, *Diary of Mackay,* February 3, 1909, 12.

16. Jacka and Jacka, *Mawson's Antarctic Diaries,* February 2, 1909, 46.

17. Pitman, *Diary of Mackay,* February 1, 1909, 12.

18. "Professor David's Narrative," 2:208.

19. Pitman, *Diary of Mackay,* February 1, 1909, 12.

20. Jacka and Jacka, *Mawson's Antarctic Diaries,* February 2, 1909, 46; "Professor David's Narrative," 2:208.

21. Jacka and Jacka, *Mawson's Antarctic Diaries,* February 4, 1909, 47.

22. "Professor David's Narrative," 2:211 (quoting Mawson).

23. Ibid., 2:211.

24. Ibid., 2:212.

25. Ibid., 2:213–14.

26. Frederick P. Evans, Narrative of British Antarctic Expedition, 8, MS 369 BJ, Scott Polar Research Institute, University of Cambridge, Cambridge, UK (hereafter cited as SPRI).

27. Ibid.

28. David Branagan, *T. W. Edgeworth David: A Life* (Canberra: National Library of Australia, 2005), 200 (quoting Arthur E. Harbord, Diary of the British Antarctic Expedition, February 4, 1909).

29. Philip Brocklehurst, Diary of the British Antarctic Expedition, 1907–09, February 4, 1908, MS 1635 D, SPRI.

30. Frank Wild, Diary of the Southern Journey, February 4, 1909, MS 944/1 D, SPRI, reprinted in Leif Mills, *Frank Wild* (Whitby, UK: Caedmon, 1999), 109.

31. Ibid.

32. Frank Wild, "Memoirs," typescript, Frank Wild Papers, MLMSS 2198, State Library of New South Wales, Sydney, 91.

33. Shackleton, *Heart of the Antarctic,* 1:353.

34. Eric Marshall, Diary of the British Antarctic Expedition, February 4, 1909, MS 1456/8 D, SPRI.

35. Wild, "Memoirs," 91.

36. Jameson Adams, interview with James Fisher, October 5, 1955, MS 1537/3/6 D, SPRI.

37. Wild, Diary, January 10, 1909, 100.
38. Shackleton, *Heart of the Antarctic*, 1:344, 346–47.
39. Marshall, Diary, January 10, 1909.
40. Wild, Diary, January 12, 1909, 100.
41. Ibid., January 19, 1909, 103.
42. Adams, interview, October 5, 1955.
43. Wild, Diary, January 19, 1909, 103. Marshall noted that the men broke through crevasses on this dash but "were carried on by the sheer weight of the sledge to which they clung." [E. S. Marshall, "An Antarctic Experience," *Medical Press and Circular*, December 6, 1943, 161.]
44. Shackleton, *Heart of the Antarctic*, 1:347.
45. Marshall, Diary, January 20, 1909.
46. Ibid., January 22, 26, 1909.
47. Wild, "Memoirs," 90.
48. Shackleton, *Heart of the Antarctic*, 1:348.
49. Eric S. Marshall to John Kendall, January 26, 1951, MS 656/1/11 D, SPRI; Marshall, Diary, January 26–27, 1909.
50. Marshall to Kendall, November 28, 1950, MS 656/19/9 D, SPRI.
51. Marshall, Diary, January 26–27, 1909.
52. Marshall to Kendall, November 28, 1950, SPRI.
53. Shackleton, *Heart of the Antarctic*, 1:349.
54. Wild, Diary, January 25, 1909, 105.
55. Marshall, "Antarctic Episode," 361.
56. Wild, Diary, February 3, 1909, 109.
57. Marshall, "Antarctic Episode," 361.
58. Ernest Shackleton, Diary of the Southern Journey, February 4, 1909, MS1456/10 D, SPRI.
59. Ibid., February 5, 1909, 109; Marshall, Diary, February 5, 1909.
60. Shackleton, *Heart of the Antarctic*, 1:354–55.
61. Wild, Diary, February 6, 10, 1909, 109, 112.
62. Ibid., February 7, 1909, 110; Marshall, Diary, February 6, 1909 ("The Lord is standing by us & sent us this breeze to assist").
63. Wild, "Memoirs," 90.
64. Wild, Diary, February 13, 1909, 112; Marshall, Diary, February 13, 1909.
65. Shackleton, *Heart of the Antarctic*, 1:354–55; Shackleton, Diary, February 13, 1909.
66. Wild, Diary, February 19, 1909, 113.
67. Shackleton, *Heart of the Antarctic*, 1:356.
68. Ibid., 1:358.
69. Ibid., 1:360–61.
70. Ibid., 1:362.
71. Wild, "Memoirs," 97.
72. Shackleton, *Heart of the Antarctic*, 1:364.
73. A. Forbes Mackay, Diary of the British Antarctic Expedition, March 5, 1909, MS 1537/3/1 D, SPRI.

74. Wild, "Memoirs," 98.

75. Shackleton, *Heart of the Antarctic,* 1:365.

76. Marshall, "Antarctic Episode," 136.

77. Wally Herbert, *The Noose of Laurels: Robert E. Peary and the Race to the North Pole* (New York: Atheneum, 1989), 262. In 2005, a sledging party led by British adventurer Tom Avery completed Peary's overall trek in roughly the same time as Peary's party, but never at anything like the rate of travel that Peary claimed on his last day north and first three days south. The overall rate claimed by Cook in 1908 also exceeded Peary's outbound rate, but, as his supporters noted, he never claimed single-day distances like those claimed by Peary.

78. Robert E. Peary, Diary, April 9, 1909, North Pole Diaries 1909, Ai/V-1/box1, Robert E. Peary Papers, National Archives.

79. Robert E. Peary, "The Discovery of the North Pole," *Hampton's Magazine,* September 1910, 284.

80. Ibid.

81. Matthew A. Henson, *A Negro Explorer at the North Pole* (New York: Frederick A. Stokes, 1912), 140.

82. Bradley Robinson with Matthew Henson, *Dark Companion: The Story of Matthew Henson,* rev. ed. (1947; repr. Greenwich, CT: Fawcett, 1969), 206–7.

83. Lowell Thomas, "First at the Pole: Lowell Thomas Interviews Matthew Henson," *Lowell Thomas Interviews* (New York: NBC Radio, 1939), 3.

84. Robert E. Peary, *The North Pole* (New York: Frederick A. Stokes, 1910), 304, 309.

85. Peary, Diary, April 11, 1909.

86. Henson, *A Negro Explorer,* 141.

87. Peary, "Discovery," September, 1910, 290.

88. Peary, Diary, April 22–23, 1909. In his final published account, Peary revised these words to read, "I have won the last great geographical prize, the North Pole, for the credit of the United States. . . . It has been accomplished in a way that is thoroughly American. I am content." Peary, *North Pole,* 316.

89. George Borup, *A Tenderfoot with Peary* (New York: Frederick A. Stokes, 1911), 185, 187.

90. Harry Whitney, *Hunting with the Eskimos: The Unique Record of a Sportsman's Year among the Northernmost Tribe* (New York: Century, 1910), 269.

91. Henson, *A Negro Explorer,* 176.

92. Robert A. Bartlett, *The Log of Bob Bartlett: The True Story of Forty Years of Seafaring and Exploration* (New York: G. P. Putnam's Sons, 1928), 204.

93. "Abruzzi to Peary: Glad You Succeeded," *New York Times,* September 25, 1909.

94. Filippo De Filippi, *Karakoram and Western Himalaya, 1909* (New York: Dutton, 1912), 327.

95. Ibid., 332.

96. Ibid., 340–41.

97. Ibid., 350.

98. "Peary Lands; Refuses Honors," *New York Times,* September 22, 1909.

99. "The King and the Explorer," *Daily Mail* (London), March 27, 1909.

Epilogue: The Last Biscuit

1. "Tributes to the Explorer and his Message," *Daily Mail* (London), March 25, 1909 (reprinting editorial comment from around the world).
2. Filippo De Filippi, *Karakoram and Western Himalaya, 1909: An Account of the Expedition of H.R.H. Prince Luigi Amedeo of Savoy, Duke of the Abruzzi* (London: Constable, 1912). There was also a second volume of photographs and maps.
3. Lieutenant Shackleton, "Full Narrative," *Daily Mail* (London), March 24, 1909. At 72 degrees of frost, the temperature would be minus 40°F.
4. "The Queen's Message," *Daily Mail* (London), March 24, 1909.
5. "Views of Famous Men," *Daily Mail* (London), March 25, 1909.
6. E. H. Shackleton to Emily Shackleton, February 12, 1907, Scott Polar Research Institute, MS 1537/2/12/15, University of Cambridge, Cambridge, UK (hereafter cited as SPRI).
7. "Lieut. Shackleton's Antarctic Expedition," *Geographical Journal* 33 (1909), 485.
8. Lecture Agency, "Extracts from the reports of the London daily papers" (agency flier), 91(08)(*7), SPRI.
9. "The Conquest of the South Pole," *Spectator* (London), March 27, 1909.
10. [News of the Week], *Nation* (London), March 27, 1909.
11. E. H. Shackleton, *The Heart of the Antarctic: Being the Story of the British Antarctic Expedition, 1907–1909* (Philadelphia: J. B. Lippincott, 1909), 2:232.
12. "University Welcome," *Sydney Morning Herald*, March 31, 1909.
13. "Professor David's Welcome," *Clarence and Richmond Examiner*, April 1, 1909.
14. "Professor David Town Hall Welcome," *Sydney Morning Herald*, April 2, 1909.
15. "University Welcome," *Sydney Morning Herald*, March 31, 1909.
16. "The Antarctic Expedition Tributes to Mr. Douglas Mawson," *Register* (Adelaide), April 21, 1909.
17. Douglas Mawson, *The Home of the Blizzard: Being the Story of the Australasia Antarctic Expedition, 1911–1914* (London: William Heinemann, 1915), 1:265.
18. Douglas Mawson, *The Home of the Blizzard: Being the Story of the Australasian Antarctic Expedition, 1911–1914*, 2 vols. (London: Ballantyne Press, 1915).
19. "'Good News,' Says Cook," *New York Tribune*, September 7, 1909.
20. Daily Mail, *The Wonderful Year 1909: An Illustrated Record of Notable Achievements and Events* (London: Headley Brothers, 1910), 82.
21. "New York Mad Over Dr. Cook," *New York Herald*, September 22, 1909.
22. "Peary Discovers the North Pole after Eight Trials in 23 Years," *New York Times*, September 7, 1909. The *Times* reprinted both telegraph messages.
23. "Says Dr. Cook Is in Error," *New York Herald*, September 9, 1909 (reprinting the Associated Press telegram).
24. "Peary Denounces Cook," *New York Times*, September 11, 1909.
25. "American Editorial Comment on Commander Peary's So-Called 'Proof' Against Dr. Cook," *New York Herald*, September 30, 1909. Turning Peary's statement against him in a racist manner, the Cincinnati *Commercial Tribune* added, "Every American with a drop of sporting blood in his veins feels like dropping into the vernacular with the exclamation, 'He ain't so blamed white at that!'"

26. "Commander Peary Repeats Challenge," *New York Herald*, September 14, 1909; "The Jeanie, with Peary Party Aboard, Arrives at Cape Ray," *New York Herald*, September 12, 1909 (includes quoted comment).

27. "Cook's Bewildered Story of Retreat," *New York Times*, September 8, 1909.

28. "Honor Is America's, Says Shackleton," *New York Times*, September 8, 1909.

29. "Nares Congratulates Peary," *New York Times*, September 8, 1909; "Melville Accepts Report," *New York Times*, September 7, 1909.

30. "Amundsen Stands by Cook," *New York Times*, December 22, 1909.

31. "American Editorial Opinion on the Cook-Peary Controversy," *New York Herald*, September 13, 1909.

32. "Press Readers Award Credit of Pole Discovery to Dr. Cook by Large Majority," *Pittsburgh Press*, September 26, 1909.

33. Benjamin B. Hampton to Robert E. Peary, November 17, 1909, Letters and Telegrams Received 1909 (F-H), Box 35, Robert E. Peary Papers, National Archives.

34. Samuel G. Blythe, "Alone at the Pole: A Typical American Drama of the Present Day in Several Acts," *Saturday Evening Post*, October 16, 1909, 21.

35. G. K. Chesterton, "The Hope of the Year," in Daily Mail, *Wonderful Year*, ix.

36. "American Editorial Comment on Commander Peary's So-Called 'Proof' Against Dr. Cook," *New York Herald*, September 30, 1909.

37. [Shailer Mathews], "Cheapening Heroism," *World Today*, November 1909, 1117–18.

38. "Duca Degli Abruzzi Arrives in Marseilles, Returning from His Expedition of Exploration in the Himalayas," *New York Herald*, September 13, 1909.

39. Apsley Cherry-Garrard, *Worst Journey in the World: Antarctic 1910–1913* (London: Constable, 1922), 1:vii. The full passage reads, *"For a joint scientific and geographical piece of organization, give me Scott; for a Winter Journey, Wilson; for a dash to the Pole and nothing else, Amundsen: and if I am in the devil of a hole and want to get out of it, give me Shackleton every time."*

40. Samuel Taylor Coleridge, *The Rime of the Ancient Mariner*, lines 59–60, 69–70.

41. A. Conan Doyle, quoted in Kathryn Schulz, "Literature's Arctic Obsession," *The New Yorker*, April 24, 2017, 88; A. Conan Doyle, *The Captain of the Pole-Star and Other Tales* (London: Longman, Green, 1890), 32.

42. R. E. Peary, *Nearest the Pole: A Narrative of the Polar Expedition of the Peary Arctic Club in the S. S. Roosevelt, 1905–1906* (New York: Doubleday, 1907), x.

43. Ibid., 45.

Credits

FIRST INSERT

Hassan cigarette card (1910) image on the top of page 1 owned by author.

Courtesy of Centro Documentazione Museo Nazionale della Montagna—CAI-Torino, used by permission: bottom image on page 1, all images on page 2, and top image on page 8.

From Filippo De Filippi, *Karakoram and Western Himalaya, 1909: An Account of the Expedition of H. R. H. Prince Luigi Amadeo of Savoy, Duke of the Abruzzi*, 2 vols. (New York: Dutton, 1912): top and bottom images on page 3 and all images on pages 4–7 (of which all photographs are by Vittorio Sella except for the photograph on page 5, which is by the Duke of the Abruzzi).

India 1909 General Map of Railways, from University of Richmond Libraries: middle image on page 3.

Photograph on the bottom of page 8 by the author.

SECOND INSERT

From Robert E. Peary, *The North Pole* (New York: Stokes, 1910): image on page 1; top left, bottom left, and bottom right images on page 2; top, bottom left, and bottom right images on page 3; all images on pages 4–7; and middle right image on page 8.

Courtesy of the Library of Congress: top right image on page 2 and top left, top right, and middle left images on page 8.

From the Collections of Maine Bureau of Parks and Lands, used by permission: middle image on page 3.

Photograph on the bottom left of page 8 by the author.

THIRD INSERT

From E. H. Shackleton, *The Heart of the Antarctic: Being the Story of the British Antarctic Expedition, 1907–1909*, 2 vols. (Philadelphia: J. B. Lippincott, 1909): all images on pages 1–5, top left and bottom right images on page 6, image on page 7, and top image on page 8.

Courtesy of the Library of Congress: top right image on page 6.

From David Starr Jordon, *The Days of a Man: Being Memories of a Naturalist, Teacher, and Minor Prophet of Democracy* (Yonkers-on-Hudson, NY: World Book, 1922): bottom left image on page 6.

From *Illustrated London News* (1909): middle image on page 8.

Photograph on the bottom of page 8 by the author.

Index